G

JESUS: The Unanswered Questions

Also by John Bowden

Karl Barth: Theologian
By Heart
Edward Schillebeeckx: Portrait of a Theologian
Voices in the Wilderness
What about the Old Testament?
Who is a Christian?

John Bowden

JESUS:
The Unanswered
Questions

SCM PRESS LTD

British Library Cataloguing in Publication Data

Bowden, John
    Jesus: the unanswered questions
    1. Jesus Christ
    I. Title
    232

    ISBN 0-334-02099-9

First published 1988
by SCM Press Ltd,
26-30 Tottenham Road, London N1 4BZ

Phototypeset by Input Typesetting Ltd, London
and printed in Great Britain by
Billing & Sons Ltd, Worcester

'O Christianity, Christianity,
   why do you not answer our difficulties?'
Stevie Smith

Contents

Foreword: Towards the Next Stage of Christian Catholicity

David Jenkins, *Bishop of Durham*

This book is a timely confession of faith which is an even more timely call to faith. All the time the reader is wrestling with, being excited by, or being depressed and bewildered by, the details in Chapters 3 to 11, he or she should bear in mind and in spirit the faith which is confessed in 'By Way of Introduction' and especially the concentrated expression of that faith on pages xvii and xviii. It is a passionate faith in God which is concerned with Jesus, truth, freedom and the possibilities of the future. Readers should also not forget that the book ends with a prayer. The whole book is thus an expression of pilgrimage and an invitation to pilgrimage, a pilgrimage which is clearly embarked on in faith and to be pursued in hope.

As the ground on which the pilgrimage travels is 'unanswered questions', and the mode and movement of the pilgrimage is to discern and pose these questions with them all focussed on Jesus or by aspects of hitherto expressed and formulated faith in Jesus, those of us whose faith in God is 'through Jesus Christ' may be tempted to dismiss the book as over-intellectual, narrowly academic and too specialized to be of interest to anyone but those who have these specialized interests. It cannot be too strongly and urgently emphasized that such a dismissal would be a deeply faithless mistake, a simple logical mistake and a dangerous practical mistake.

The inescapable point of Chapters 3 – 11 is that the questions are there and that they are posed from a variety of possible and sustainable viewpoints, maintained by a variety of serious arguments and built up over many years of careful scholarship on the one hand and careful scrutiny of actual events and discussions on the other. To judge by the ways in which much current controversy is conducted many self-styled faithful people repeatedly and deliberately ignore these questions, thereby displaying their little faith. For the questions will not go away because some among that minority who claim to be Christians go on trying to cling to outmoded rules of the game and claim that *they* (we ?!) have such a revelation from God that we are authorized to tell the rest of the world, on our own terms, what is a proper question, what is a proper answer and what is a proper procedure for dealing with questions.

Such an attitude is Bourbon-like in its refusal to learn anything from the present with a view to the future and its refusal to forget anything of the limited and rigid views inherited from (or imagined from) the past. It is also a misunderstanding both of the way revelation has in fact been received and developed in the past of the Christian tradition and of the claims made within, and on the basis of, that received revelation. As any informed study of the Old and New Testaments makes clear, the vehicles, contents and claims of revelation have always been shaped by contemporary culture, events and understandings. This has been carried forward into the history of the church, of the churches, and of all those groups of groups which now extend the Christian faith and Christian exploration over the whole world. To claim an arrested development somewhere in the history of the middle or late mediaeval Mediterranean, focussed on Rome and Byzantium, with a further focus, in some interpret-ations, in Geneva is neither consistent nor plausible in the light of the way things have actually gone on.

It is further to deny the content of the revelation so far. For the revelation is about the being and the dealings of the living and universal God, 'creator of heaven and earth'. It is inconceivable that the content, impact and understanding of the revelation, therefore, should not be altered and expanded by the moving out of believers to all parts of the world and by the encounters of that world with facts, horizons, possibilities and demands which have never before been dreamed of.

If the revelation which the Bible reflects is a revelation proceeding from a living God and has to do with living engagement with this God then all questions which arise as the human story develops have to be faced. And to be faced as material for revelation, discovery and obedience. There can be no 'no go' areas for God, so there can be no 'no go' areas for faith. Pilgrimage does not stop with the seeming safety of the apparently known or rest in the waning security of the apparently established. It did not do so in the Bible; why should it do so now?

So, it would be faithless to turn aside from the questions assembled in this book. It would also be a mistake in the logic both of faith and of the discussion, exploration and commendation of faith. For a principal contribution to this book's timeliness is that it puts all (or most !) of the unanswered questions about Jesus side by side and requires nine separate chapters to do so. This serves to show that logically we who continue, with confidence and conviction, in that way of responding to God which lies 'through Jesus Christ' must face the pressing practical question of authority and find a new and renewing way of living with it and thus developing and commending our faith. When questions come up about Jesus and his significance the tendency is to fall back on one line of authority such as an appeal to the Bible, or to doctrinal orthodoxy, or to the obvious moral superiority of Jesus, or to a simple statement of uniqueness and finality. Which ever is the main ground of appeal and argument is then held to be backed up, even if in a subordinate way, by the other lines of appeal and argument. But, as the chapters in this book show, each of the lines is itself shaky and rests on presuppositions which are genuinely questionable. Now, logically a combination of questionable arguments does not build up to probability higher than the probability of each of the separate arguments but to an overall probability which is lower than the partial probabilities of each of the separate arguments. This may seem a rather technical point, but its practical effect is very far-reaching. It means that with regard to faith in God expressed and explored through, in and around Jesus Christ no triumphalist, dominating or, in any sense publicly enforceable authority is viable. Too much at each and every turn is questionable and uncertain.

Further, although this goes beyond the logical point, some of the issues raised put very proper moral questions to the assumption that Jesus is evidently morally superior or triumphantly unique. Or, at the very least, there are sharp questions raised about the way believers have made use of these assumptions and claims. This is to say that assumption by Christians that the place we habitually give to Jesus is obviously logically sustainable or obviously morally superior is demonstrably false – when the various sets of 'questionability' are put side by side. This is a particularly timely demonstration when we are confronted with so many strident demands for 'moral authority', so frequent refusals to argue, and so much religious extremism and regression. The simple truth is that the posturing and postulating Emperors of religious certainty and moralizing absolutism have no clothes. They may refuse to recognize this and it is necessary to have a sympathetic understanding of those forces of fear and uncertainty which encourage such attitudes. But it is humanly, healthily and spiritually essential to maintain the patient demonstration of the evidence that at any rate in the sphere of Christian faith (and, surely, evidently in all spheres of human enterprise and exploration) such claims to such authority have neither logical nor historical foundation.

This is why pushing this book to one side would be a dangerous practical mistake. Many people seem to be out to capture religion for their own comfort, confirmation and profit. But Godliness is to do with the uncertainties, the sufferings and the openness of Jesus, reaching out to the whole wide world and to the immense varieties of human beings and human experiences which are still continuing. So the future of a true Christian faith must lie with an exploration that persuades, a love that serves and a vision that combines an ever-expanding realism with unquenchable hope. As a challenge to return us to and renew us in such a search and such a faith this book has an important part to play.

David Dunelm:

Preface

This is a book of questions. They arise out of a wide variety of areas of Christian thought, practice and experience: study of the Bible, doctrine, ethics, the history of Christianity, liturgy, personal prayer, pastoral work, the use of Christian belief as a source of manipulation within society and the relationship between Christianity and other faiths – to mention the main ones. Few of these questions are ones that I have thought up myself; some are more sophisticated than others, but they can all be found elsewhere, often discussed at great length.

However, they are all *my* questions, and those of a large number of people with whom I have talked over the years. Particularly in the present climate, I must make it quite clear from the very start that this is a book which has arisen out of widespread discussion over a considerable period and in a number of different contexts; it is not the result of solitary communing with books and a word processor but of attempting to be sensitive to what is in the air and what concerns a not insignificant number of thinking Christians.

Of course books come into it a great deal – lots of books, which will appear in the quotations and in the footnotes. But they play a rather different role from the books which are cited by other authors on their pages. For my work over more than twenty years has been primarily that of a theological publisher, so many of my references are to books with whose appearance and reception I have been closely involved, written by authors from whose friendship, learning and experience I have come to know far more than can be conveyed on any written page. The books mentioned here are only the tangible sign of something much deeper which underlies them.

I know, of course, that the same sort of friendship and sharing is also be found in the academic community, but since publishers are faced with the whole range of theological subject-matter and cannot keep to a particular specialism, in time the picture which is there for them to see becomes wider – and, as in my case, the number of questions inevitably increases.

In one public debate over some of the issues we shall be considering I was told by a distinguished professor of theology that my questions were 'scholar's questions'. However, the substantial audience did not seem to think so, and made it quite clear that they were their questions, too, and that has always been my experience. The questions that I have brought together are not in fact academic ones, questions which one thinks up in a mood of innate scepticism, though some have arisen first within an academic environment or as a result of the relentless pressure for honesty and clarity which academic criteria exercise. They are above all questions which arise out of a personal search for truth, which I still believe also to be a search for God, out of a response to what I believe to be signs of and pointers towards that God one of whose means of communication St Augustine so movingly described as being the instilling of a sense of restlessness.

Twenty years ago I would not have had to spend so much time simply justifying the asking of questions – I would simply have asked them. But things were very different in those days and that is something else with which I have constantly to struggle. Looking back at what I consider to be the best of the theology and biblical and historical research over the last twenty years I can see many signs of progress and positive development – not just in the more detailed knowledge that has been acquired in hitherto obscure areas but also in understanding the limitations of the scholar, accepting our ignorance in so many areas and the sparseness of our material. There have been welcome signs of increased interest in Christianity from scholars working in other fields, which in particular have helped us to see the degree to which economic, political and cultural influences have made their mark on Christian thought, life and organization. But the life of the churches has manifestly been moving in the other direction. The level of theological and historical knowledge and insight has – to judge from public debates – fallen appallingly and attempts to ask questions are largely frowned on. Instead, we are told that there is a 'turning of the tide', and that there is nothing wrong with traditional beliefs (seldom defined in any detail), which need only to be restated with renewed conviction and faith.

This affirmation of 'the turning of the tide' is, of course, made at a time when the churches in England have never been numerically so weak (recent statistics indicate an active membership in the Church of England of about 3% of the population) and the decline in numbers of ordained clergy has never been so great (in the Roman Catholic church, of course, it is catastrophic). So it represents the standpoint of an embattled minority who make their point by drawing on a limited range of evidence and appealing to those who still have no difficulties with the churches as they are.

But this is to ignore those who once were at least peripheral members of the church but are no longer so (clearly a growing number) or those – to be found in so many congregations – who still cling on to Christian practice by the skin of their teeth in the hope that somehow, some day, things will get better. Why is it that so many people have left the churches? Why is it that so many people one talks to are so dissatisfied? Is this all the result of an inevitable process of secularization? Are *all* these people seduced by the materialism of modern society? Might not there also, as one element, be the failure of the church to submit its own beliefs and the practices arising from them to that scrutiny which alone can prevent them from ultimately looking like superstitions with inadequate intellectual support? Might the churches not need a much greater concern for thinking which might one day bring back the doctors, teachers, social workers and others, so few of whom now have much time for the churches?

So this is a book of questions – my questions and *our* questions, those of scholars and ordinary Christians, thinking Christians, who do not believe that the deep problems raised by Christian claims are now being taken seriously and, far from feeling that the tide has turned, are afraid of the flood of anti-intellectualism in the churches which seems to be rushing up to engulf us all, and want to try to do something about it before it is too late.

The questions are all focussed on Jesus, because on any account Jesus of Nazareth and the developments to which he gave rise are the focal point of Christianity, and it is around the interpretation of his person, christology, that so many problems cluster. Because this book brings together the questions of a wide variety of people, it lays no claim to originality. What it does do, however, and what no other book I have come across does, is to bring questions from a great many different fields within a single volume and allow them to make their impact all together, so that there is no escaping from their cumulative effect.

This is important, because another disturbing feature of our time is that both the life of the churches and theological study have become highly compartmentalized. For example, the recent revisions of liturgies in, say, the Anglican and Roman Catholic churches have tended to disregard the work of biblical critics.[1] Christian doctrine is still largely treated as the Bible used to be two centuries ago, presented as having such unique authority that it must have been made in heaven, rather than being the work of thinkers and negotiators at particular periods during church history, and therefore open to historical criticism and the problems of cultural relativism.[2] Those discussing the relationship between Christianity and other religions often seem to leave totally out of account the major crisis that has developed *within* the Christian tradition as to the nature and criteria of Christianity and the way in which the Christian tradition has in so many respects turned into secular Western technological and economic expansion all over the world.[3] Feminist theologians and liberation theologians seem to base some of their claims on wishful thinking about the support the Bible could provide for their views, and have not really grappled with all that the Bible says – or does not say.[4] Some generations of clergy, teachers, students with theological training have developed as it were split personalities, with little relationship between heart and head, recognizing the existence of the findings of modern research with part of themselves, but then bracketting it off in their personal devotion and the life of the church to which they belong; others have found a way of simply dismissing the questions that the modern world poses to their beliefs.[5]

But we must surely accept that we live in one world. It is manifestly unhealthy to be one kind of person in the role of believer and another in other areas of life. There cannot be one kind of religious truth and a completely different kind of secular truth. So Christianity, if it is to be a coherent faith at all, must relate all the aspects I have mentioned to one another without gross conflict between them, and therefore this compartmentalization can only be seen as a transitional stage beyond which we need to progress.

That means that there must be more interaction between the churches where Christian faith is still lived out and practised and those areas where the study of religions is carried on within secular colleges and universities, by scholars and students who either have no personal religious commitment themselves or who regard that commitment as something quite separate from their studies. Each needs the other if Christian belief is to be something which claims the whole person. Judith Herrin quite rightly points out that 'the history of faith is far too important to be left to adherents alone',[6] and we need to know that history as fully as we can, if only to rid us of some of our fond illusions. But there is also a future to be worked towards, and that also involves living out a faith in the present. Interest and concern in religious belief is more than intellectual curiosity or interest in an academic discipline; it is not just a matter of looking at, but also of belonging to, sharing in the quest of, communities of believers or would-be believers.

For all its questioning, this book is written out of a deep and positive faith in God, to whom I cannot say no, a faith which I have to acknowledge originated through the Jesus about whom I ask so many questions. I have to ask the questions, because they are there to be asked, and if God is, then God is to be found, or to find me, through those questions and not by avoiding them. Jesus is extremely question-able, but nevertheless he is somehow worth bothering about because by asking all the questions one comes up against the reality of how things still are. At least many people do. So that is a first reason for asking all the questions.

A second reason for writing it is a passionate concern for the truth of things and what I would dare to call a love for the God of truth. The truth of how things are does not appear very often these days as an issue in the more publicized religious controversies, but all down the centuries there have been many Christians for whom that truth has been the only thing that matters. I was trained in what nowadays would be regarded as a rather old-fashioned and 'liberal' tradition, and that has left its mark indelibly on me, but I have no regrets, for it stood – and still stands – for values which mean an enormous amount to me. That the tone of what I have written is rather more passionate and involved than this tradition tends to approve of is because since I was brought up in that tradition I have changed, and I can also see, perhaps not clearly enough, some of those things which it lacks, above all a sense of what forces in practice shape the face of the world and its religions and how it is important to do more than just analyse them, important to play a more active role in changing society and the churches.

Thirdly, there is no doubt that questions have an enormous power to liberate. Questions uncover the half-truths which in the past have been used to dominate and control, to instil fear and endorse social and sexual inequality, to perpetuate institutions which have outlived their day and to postpone change. Such questions may lead to liberation movements, in the churches or in the wider world, which make use of even more powerful forces to bring about change; but then as they too come to get above themselves, questions once again can redress the balance. Questions are dangerous, and people have regularly been killed for asking them; but they are a sign of human freedom, and it is an unhealthy society, religious or secular, in which they cannot be asked – provided, always, that they are genuinely in search of an answer and do not lead to an apathetic scepticism.

Fourthly, it is only by asking questions of our own religious tradition that we can hope to engage in constructive discussion with people of other faiths who are also part of our one world. For example, especially in Britain, there are those who, despite the evidence to the contrary, insist on maintaining that society is still Christian, rather than post-Christian or pluralist, and that a narrowly Christian attitude to faith and morality is the only way towards national salvation. Such attitudes almost rule out constructive debate from the start, or encourage retreat into an irrational and anti-intellectual fundamentalism, from which it is impossible that a healthier and more open society can develop. Whereas a realization of the way in which religious traditions have grown up in history and of the cultural influences that there have been on them, which because of the historicality of our very way of thinking (as we shall see) is the fact which this questioning brings home to us, can do a great deal for tolerance and mutual understanding.

The questions raised here first took sufficiently coherent form to be raised in public about ten years ago, and a number of them appeared in a series of lectures entitled 'Christianity without Christ?' which I was invited to give at the University College of North Wales in 1978. Later they were distilled into a single lecture which I gave to substantial audiences at gatherings arranged by the Southwark Ordination Course in London and the University Extra-Mural Department in Birmingham, two shining examples of places where thinking is still going on and theology is still presented in a positive, exciting yet questioning way, and to a number of smaller groups. It was the initial response to this paper at Southwark Cathedral that led directly to the first draft of this book. I had suspected that the paper would provoke protests and agitated outcries from the audience and I was surprised that, far from being shouted down, what I said, or rather asked, seemed to fall on sympathetic ears and led to a constructive discussion and even requests for a book along its lines. By expanding the outline of the paper and making chapters out of its paragraphs, I have produced what I hope are a whole series of starting points for widespread but inter-related conversations and discussions.

For it is such conversations and discussions, in many different forms, that are needed if the Christian churches are to escape from the anti-intellectualism to which so many of them are in thrall and rediscover a richer and truer faith, and if it is to be possible to re-establish the links between Christianity and the wider cultural world which were once so strong, and thereby recover a feeling that the Christian tradition still has a creative future.

The book has been particularly difficult to write and I am aware of its many flaws. There is much to be said against the writing of books by publishers. For one thing, writing a book feels just like being an overworked midwife who is herself having a baby at the same time. For another, it is just not possible to spend time researching in libraries or tracking down all the books that ought to be read, and opportunities for reflection at leisure are limited. Publishers do not have 'long vacations'. Nevertheless, here is the book, for better or for worse. Babies, even metaphorical ones, once conceived, grow of their own accord, becoming more uncomfortable the further advanced they get, so that one longs to be delivered of them. There will always be gaps and inadequacies in any book which attempts to cover a wide area, and I think that the fairly extensive documentation in the footnotes legitimates at least the broad outline of my case.

The footnotes are particularly important. It has not been easy to know how much knowledge to presuppose on the part of the reader; in particular I have become more and more aware of the degree to which those who have not engaged in first-hand study are ignorant of the complexity of the records of Jesus in the Gospels. And biblical scholars are often woefully ignorant about the course of discussions on issues like cultural relativism or the relationships between world faiths. Those who read earlier drafts of the typescript told me that certain passages were particularly dense. I have tried my best to make them clearer, but have doubtless often failed, in which case the footnotes indicate a way of shedding more light on them by further reading.

I have many people to thank for their help, encouragement and support, beginning with those correspondents who since I wrote *Voices in the Wilderness* in 1977 have reassured me that I am not just a lone and unrepresentative voice and those who joined in the discussions of the lectures which led to this book. For their comments on earlier drafts, as well as my wife Rachel I must thank my son Hugh, who made me write on the topics covered in Chapter 8. Robert Carroll, Leslie Houlden, David Lindsay, Dennis Nineham and Alan Race all made invaluable and often critical comments from which I have benefited a great deal. The remaining faults are all my own. There would have been even more faults had I not had the support of all my colleagues at SCM Press, who have done me the service of treating this as one more book – with the care and attention they devote to everything that we publish. Invidious though it is to mention names I have particularly valued the comments of Linda Foster and Susan Molyneux; Mark Hammer has produced another of his superlative covers; and Margaret Lydamore has made this book particularly her own, combining in equal measure encouragement to get down to it and finish it with unsparing criticism of what does not live up to her standards or attempt to answer her questions also.

As I began by saying, for many Christians now is not the time for asking questions and I am quite prepared for what I have written to be ignored, dismissed or rejected. I, too, can read the signs of the times clearly enough. I have thought very hard indeed about whether a book like this should be published at present or at all, and I have taken a good deal of advice from a range of people before putting the book forward for publication. I was still entertaining a few niggling doubts when I received a postcard imitating that Jewish saying immortalized by Primo Levi, 'If not by you, by whom? If not now, when?'[7] So here it is.

At proof stage the book has acquired a Foreword by David Jenkins, Bishop of Durham.

I begin the first chapter by describing how at university I came to read theology and was started on the process of questioning faith which has gone on ever since. Reading theology in my college at that time also meant being taught by David Jenkins, and my tutorials with him marked the beginning of a friendship which has steadily deepened over the years in a way which I have found a great strength.

What some readers may find my surprising confidence in God (despite my questions about Jesus) has regularly been fortified by what David Jenkins has said, from the sermon (delivered in 1956 in Pusey House Chapel) on 'There is No God', which I can still remember as though it were yesterday, through the Bampton Lectures of 1966, *The Glory of Man*, to the first chapter of that *Dark Night of Our Institutions*, the whole of which I hope that he will soon have time to complete. Even more, it has been fortified by what he has been and is, for me and so many others, and so it is right that the last word of thanks in this preface should go to him.

1 | By Way of Introduction

It was in an Oxford college chapel that I first heard some words which, consciously or sub-consciously, have haunted me ever since. 'What is bothering me incessantly is the question what Christianity really is, or indeed who Christ really is for us today.'[1] For a great many Christians, the sentence will need no further identification; as soon as they hear it, they will recognize it as easily as the theme of a great symphony; and like such a theme, it will have all sorts of associations for them.

Here is Dietrich Bonhoeffer, in a German prison in 1944 and soon to die, stretching his thought to the limit as he tries to picture Christian belief in the future, after the war, in a world from which God has been forced out, a world in which human beings have to stand by God, rather than God standing by them: a world of religionless Christianity.

Bonhoeffer's words grew familiar through the paperback of his *Letters and Papers from Prison*, which sold tens of thousands of copies and has become a classic of modern devotion as well as a testimony to radical, pioneering thought in the most oppressive of circumstances. That became even more so as a result of the way in which his musings were taken up by John Robinson, whose *Honest to God* so caught the mood of the early 1960s, when it looked as if the post-war world really was going in the direction in which Bonhoeffer expected. But when I heard Bonhoeffer's question 'Who is Christ for us today?' the year was 1956, seven years before *Honest to God*; *Letters and Papers from Prison* had appeared in English, in hardback, only in 1953, and the famous paperback had still to make its mark.

I am not even certain whether by then I had decided to attempt to become a theologian (I had gone to Oxford to read classics); but it was around that time that I decided to study theology. I am still not quite sure what prompted my decision: it was not Bonhoeffer at that stage, though he meant a lot to me subsequently. Perhaps the most important factor was my then college chaplain and theology tutor, Christopher Evans, who went on to become a distinguished professor of New Testament in Durham and in London before his retirement. It was characteristic that he should have preached about Bonhoeffer well before most people had heard of him, and his thoughts, like Bonhoeffer's, went disturbingly beyond the accepted commonplaces (as we shall see in due course, since I shall have occasion to refer to his work later in this book).[2] With his ruthless sense of integrity he would insist that where questions were called for they should be pursued to the end, and not fudged. He became my tutor, and the habit of questioning stuck.

By him, for the first time in my life, I had my nose rubbed in (no other phrase will quite do) the Gospels, especially the first three of them. The basic book which we used as students was the synopsis: the texts of Matthew, Mark and Luke printed in three parallel columns, in Greek, in such a way as to bring out what material is shared (as it is) by two or all three of them, what material is peculiar to an individual evangelist, and how the later evangelists make changes to the earlier. Simply looking at the differences in wording between one version and another of an episode in these Gospels raises an endless series of questions.[3] And in addition, week by week we had to make our own attempts at coping with some of the most difficult questions any New Testament scholar can face: 'Why and what did Jesus teach in parables?' 'What did Jesus mean by the Kingdom of God?' 'To whom was Jesus referring when he used the phrase Son of Man and what did he mean by it?' 'Did Jesus foresee his death, and if so what significance did he attach to it?' 'What does the Gospel evidence tell us about the resurrection of Jesus?' Then we were introduced to the Gospel of John, and had to consider why that was so different from the other three Gospels and what we were to make of the difference. We discovered just how desperately hard the problems with which we were confronted were to answer satisfactorily, indeed how some of them were virtually unanswerable (why, we shall see in Chapter 3). And inevitably, in many of us this produced a great sense of frustration and uncertainty.

It was, of course, possible to treat all this as an academic game, one of the hurdles to be overcome before getting down to the serious work of being ordained, joining in the life of the church and preaching the 'real' gospel, and many people did just that. Moreover they had some justification, for the work in which we were engaged was merely that of dissection, taking to pieces, without really much indication of how, if at all, the pieces could be put together again. We were being asked to read what was actually there, the words the evangelists had written in the language in which they had written them, with someone who would go on questioning us about both what we had seen and what we had failed to see but whose task was not to provide the answers. Those were for us to find for ourselves, if we could, and more often than not we couldn't. However, because one couldn't become a clergyman or a teacher two or three years later without some answers to give, there was a temptation to fall back into pre-critical attitudes, to betray what one had learned or at least to keep it in a separate part of one's mind, as though it did not really affect the rest of what one was doing, or going to do. Yet all the time there was also the inescapable realization that to retain any sense of integrity it was essential for us not to go back on what we had learned and to hold it in tension with the rest of the Christian tradition.

This tension, with which Christians have had to live for well over a century, is often insufficiently understood and certainly underestimated, and it is felt by teacher as well as by pupil. As one looks back on the whole approach, its weakness as a training method for clergy and teachers seems all too obvious, and that more attention was not paid to this at the time is a marked weakness of the liberal tradition in which it was practised, so marked as to have led more recently to talk of the 'bankruptcy' of historical method. However, it is hardly the method that is bankrupt, though biblical study has moved on since the 1950s and takes into account a whole new series of factors, ranging from sociology to the insights of literary criticism. The problem lay, as it still lies, in the tension between the pre-critical understanding of the Bible so deeply embedded in the Christian tradition and the demands of truth in the modern academic world.

Evidence of the tension is clearer in the nineteenth century than it is today and we can see at first hand how at least one distinguished biblical scholar was led to resign his position as a result. As a professor at Greifswald in Germany, Julius Wellhausen was also responsible for training candidates for the ministry; by 1882 he found the pressures on him caused by the clash between academic study and training for the church so great that he gave up his chair. As he wrote to the Prussian Minister of Education:

> Your Excellency will perhaps remember that in Easter 1880 I requested, if it were at all possible, to be transferred into the Faculty of Theology. At the same time, I tried to set out the reasons for my request. I became a theologian because I was interested in the academic study of the Bible. It then gradually dawned on me that a professor of theology also has the practical task of preparing students for ministry in the Protestant church, and that I was not up to this practical task. Despite every restraint on my part, I was making my pupils more unsuitable for it. Since then, my theological professorship has been a heavy burden on my conscience.[4]

He had to become a mere lecturer in another university, and it was three years before he became a professor in a different discipline, and then only after a bitter struggle.

But running away from the conflict is no answer either for those who teach or for those who learn from them. As I said, the conflict produced by New Testament study is inescapable, both because of the nature of the Gospels themselves and because of the nature of the method with which we find it natural to study them, namely as historical documents (and the historical method, as we shall see, causes conflicts over a far wider area of the Christian tradition). We shall be looking more closely at this method later, but it is one which is all-demanding: as Ernst Troeltsch, another great German professor, once put it, 'Give it your little finger and it will require your whole hand', adding wryly that in that way it resembled the devil.[5]

I have stressed all this because it is important to realize from the start, as I was made to, that considerable problems arise simply from sitting down and reading the Gospels carefully and critically and trying to make sense of what one sees. And everything else goes back to that Gospel evidence and must be explained in relationship to it. That is why when we come to the specific questions about Jesus we have to begin by looking in more detail at the Gospels.

In addition to similar critical study of the rest of the New Testament and the Old Testament, basic university theological training in the 1950s had just one other component: the history of Christian doctrine up to the year AD 451. That was the year of the Council of Chalcedon, the gathering of bishops of the church which is widely reckoned by Christians to have made the classical statement about the nature of Jesus Christ, known as the Chalcedonian Definition (which we shall also be looking at, in Chapter 5). For me, at any rate, patristics, as the study of the Church Fathers is called, was a strange world to come to after biblical criticism, simply because the world inhabited by the Fathers was so different and unfamiliar and approached by those studying it in such a different way. Here was a world of theological reasoning, philosophical argument and a use of the Bible (and a world of church intrigues of a kind familiar to any age), through which we traced the way in which a great edifice of Christian orthodoxy came into being in the four centuries after Jesus' death. We came to know who were 'good' and who were 'bad', to discover the views of 'Fathers' and 'heretics'. But we were asked only to trace developments and to try to understand the workings of a different cultural pattern from our own. In no way were we encouraged to approach all this material with the questioning attitude which was so familiar from Gospel criticism. We were not encouraged to dispute the conclusions reached by the Fathers; they were a given. In fact, it may be said in passing, at that time many theologians seem to have felt able to be quite radical in their questioning of the Gospel record because they felt secure in having the support of traditional Christian doctrine (and the church's liturgical tradition) behind them, which they took almost completely for granted.

However, over the past twenty years, scholars have increasingly been arguing that in patristics, too, a much wider range of questions needs to be asked. The authority and content of the doctrines worked out by the Fathers also needs to be questioned, in just the same way as the authority and content of the Bible. In this way, slowly and of course with some reluctance (slowly, because early Christian doctrine does not intrinsically have quite the perennial attraction of the Bible; reluctantly, because the implications are so daunting), biblical criticism has been joined by doctrinal criticism,[6] and substantial doubts have been cast on the validity of the two major doctrines of the Christian church: the Trinity and the Incarnation. Here too, countless questions have been asked about the nature and identity of the Christ believed in and worshipped in the churches.

In describing my theological studies I have also been writing about two areas in which all Christians, of whatever age or background, are involved in one way or another. At least every Sunday in church the Gospels will be read and the creed recited, and unless they are simply listened to with half an ear or repeated parrot-fashion they call for some thought and prompt some questioning. Moreover, in many churches both these activities will take place within the framework of the eucharist, the mass, holy communion (whatever name is used for the celebration of 'the Lord's supper'), and that liturgy has its roots in the life and ministry of Jesus of Nazareth. Hymns about Jesus are sung, the authors of which may well span almost the whole of Christian history, from earliest Christianity, through the Catholic Middle Ages, the Lutheran Reformation and the great hymn-writers of the Methodist, Baptist, Congregationalist and Presbyterian churches to the present day. If the sermon touches at all, as may well often be the case, on questions of personal and social morality, then the teaching of Jesus is likely to be referred to. And in addition to all that there will be the personal worship and prayer 'through Jesus Christ our Lord' of the individuals who make up the congregation.

So every Sunday, at least in principle, has a focal point which can prompt thought and questioning about Jesus in relation to biblical criticism, Christian doctrine, worship, ethics, images of Christ down the ages and personal devotion. And the Sunday service is only one part of the church's life. In asking questions about Jesus, therefore, in one way or another we shall have to consider all these areas if we are to gain a picture of the place of Christ in the Christian tradition and the problems raised by it. Nor must we forget that Jesus is known, talked about, argued over, admired, criticized, revered far outside the Christian churches, both by those forced to the fringes of the churches or those who, while unprepared to identify with the churches, yet would not want to dissociate themselves from the movement Jesus began, and those of other faiths – or none – who know a great religious teacher when they see one.

So far in this chapter I have been referring both to 'Jesus' and to 'Christ', and before we go any further something should also be said about this alternation. 'Jesus' is the Greek version of the Aramaic/ Hebrew name Jeshua/Joshua which was borne by the man 'from Nazareth' who lived and died in Palestine during the first century of our era and about whom the Gospels were written. It was a traditional name going back to the Old Testament hero Joshua the book of whose exploits is, of course, entitled 'the book of Jesus' in the Greek Old Testament, the Septuagint. 'Christ' is the Greek equivalent of the Hebrew 'Messiah' and was used as a title of honour for Jesus from the earliest Greek-speaking communities on. ('Christian' is, of course, derived from Christ; oddly enough it seems to have been used first by outsiders as a term for a member of the first churches; it may even have had contemptuous overtones to it.[7])

Now with these two different names go two rather different worlds. As we shall see in Chapter 3, it is almost unanimously recognized by New Testament scholars that Jesus never used the title 'Messiah' ('Christ') of himself – at most he seems to have spoken of a mysterious 'Son of Man' who had a relationship to him over which there is still argument. The title 'Christ' was used of Jesus after the resurrection by the earliest churches, the first direct evidence for which comes to us in the letters of Paul. It has long been clear that to move from the Synoptic Gospels to the letters of Paul is to move from the life of an itinerant Jewish preacher and his followers, active in Galilee and Jerusalem, with a message and a life-style coloured through and through by that world, to the cosmopolitan life of Greece and Hellenized Asia Minor and with an eye to Rome; it is to trace a movement emerging from a backwater into the civilized world of the time. With that move the message changes. The centre of Jesus' preaching is the kingdom of God;[8] the centre of Paul's preaching is Christ crucified and risen, to such a degree that the believer is said to be 'in Christ' (the meaning of which was another essay topic which once caused me no little trouble!).[9] In other words, the Jesus who *has* a message changes into the Christ who *is* the message. (Of course there is not a total discontinuity, since we often find both names together as Jesus Christ: the 'Jesus Messiah' of some modern renderings is misleading, because when the title Christ came to be used of Jesus in the Greek-speaking world it had much wider connotations than the Jewish 'Messiah'.)

Among theologians it has long been conventional to use 'Jesus' predominantly to denote Jesus of Nazareth as he was in his earthly life, and to use the term 'Christ', which soon virtually became a surname, to describe the church's Lord. Thus study of Jesus as he was in his lifetime has often come to be called 'the quest of the historical Jesus' and study of the views of the nature of Christ, as expressed, say, in doctrinal discussions, is known as 'christology' – the neologism 'Jesuology' has, fortunately, failed to establish itself. Of course it is impossible to draw a hard and fast distinction between the two and usages are not always precise, but that is the usual pattern.

Particularly during the last century, when historical research had raised hopes that Jesus might be rescued from the alleged over-interpretation to which the church had subjected him and rediscovered him 'as he really was', much was made of the contrast between 'the Jesus of history' and the 'Christ of faith', and the latter was challenged in the name of the former.[10] The historical researchers claimed that their Jesus would be the new source of inspiration; some opponents accepted the contrast that they made but argued that if the critics' picture of Jesus differed from the Christ of the churches, the latter was the real Christ because his had been the impact. But this contrast did not prove acceptable for long, because it was rightly pointed out that since the Gospels are the church's books and in them Jesus is already portrayed through the eyes of faith, i.e. the portraits of him in them are theological portraits painted by members of first-century churches, it was an illegitimate one. The Jesus was as much 'of faith' as 'the Christ'. And so the contrast tended to fade away in mainstream scholarship.

However, while I have been thinking about and writing this book I have become increasingly convinced that to dismiss the recognition of the tension between Jesus and Christ so quickly is a mistake, and that this recognition is an important insight into what has happened down the church's history. Time and again, well before the rise of modern criticism, the church (and the Christ it has worshipped) has been challenged in the name of Jesus. Reform movements, many of which were ruthlessly persecuted by the church, used what they read in the Gospels about Jesus to question the life of the church when they felt that it had gone seriously wrong in some respect. And this kind of protest is still carried on today, with the same basically pre-critical attitude, not only within the churches but also by those outside them, who may be heard to say that they have time for Jesus, but not for the church.

So it would seem that to describe continuity between Jesus of Nazareth and the Christ of the church (in any case, to be accurate one should say 'Christs', and there, as we shall see in Chapter 4, the difficulties mount) in some such terms as 'Jesus who is the Christ' is somewhat naive and simplistic. What we see in the history of Christianity from the beginning to the present is the life of the churches (often accompanied by the rise of breakaway movements and their sympathizers) revolving round two focal points, not one: 'Jesus' and 'the Christ'. Of course these two focal points are intimately linked, but at the same time they are distinct enough to be set in opposition the one to the other and therefore really are two. (In Chapter 5 we shall be looking in more detail at the way in which 'Christ' developed from being merely the Greek equivalent of 'Messiah' to denote a cosmic figure.) It is not least the possibility of being able to appeal to 'Jesus' against 'the Christ' which has made the series of questions on which we are about to embark so complicated.

To give some indication of the way forward at this point: before we begin at the beginning with the Gospels and ask why there is so much dispute about precisely what Jesus said and did, it is important to try to establish some ground rules for the questioning and arguments. Arguing about religious beliefs is never a simple matter. All too often discussions get hopelessly bogged down because basic premises have not been made clear or complex concepts or factors are used as though they are basically quite simple. 'Ah,' the other party may say triumphantly when apparently forced into a corner, 'but what about the Holy Spirit?' Or, 'But you've left faith entirely out of it', 'but that's a mystery', and so on. Nor should we forget for a moment the darker side of the Christian tradition which has been there from the beginning: the way in which force has been used to suppress arguments and manipulate doctrine and doctrine has in turn be used as a means of manipulation.

I do not expect to convince every reader that my approach is the right one or the only possible one, but in the next chapter, about theology and truth, I have at least tried to indicate what that approach is. To sum it up, we cannot leave out of account the way in which at a certain point in history (say towards the end of the seventeenth century; I mention the Dutch Jewish philosopher Spinoza as a symbol), the status of the Christian tradition dramatically changed. Up to that point, the burden of proof had lain with those criticizing established religious tradition because that tradition could still in one way or another defend its claims to possession of the truth, but from then on the burden shifted so that it was for those defending particular traditional religious beliefs or institutions to explain and justify them in terms of a world-view the foundations of which had shifted from religious authority to the sciences in all their forms.

After the chapter on the Gospels, Chapter 4 looks at the kaleidoscopic variety of ways in which Christ has been presented down the centuries and at how Christianity itself has taken different shapes and has been preoccupied with different beliefs and styles of living in different periods, to such a degree that one can legitimately ask what the substance of the Christ of the church is and indeed whether Christianity has preserved an identity throughout. Chapter 5 explores the problems that are associated with the doctrine of the Incarnation, and shows the pressure under which it has come in recent years, along with the problems attached to attempts made to establish the uniqueness, finality or divinity of Jesus on a different basis, e.g. the assertion of the moral perfection of Jesus. The problems in Chapter 6 are those which go with the claim that Jesus is the supreme representative of humankind; the chapter goes on to examine the problems of putting Christ at the centre which are experienced by marginalized groups, particularly those as large as women and black people. Then it criticizes the view expressed in such terms as 'Whatever you may be suffering, Jesus suffered too, because he took the whole of humanity upon himself', and finally takes up the Stevie Smith quotation with which this book begins.

Chapter 7 looks at ethical questions connected with Jesus. Could his behaviour be said to have been perfect? Should Christians do as Jesus teaches? But what does he teach? And why does so much Christian moral teaching, from the New Testament on, seem to get along quite happily without referring to Jesus at all? Chapter 8 moves from this to the use of Jesus as a figure in the world of politics and power; it sees this tendency at work already in the New Testament, and with the official recognition of Christianity substantially reinforced in a variety of forms from the political theology of

Constantine to the very different political theologies of the present day. Chapter 9 is concerned with the common tendency to 'modernize' Jesus, to treat him as though he belonged to our age. How can a man from first-century Palestine possibly speak to our age and at the same time remain in his own, as he must, if we are to begin to understand him as a historical figure? Chapter 10 discusses some of the difficult problems relating to historical and cultural relativity. If the historical consciousness which is now part of our make-up introduces the problem of relativity by highlighting the changes between different periods and their world-views, and shows how ideas emerge through history, what is the authority of Christian doctrine? Chapter 11 looks at further Christian claims for the 'finality' of Christ, notably that he is the ultimate and supreme revelation of God and therefore that Christianity is the ultimate and supreme religion, along with the problems that go with those claims, in particular against the background of the world faiths.

By this stage a complex set of questions and problems will have been brought up, to which the mainstream Christian tradition has not produced satisfactory answers. Because these questions and problems are so complex and interrelated it was difficult to know, after looking at the Gospel evidence, in what order to discuss them; none of the possibilities I have considered has seemed entirely satisfactory, simply because of the complicated nature of the issues, and the present approach is not without its disadvantages. You may therefore find it more helpful, and indeed necessary, at this stage, to read some of the earlier chapters a second time in the light of what is said in the later chapters, in order to feel the full impact of the many dilemmas which have arisen. The end of Chapter 11 is a kind of watershed, and though Chapter 12 introduces one more question, from that point on the book becomes more positive. I have tried to end the book by reiterating the conviction which I expressed in the introduction that the asking of questions can be a positive contribution towards liberation from half-truths and towards greater understanding between those of differing faiths, and by indicating my own views of how one goes through, or lives with, or perhaps simply abandons as pointless, some of the problems and to suggest the way towards some answers. However, I want to make it quite clear at the start that the first eleven chapters of the book are different in status and content from the last two. The questions are all there independently of my choice of them, there for everyone to take note of or ignore, but there nevertheless. The answers are ones that I have chosen and which make sense to me, but others may not find them enough. I too may find them inadequate in due course, or may be able to replace them with better ones, but that is a different matter.

It is undoubtedly foolish to attempt to cover, even in passing, so many complicated questions in such a relatively short book. Many of them are discussed, and indeed answered, with enormous sophistication elsewhere, at very great length, and scholars will inevitably criticize me for being naive and superficial. My problem, however, is that I do not even begin to understand many of these complex, long, sophisticated (and also, it has to be said, often mutually contradictory) explanations – and I am not ashamed to say so publicly. I have tried to write a book that anyone who wishes to read has the possibility of understanding, as clearly and simply as I can do so. If that has disadvantages in other respects, then so be it; there is never any harm in simple questions, and indeed there is a classic simple question which I always associate with christology: 'Where are the emperor's clothes?'

While the main discussion of the relationship between Christianity and other faiths comes in Chapter 11, I want to end this chapter by saying something about Judaism. For Judaism is more than just an 'other faith'; it is the tradition out of which Christianity grew, and the links between it and Christianity are innumerable and close. Over the past two or three years I have been regularly involved in a Jewish-Christian discussion group which means a great deal to me, both for its friendship and also for the way in which its Jewish members have made me stand in their place and see Christianity through their eyes. I have not liked a lot of what I have seen of the Christian churches from their perspective, not least the way in which the man on the cross has been transformed into an all too imperialistic-Christian 'Lord of heaven and earth', and the way in which the Christian language of suffering, humility and sacrifice can so often (though not always) ring hollow against the experiences of the Jewish people, notoriously also at the hands of Christians themselves. Christian imperialism is a danger which takes a great many forms and is to be avoided like the plague.

I have also been made increasingly aware, above all by reading two or three recent books,[11] of the terrifying amount of antisemitism that there is within Christianity, beginning from the very pages of the New Testament, and taken over from there into so much of Christian liturgy and spirituality. At a time when we are being urged in some quarters to recover the 'traditional' faith in all its richness, it is worth remembering some of the 'richness' which that faith contains. Along with the virgin birth comes the argument from the 'prophecies' to Christ in the Old Testament, repeated each year at Christmas in countless carol services, an argument which infers that the Jews were blind and deaf because they could not see the Messiah who was prophesied so clearly in their own scriptures. It does not take much historical research to see where that leads.[12]

As I have said elsewhere,[13] if there is one thing which I miss in the Christian tradition that I find – always to my amazement, given its background – in the Jewish tradition, it is a touch of humour, the sound of laughter. By virtue of its subject matter this really is going to be a very serious book, and as I have written it I have felt saddened by the belligerence and earnestness of so many controversies over areas of which no one can know anything anyway, and regret that Christians never developed anything parallel to that great body of Jewish humour in the face of the most terrible absurdities. That could well be one of our greatest failings. Laughter is something which those in power can least afford to encourage, particularly when they are not certain of their authority. Its absence from the Christian tradition is a serious weakness.

One of the more illuminating recent systematic discussions of the nature of theology contained the comment that all Christian theologians should write as though they had a Jew looking over their shoulder.[14] Along with everything else, I have also tried to do that. I have also looked over a few Jewish shoulders myself, since I have often found Jewish reflections on our modern world more helpful than many of those by Christians, and it is with two of these that I want to end this introductory chapter. The first is from a Jewish psychiatrist reflecting on wholeness in the context of Judaism, but what he say applies equally to Christianity and anticipates a theme to which we shall be returning at the end of the book, though I discovered these words after I had written my final chapters:

In an epoch when all traditional communities throughout the

industrialized and industrializing world have been falling apart under the impact of revolutions, industrial, social and political, in a period when families are breaking up at a rate never before seen, and the lonely crowd is the metaphor of our time, it is no wonder so many break down and their lives fragment.

There never has been such a time when traditional answers have been found to be so wanting, and so many have been thrown back on their own personal resources. There never has been such a time when so many have found themselves forced to find their answers from their own resources, and so many feel their resources inadequate.

But, there is no going back for any of us, Jew or Gentile, no going back to the security of the old communities and the certainties of the old formulae and their repetition, though there are those who are trying, and the growth of fanaticism is an expression of this, as Nazism was the expression of an attempt to return to the mythical certainties of Teutonic tribalism.

This is a terrible time, a testing time, a time when God seems not here. Does he exist, or has he withdrawn, or has something happened to our consciousness that we no longer experience the Presence as our forefathers did? People try to storm heaven with drugs or meditation, they make strange fire and who can blame them?

This is a time of growing up, when the children must learn to be alone. All the excrescences are stripped away, and we are left naked and alone. We can shiver to death, or we can accept the challenge. Who will survive?

Yet, though we are naked we are not left with nothing. Enough remains for those who are desperate and determined and not too proud to learn. 'Who is wise? He who learns from all men.' If we are prepared to allow ourselves to be called into question... in fear and in trembling, swinging between doubt and certainty, a new garment can be woven, a seemly garment for each.

There are no collective solutions, only people tested in the fire of their painful search for truth, co-operating in the light of their experience of it. Out of this alone can grow a new experience of community.[15]

The second quotation comes from Dr Jonathan Magonet,

Principal of Leo Baeck College, London:

> At a time when revelation is not immediately apparent, then at least we can try to go for an honest evaluation of our situation today. If a Kafka, a Freud, a Karl Kraus tell us the truth about ourselves, then theirs are the voices that should be added to a contemporary religious consciousness... We cannot go back to nineteenth-century naivety; we know the risks of giving in to a contemporary barbarism – the religious task is to find the synthesis that re-establishes the balance between intellect and emotion, between self-centredness and altruism, between an anchoring in this world with its duties, responsibilities and enormous possibilities and a transcendent reality that gives perspective and meaning.[16]

This is the world against which the interpretation of Jesus of Nazareth has to find a meaning. And since it is our reality as sensitive, thoughtful, visionary men and women see it, it is in terms of the questions raised by that world that this interpretation must be made, not in terms of some past age that we may not even have understood properly. Moreover while those who have already found in Jesus a clue to how things are will want to pursue that clue – and it is no more than a clue; it is not an illuminated motorway sign – they also can never forget the question of those who have not found it: 'Why bother?'

2 | Christianity and Truth

In the Gospel attributed to St John, Jesus is made to say: 'I am the way, the truth and the life, no man comes to the Father but by me.' Over a long period, though within an increasingly restricted area of subject-matter, that statement has been understood to mean that all truth, in terms both of knowledge of God and knowledge of how to live an authentic human life, is to be found in Jesus. Jesus is the criterion of the truth, the truth of how things are. That truth may not yet be available fully, for there is a Spirit who will 'guide you into all truth', but that truth will be the truth that is to be found in Jesus, 'for he will take what is mine and declare it to you'. These words have exercised enormous power down history and still have great emotive force for Christians today; indeed, Christianity is flourishing – or at any rate declining less – precisely among those who are moved by them and confidently declare them to be 'gospel truth'. They have been, and still are, a source of confidence and certainty that to be a Christian is to be right. A corollary of this is the view, held with varying degrees of sophistication, that all those who are not Christians fall short of the truth; that if they are of another faith that faith is somehow inferior; that if they have no faith at all they are lost; and that everyone will have to come round to Jesus Christ in the end. Of course, in these days of inter-faith dialogue and within a multi-cultural society, the more sensitive Christians do not put it quite like that; but under the influence of John 14.6 and John 16.13ff. and the even stronger affirmations to this effect that can be found down Christian history, their reticence is often politeness. Press them hard, and they will not go back on the basic conviction: Jesus is *the* truth.

But the question 'What is truth?' is not the monopoly of the cynical Pilate in the same Gospel.[1] It is a legitimate question to put to the Christian tradition. Ask how the statement that Jesus is 'the truth' works out in detail over a variety of different areas, and difficulties begin to emerge. Some of them have been there from the start, and over long periods have been kept at bay by Christians who have used social sanctions, censorship and violence to suppress them; others have emerged particularly as a result of the rise of modern science since around the seventeenth century. And they have led to a crisis within the churches. Those who want to go on making the traditional Christian affirmations and to go on believing that these affirmations actually contain final and unchanging truth, which only needs to be reinterpreted, are faced with other practising Christians who feel that the world has changed to such a degree that what is said about Jesus and Christianity generally must change also, and that this is only to be expected, since all we ever have at our disposal is fallible knowledge and approximation, 'through a glass darkly'.[2] The latter also believe that they are in search of the truth, but believe that in seeking that truth they must be led in the direction indicated by the development of modern thought, research and knowledge, even if it points to the need for substantial change. Nowhere, inevitably, is the problem more acute than in connection with Jesus – as has been evident from the degree of controversy in Britain recently over issues like the virgin birth and the resurrection.

It would have been healthier if this clash had been and could continue to be argued out within the churches in more depth. As it is, the churches have allowed the crisis to fester in an unhealthy way by attempting to keep out the expression of questioning and doubt with dogmatic assertion and protest, coupled with a kind of 'not in the street or you will frighten the horses' mentality. The churches often show signs of a double standard. Too many public Christian statements, and therefore those who make them, seem to have that characteristic which Adrian Hastings attributed so nicely to Randall Davidson, Archbishop of Canterbury: 'His weakness... was reluctance to state in public what he felt and even wrote in private.'[3] The criticism is often voiced that a particular view is something that could be said by a university professor but not by a bishop; is all right for the study or the university lecture room but not for the pulpit; acceptable in a hardback book but not in a paperback. And such comments are made not just on statements relating to peripheral matters; they are made on statements relating to the very heart of Christianity and its most important claims; in short, to its truth.

Here is a particularly striking example, to which I was a witness. A distinguished professor of theology who that year held the senior position in his church, took the opportunity of an official visit to London to address a university seminar. In the questions following his paper, the discussion got on to the knotty problem of criteria for truth in theology. 'When theology students first come to my class,' said the professor, 'I put a five-pound note on the desk and say that I will hand it over to anyone who by the end of the term can produce one satisfactory criterion for theological truth. It has yet to be taken.' His comment evoked no surprise within the seminar, but if he had put down his five-pound note at the main assembly of his church...

Another way of putting it would be to say that Christianity always runs the risk of being turned into a less than desirable ideology, in the bad sense of the word, and that the present is a time when that risk is very considerable indeed. Ideology is not a particularly easy word to define, but it is an extremely useful one here, so I shall try to explain what I understand by it. 'Ideology' is widely used in political contexts, and the term is particularly associated with Karl Marx, but it can be used in a much wider sense. Here it denotes any systematic view of the world, any description of reality, whether it is political, religious or scientific; it can denote not only the content of a belief or world-view but also its framework and the way in which it is presented, and since an ideology always goes with a particular group of people who hold it, it has sociological connotations as well.

In some contexts, 'ideology' can be a neutral word, but in the way in which I am using it, and in which it has most often been used, it has negative, pejorative connotations. Here ideology is used to denote the way in which a group (usually, for obvious reasons, a group with which one disagrees) disguises in its thinking and attitudes the real nature of a situation, since to recognize that reality would not be in its interests. If you are not a completely convinced member of that group which you accuse of being ideological, it is easier to notice what the group overlooks. Its members are convinced that the way they look at the world is the way things always have been and necessarily are; whereas outsiders are much more aware of the extent to which the ideas by which the group lives are social, historical products. The outsider, then, sees the group as claiming absolute and universal truth for views which seem to be held on the basis of illusions and illegitimate arguments and to be backed up by social pressures within the group.[4]

It is possible to illustrate what this general statement means specifically in terms of Christianity: liberal and radical Christians will readily recognize, say, the claims of fundamentalists or creationists as ideological in the way I have outlined. One could take this even further and argue that the institutional church as it now is runs the risk of being as alien and incomprehensible in its thought and actions to those who recognize the contribution of modern knowledge, research and insight as, say, Plymouth Brethren, Jehovah's Witnesses and other forms of sectarian Christianity are to most Anglicans and Roman Catholics. If that is the case, as far as its claims to truth are concerned, traditional Christianity appears to those looking at it from the outside to be in precisely the same boat as Marxism, Fascism or any other ideology; indeed some of the parallels between it and them become dangerously close. Christianity, too, has rewritten history to suit itself; Christianity, too, has exterminated opponents in large numbers. On such occasions has its justification been any different from that of totalitarian states? At the least these are questions which Christians have to answer; and they have to answer them by defending and explaining the nature of their truth-claims.

Those who have written at length about ideology have also made another important point about it. Ideology is not sheer error or illusion. In his *Ideology and Utopia* Karl Mannheim said that ideology occupies a position between 'a simple lie at one pole, and an error which is the result of a distorted and faulty conceptual apparatus at the other. It refers to a sphere of errors, psychological in nature, which, unlike deliberate deception, are not intentional, but follow inevitably and unwittingly from certain causal determinants.'[5] Nicholas Lash said virtually the same thing in a slightly different way; he defined ideology as 'a cognitive grasp on reality unwittingly distorted through the influence of power and particular interests'.[6]

One can again illustrate this in a Christian context, for example that of fundamentalist evangelical Christianity: if a person has a conversion experience of 'Jesus as Lord and Saviour' he or she is likely soon to gravitate to a close-knit group of like-minded people (if indeed the experience itself was not a consequence of membership of such a group). That group will hold distinctive views about biblical inspiration, about the person of Jesus, about moral behaviour, the marks of a Christian, and so on. The person joining the group will take over such views, not as a result of having examined their soundness and viability, but simply because they are the watchwords of the group, the passwords of membership. To question them is not just to ask intellectual questions, but to threaten the cohesion of the group. In this kind of situation, it would seem by most criteria that ideology as I have described it is in control and that the question of truth gets short shrift.

I hope that by now it has become clear what I mean by talking of Christianity in terms of being an ideology in the bad sense of the word and also why the question of the truth of Christianity is so important that it must occupy us right at the beginning of this book before we get on to the more detailed questions about Jesus. But again, what is truth, and how is it that Christianity can even begin to run the risk of being regarded as an ideology by those looking at it from an uncommitted, outsider's historical or sociological perspective when it contains within its tradition such strong assertions of its truth and finality?

As I have indicated, the present problems over Christianity have been caused by its inability to cope adequately with intellectual challenges to its views and its tendency to fudge the issues, as though the challenges had not been made in the first place. Since at least the middle of the last century Christians have been manifestly faced with the need to answer an enormous number of new questions about their beliefs and practices: from the natural sciences, above all with the theory of evolution; from biblical criticism and all that arises from realization of the nature of our historical consciousness, along with the sense of relativism which that brings; from Marx and Freud and the extensive critiques which have followed from their pioneering work in political theory and psychology; from sociology; from closer contact with, deeper knowledge of and indeed social pressure from other religions. And all these come on top of earlier questions, left unresolved, extending well back before the Reformation (which, though it is so often presented as a great watershed, is in fact far less significant than two other milestones at which we shall be looking shortly).

As I indicated earlier, the crisis which these complex developments have created for the churches is that rather than being able to assume that Christianity continues to be true unless proved otherwise, they must now explain how Christian belief is still viable and what form it may truthfully take in the light of the accumulation of insights in the areas of science, history, psychology and so on over several centuries. So great and so all-pervasive has been the change brought about by developments within these disciplines that we even look at the world (including Christianity) in a different way. For example, an ongoing theme of this book will be the way in which, when confronted with the question of what something is (that something can range from Christian belief, Western society, the scientific world-view to the papacy or the Anglican communion), the automatic tendency is to reply in terms of how it came to be.[7] In those terms, many complex questions can be answered – provisionally, and subject to constant revision – by outlining the details of a historical development. On the assumptions that underlie this historical approach, we live in a society the science and technology of which has opened our eyes to new dimensions of the universe and improved the potential quality of our lives out of all recognition, and in the process has challenged authoritative statements made by the churches and proved them to be unsound. (I am not forgetting the cost at which this has been achieved nor how a minority of the world lives at the expense of the majority, but to dwell on that does not alter the point under discussion.)

The doubts over the truth of Christianity and its claims about Jesus to which this led are so strong specifically because they are prompted by an independent quest for how things are. This quest has relied on its own criteria for investigating the claims of the churches, and because it has so often found those traditional claims wanting where they can be checked (e.g. in the realms of history, geography, science), it has become increasingly sceptical of them where they cannot. It is because there is that by which Christianity can be tested – and found wanting, because there is now another independent, alternative source of truth-claims – that Christianity can be accused of being an ideology. Shortly, we shall see in more detail just where the two sources of truth come to clash. For the moment, I want only to recall just how the second source of truth came into being. For that we need to take ourselves back roughly a thousand years.

In her book *The Study of the Bible in the Middle Ages*, Beryl Smalley portrayed a world in which the Bible, and the tradition based on it, was the sole source and focal point of all knowledge. This world was indeed a narrow and constricted one, rather like the waist of an old-fashioned hour-glass or egg-timer with the wider world of classical and Hellenistic antiquity above and the even wider post-Renaissance world below. However, since the mediaeval world determined so much of later Christianity, whether positively or negatively, and in the West Christianity has come down to us through it, it is one that still concerns us.

In the Middle Ages the Bible was a school book and the source of teaching for liberal arts, the devotional book of the religious, the authority for professional theologians. The Old Testament influenced ideas on Christian priesthood, not least prompting the activities of popes, bishops and priests in the political sphere, so that indirectly it also influenced princes and politics; the New Testament was an inspiration for many reform movements, inside the churches and outside them.[8] Indeed the Bible was all in all. From St Augustine onwards it had been accepted that 'the book of mysteries was also an encyclopedia which contained all knowledge useful to man, both sacred and profane'.[9] There might have been many differences over how it should be interpreted, but no one doubted its essential truth, and even had they done so, there would have been no convincing way of substantiating such doubts. The Bible was thought to contain authoritative information about everything from astronomy to music. It reigned supreme. The Bible and its view of the world dominated all study of history, geography and astronomy, to mention just three areas which we shall be looking at more closely.

However, as the Middle Ages came to a close the situation changed dramatically. The two areas in which the pressures first arose that were to shatter the biblically-based view of the nature of earth and heaven and as a result to cause a revision of the range and more particularly the duration of human history were astronomy and geography.[10] There were good reasons why these areas in particular raised problems. Both as a result of an age-old interest in astrology and because of the use of the stars in navigation, astronomy was the science which had accumulated the most important collection of data from observations and accurate mathematical methods, capable of being used for the construction of hypotheses. Navigation and exploration were motivated by the quest for new lands which could be exploited for profit.

Nevertheless, so well established was the traditional Christian view that it took a long time for major changes to come about, although the information on which they were to be based was already available. How long these changes took depended on local religious and cultural conditions. There was often great reluctance, and as was to be so often the case later, every kind of device was adopted in defence of the old view before the new one was grudgingly accepted. In astronomy, for example, imaginary circles (epicycles) were introduced into the paths of planets to rescue the old Ptolemaic theory,[11] until pressure became too great to prevent the 'paradigm-shift', that point at which pressures on one apparently coherent complex of explanations becomes so great that the whole complex has to be abandoned in favour of a new perspective and a new organizing principle.[12]

To illustrate how a final, last-ditch attempt was made, both in astronomy and in geography and history, to reconcile the new discoveries with what was said in the Bible and thus to avoid the problem of two conflicting sources of truth, I have chosen two representative seventeenth-century figures in whom we can see the beginnings of the problem with which Christianity is still vainly wrestling, one of whom is far better known than the other: Galileo Galilei and Isaac de la Peyrère. They are worth dwelling on, because what happened in the seventeenth century is still comparatively unknown to Christians and is, as I have already said, far more important in the long run than the Reformation, over which so much ink has been spilt.

Galileo Galilei has become the symbol of the new, Copernican astronomical view of the world, and his condemnation by the Roman Inquisition in 1633 has not only been much discussed but even dramatized.[13] Whether he or the church which condemned him were as dramatic subjects as Bertolt Brecht makes out is, however, another matter. It would certainly be wrong to cast the Roman Catholic church as the villain of the affair and to accuse it of having shown special intolerance, since the new astronomical theories began to be condemned in Protestantism at around the same time.[14]

The threat of these new theories was seen to be directed at all of the Christian tradition. Secondly, it would be wrong to regard Galileo as a zealous opponent of the Catholic church. He was not. Thirdly, of course, at that time the evidence was still far from conclusive – which makes what actually happened all the more tragic.

Galileo was a man utterly convinced of the truth of the new system, but at the same time aware that it went against the teachings of the Bible and the church. So he was concerned to find a way of reconciling two apparently conflicting truths. That is what gives him symbolic value in the history of theology as well as in the history of science, because he was virtually the first representative of the many who were to face similar problems over the years to come. How Galileo attempted to resolve his dilemma is shown in an open letter which he wrote in 1615 to Christina, Grand Duchess of Tuscany, the mother of Grand Duke Cosimo II in whose service he was employed as court mathematician. It has been said to be one of the most remarkable documents in the history of biblical criticism.[15]

Galileo begins by stating his problem. The Bible often says that the sun moves and the earth stands still, and the Bible is inerrant and does not deceive. On this basis any view to the contrary is to be condemned. How is this problem to be resolved? His reply is fascinating. Scripture and nature both proceed from the word of God, but nature is inexorable and immutable, whereas the Bible often speaks figuratively to accommodate itself to human understanding. Once evidence emerges in the scientific sphere as to a particular state of affairs, that must be accepted; the authority of the Bible may not be made binding on scientific questions. But Galileo pleads for a recognition of the difference between knowledge which has a demonstrable basis, which does not depend on interpretation, and knowledge over which argument is legitimately possible, where interpretation is involved. There is no way of suppressing the former kind of truth, whether by silencing individuals, banning books or even prohibiting the study of authority altogether. Even the Pope is powerless here.

The letter is important because it contains so clear a statement that the new developments in astronomy represent a second source of knowledge. From now on, theology and the church also had to take note of new established facts, facts which conflicted with what had previously been asserted as true on another basis. Galileo hoped that the new discoveries would be capable of reconciliation with the church's teaching and interpretation of the Bible. But that was not to be. The church responded in a way which was all too familiar. He was condemned, and the problem which he had discovered was thus made infinitely more serious in the longer term. And sadly, as we shall now see, virtually the same thing was to happen in a different field with Isaac de la Peyrère.[16]

Although a wealth of new information about the geography of the world flooded in throughout the sixteenth century as a result of the voyages of discovery, it began to make its impact only around the latter period of Galileo's life. Until then the geographical view of the world had remained essentially that of the Bible. The inhabited earth was understood to be surrounded on every side by the ocean, beyond which was the darkness. Palestine lay at the centre, with Jerusalem as its navel, and the earth was divided into three continents: Asia, Africa and Europe, inhabited by the three sons of Noah. The maps on which this geography was portrayed were circular. As the new discoveries were made, the maps changed; it took longer for the consequences to be realized and stated.

The geographical problem was that the new areas which had been discovered had inhabitants of which the Bible was quite ignorant, and these seemed to have no connection with the history recounted in the Bible and no religion which could be related to the God to whom that Bible bore witness. This increased the pressure to challenge the biblical account of history and with it the biblical chronology, which the Reformers, for all their questioning of Christian tradition in other respects, had retained. Luther, for example, did not hesitate to correct other chronologies of the world by the Bible because he regarded it as being the most reliable source.[17] The Bible proved history; conversely, history supported and explained the Bible. Such importance was attached to maintaining the accuracy of the biblical record that in some quarters preposterous solutions were sought. For example, the difficulty caused by the discovery that on traditional datings based on the Bible Pharaohs had been reigning even before the creation of the world was solved by arguing that the Egyptians had simply invented the first eight dynasties to enhance their glory.[18] However, such desperate expedients hardly proved convincing: Chaldaean and

Chinese chronology raised precisely the same difficulty, and it was impossible to assert that these chronologies had also been falsified.

The more doubt was cast on biblical chronology, the more questionable became the biblical account of the whole history of the world, and above all the geography which it presented.[19] This is where Isaac de la Peyrère saw contradictions which he attempted to resolve. De la Peyrère was a Frenchman who lived in Bordeaux. Writing around twenty years after the condemnation of Galileo, he listed the sources of his suspicions of biblical history. 'Ancient Chaldaean calculations, the earliest documents from Egypt, Ethiopia and Scythia, newly discovered areas of the earth including those unknown lands to which Dutchmen had sailed and whose inhabitants probably did not descend from Adam...':[20] all seemed to tell a different story from that recorded in the biblical account. How was this new information to be reconciled with the traditional story?

The title of de la Peyrère's book, *Pre-Adamites*, written in France but for safety's sake published anonymously in Holland, indicates his solution. Like Galileo, he could not doubt what had been discovered, but equally he wanted to preserve the authority of the Bible so that there were still not two sources of truth but one. He expressed his aim in a rather moving way:

> To reconcile Genesis and the gospel with the astronomy of the men of old, the history and philosophy of the most ancient of peoples. So that if the astronomers of the Chaldaeans were to come, or the Egyptians with their primaeval dynasties, if Aristotle himself were to come and with him the chronologers and philosophers of the Chinese, or if an at present unknown but perceptive people were to be discovered in the south or the north who had an ancient culture and tradition extending over tens of thousands of years, each from his position could readily accept the creation stories and happily become Christians.[21]

Or, as he put the aim from another perspective, it was to 'reconcile faith with reason'.

In his book de la Peyrère was so diplomatic and conciliatory that he actually put his solution first. The Bible itself suggests that there were men before Adam and Adam was the father only of the Jewish race. De la Peyrère took as his evidence St Paul's Epistle to the

Romans, 5.12-14, the passage beginning 'as sin came into the world through one man and death through sin, and so death spread to all men...'; having convinced himself that this passage was a reference to men living before Adam he could reinterpret many passages in the Bible to support his theory (e.g. who were the men of whom Cain was afraid after he had killed Abel?).[22] His whole argument is a mere curiosity to us now; but the discovery of what de la Peyrère thought to be a solution enabled him to look the real problems straight in the face, and to take many of the historical statements of ancient authorities more seriously than had been done before.

However, all this was to no avail. De la Peyrère suffered very much the same fate as Galileo; on a visit to Holland, which was at that time under Spanish control, he fell into the hands of the Inquisition and was forced to issue a recantation. The publication of his book had unleashed a storm of indignation and protest: it was publicly burned in Paris by the city executioner. Nor, as in the case of the new astronomical theory, was the Roman Catholic church his only ecclesiastical opponent: Lutherans and Reformed alike joined in seeing his views as 'the most pestilential theory ever held in the church'.[23] The disadvantage of this reaction was, of course, that since there was no possibility of de la Peyrère's solution being accepted, it disappeared, and all that remained was his clear statement of the problems. Since accommodation did not prove possible, here the only conclusion that could be drawn was that of the existence of two conflicting sources of truth.

There had been clashes between two apparent sources of truth before the seventeenth century. A more sophisticated account of developments in Christian thought before Galileo and de la Peyrère than I have given would have had to note in some detail the relationships between Christianity and the dominant philosophies of particular periods: first Platonism and then Aristotelianism.[24] The latter, in particular, caused many difficulties. But when there was a difference between Aristotle and Holy Scripture, this was simply a matter of maintaining one conviction against another, and since on the scriptural side the conviction was one backed up by divine revelation, whereas the other had been gained by inductive argument, in the Christian world there was no doubt as to which would emerge victorious. There was no lasting difficulty because neither position could be proved – or disproved – in the strict sense.

All this had to change in the end, whatever the difficulties and the opposition, once mathematics and empirical evidence came into the picture. Galileo and de la Peyrère were not defending their own opinions against others; they felt confronted with 'laws', with evidence quite independent of their own personal views. And so began that long process which is the beginning of all those problems that we still face today.

The story of this break-up of the old view of the world and the undeniable development of two conflicting sources of truth, the Bible and the world of the sciences, thus begins much earlier than is usually realized, and not in fact in that area which theologians so often see as the cradle of scepticism, Enlightenment Germany.[25] The next important chapters in fact take place in England: the scholastic-type theology of Lutheranism put a brake on developments in Germany, which is often thought to be the pioneer in this area.

It is important to realize just how wide the area of controversy had become by this stage, at the end of the seventeenth century and the beginning of the eighteenth century. It was not just theological and academic in a narrow sense, but political and constitutional. The Bible was so to speak entangled in a whole nexus of contexts. For example, the Old Testament had long been thought to offer guidance about 'king and state, about a commonwealth organized under divine statutes, about law and property, about war, about ritual and ceremony, about priesthood, continuity and succession... because these were controversial matters in church and state they generated deep differences in biblical interpretation. It was precisely because the Bible was assumed on all hands to be authoritative that it stimulated new notions about its own nature. It was because men sought answers to problems of life and society, as well as of thought and belief, that the Bible itself stimulated critical modes of understanding itself.'[26] It was from these areas that the Bible slowly became disentangled, to such a degree that it is difficult for those brought up in the secular second half of the twentieth century to realize how great was the role it once played in society as a whole, as well as in the more familiar areas of history and doctrine.[27]

Finally, at a relatively late stage in the controversy, in Germany in the second half of the eighteenth century, against this background of the dissolution of the old order there were raised those first questions about the real nature of Jesus which mark the beginning of what is now almost universally referred to as 'the quest of the historical Jesus'.[28]

I have introduced this rather more general discussion about Christianity and truth, along with the briefest of outlines of the coming into being of two conflicting sources of truth, because, as I said in the previous chapter, it seems to me important that discussion about Jesus should take place within some sort of ordered framework. Concepts have histories; cultures change; and therefore even the same statement repeated down the centuries will be understood differently, depending on the background against which it is set. The problems of history and Christian doctrine will occupy us more fully in Chapters 5 and 10, but right from the beginning we must recognize that Christian belief does not exist in a vacuum but interacts with its environment and changes from age to age.

To talk, for example, of the uniqueness of Christianity and the finality of Christ against the background of the first-century world was very different from making the same claims against the background of our world. Between us and Jesus there is a great gulf fixed, and our world is separated from his by the revolution of which I have been describing the beginnings. To suppose that we can move readily between the present and the Graeco-Roman world of the first century and its immediate sequel is to delude ourselves.

Theologians in particular and those who appeal to a traditionalist kind of doctrine often seem less aware of this than they should be, and it is perhaps a reflection on their lack of insight here that to find a telling description of the impact of the revolution we have just touched on we do best to go to some comments by Lord Hailsham, published in *The Times* in the mid-1970s.

Obviously the allegedly miraculous, whether it be the Virgin Birth, the feeding of the five thousand, or the resurrection itself, presents difficulties of credibility to the scientifically-minded modern man. But far more serious to my mind is the time-scale which the Bible presents, which underlies its whole view of human history. It is not the talking snake and the miraculous trees which puzzle one about the Genesis story of the creation, nor the difficulties of accommodation in the overcrowded ark. These can easily be explained as allegory or myth or a mixture or both. But to think of the world as about 6,000 years old enables the facts of the New Testament to be regarded easily as a culmination (as it was presented in the first century) or relatively easily as the prelude to a climax (which it has become between the second and the twentieth). And when it has come to be believed that the human race has been present on the planet for millions of years and may, for aught we know, continue to be present for an indefinite time in the future, the uniqueness of the Christian religion requires to be demonstrated in quite a different way.

That again is something to which we shall be returning in a later chapter.

But perhaps it is not fair to end this chapter by blaming the theologians. Rather, we might pause for a moment to consider at just what cost the pioneering figures among them have pressed forward their researches. We have already seen how Galileo and de la Peyrère suffered excommunication for their views. That such persecution was not just a Christian monopoly emerges from the way in which before the end of the century the Jewish philosopher Benedict de Spinoza of Amsterdam, among many other things himself also an early biblical critic, was expelled from the synagogue by his fellow-believers.[29] By this time the evidence in favour of that source of truth which is not the Bible had grown so quickly that, as I said earlier in passing, it was no longer a question of taking one's stand on the Bible and seeking to explain new phenomena in a way which did not contradict it. One took one's stand on the world-view that had emerged from science and greater knowledge of the world, and questioned everything, Bible and 'revealed' religion included, from that. The burden of proof had shifted, the perspective had changed, and from then on Christians – and indeed those of other religious traditions – had to face the possibility that in reality there was again only one source of truth: and this time it was not the Bible or any religious authority. Our world is very different from that of Spinoza – the various sciences have brought countless changes of perspective in between – but the basic problem has not changed.

Galileo, de la Peyrère and Spinoza were not arguing in a forum in which there was freedom to present one's views, a forum in which the force of argument was the only one that prevailed. Before them countless predecessors had been burnt at the stake or otherwise executed for their views. After them the pressure was to go on in a rather milder way – if you can call mild being compelled to resign your university chair for views which in the long run inevitably had to be accepted, being excommunicated from a church which had trained you in a celibate life to devote your whole self to it, or being subjected to other forms of ecclesiastical pressure. A modern-day version of Hebrews 11, listing the heroes of the quest for a new understanding of the Christian faith, could select a long list of names from the nineteenth century including those of David Friedrich Strauss,[30] F.D.Maurice,[31] Robertson Smith,[32] Alfred Loisy[33] and George Tyrrell,[34] whose views before long became widely current within, and even officially recognized by, the churches. And even today the names of theologians like Hans Küng,[35] Edward Schille-beeckx,[36] Leonardo Boff,[37] Jacques Pohier[38] and John Hick[39] still appear in the headlines in the same cause for views which will doubtless eventually be accepted in much the same way.

But as Galileo told the Pope of his day, no matter how much of this goes on, it cannot stop the truth; and it certainly cannot help us over the questions we ask about our authentic nature and destiny, of which Jesus has been the paramount symbol. Of course it is possible to build up a religious tradition on a set of beliefs which must be adhered to on pain of being rejected from the community, and it is even possible within such a tradition to find a good deal of warmth, comfort and security. But the religious quest has always been about something more than warmth, comfort and security, and it has always involved a vision greater than of that which is made by human hands.

However, for long that quest has been associated above all with the person of Jesus, who has been its paramount symbol. How does that symbol stand up to modern questioning? It is to that issue that we now turn.

3 | What can we really know about Jesus?

There is a good deal that we probably do know about Jesus; the trouble is that we can rarely, if ever, be sure precisely what it is. Though that comment may sound somewhat cryptic, it seems to me to be the best description of the present state of research into the Gospels.[1] Because of the very nature of historical research, discussion about Jesus always contains countless approximations, and one of the most confident of recent studies nevertheless concedes that 'it can still be argued that we can have no reliable historical knowledge about Jesus with regard to anything that really matters'.[2] Parallels to such a verdict could easily be found in a variety of other modern works.

That may be the conclusion of many New Testament scholars, but before accepting it we need to know rather more about how it is arrived at. Unfortunately, however, I know of no book to recommend which spells out the difficulties that make such a conclusion necessary, taking the reader through them step by step, though it is easy to see why such a book has yet to be written, because the issues – and the evidence – are so complicated. So I must attempt an inevitably brief and summary account. But where does one begin?

I have chosen as a starting point a classic book by the present Bishop of Salisbury, John Austin Baker, entitled *The Foolishness of God*. It has been much praised ever since its first appearance in 1970 and is generally still regarded as a positive statement of Christian belief. Certainly John Baker is not a radical. This is what he says:

If it could ever be proved that the Gospels consisted throughout of completely accurate material for a biography of Jesus, the traditional Christian faith would collapse in ruins. This can hardly be stressed too strongly, especially to those Christians who are convinced that an orthodox faith rests on the factual reliability of the Bible in general and on the status of the Gospels in particular as precise records of the words and acts of Jesus, and of the incidents of his life. Such a conviction is very nearly the reverse of the truth.[3]

To illustrate this point, he takes three fundamental elements in traditional Christian belief about Jesus: his sinlessness, his infallibility and his awareness that he was God made man. After advancing powerful arguments against all these elements he concludes:

Any attempt to treat the Gospels as in their entirety an accurate factual record would both make it necessary to abandon any doctrine of true incarnation and at the same time render it impossible to resolve the contradictions of the texts in any rational manner. In fact the conflicts of evidence are such that the Gospels cannot be said to give united support to any view of Jesus, orthodox or heterodox. The total picture does not hang together; and unless we are prepared to believe in a Jesus who was both confused and confusing cannot be correct.[4]

John Baker's remarks, which would be accepted by most theologians, tell us clearly two things. First, that there is tension between traditional Christian doctrine and the Gospel record; and secondly, that there is a considerable amount of contradiction within the Gospel record. The tension between the Gospel record and Christian doctrine is something that we shall look at in more detail in Chapter 5. Here we shall be concerned with the contradictions within the Gospels. As John Baker tells us, these contradictions are what makes the 'quest of the historical Jesus', the attempt to arrive at some firm conclusions about who Jesus was, really imperative.

There is no question that we do know a great deal more about the background to the life of Jesus than we did, and that that background knowledge is steadily growing. The work of Jewish and Christian scholars and specialists in classical antiquity, with new material made available through archaeological exploration, is constantly enlarging and clarifying the world of the first century of the Christian era. And the questions that are being asked are becoming increasingly sophisticated. They are more open than they used to be, and they are no longer so dictated by a concern to keep the biblical Jesus in line with traditional doctrine. But whatever advances have been made, scholars have to agree on one necessary limitation: the evidence for Jesus is always going to be limited to the Gospels themselves. No one seriously doubts that Jesus ever existed, though that has been argued from time to time; but historical sources outside the New Testament are so scanty that their information could easily be written on a postcard[5] and they do not tell us anything of substantial interest. So the 'quest for the historical Jesus' is essentially about how we read the Gospels.

The tension between the Jesus of history and the Christ of faith at which John Baker first hints has come to be symbolized by the writings of Hermann Samuel Reimarus during the second half of the eighteenth century. Reimarus was a teacher of oriental languages in Hamburg who, in a book published (safely!) after his death, claimed that he could distinguish the real life and teaching of Jesus from the 'false account' which had come down through the church.[6] Perhaps he would not have achieved such prominence in our century had he not been seen as a kindred spirit by Albert Schweitzer. Schweitzer, as well as being a gifted musician and doctor, made Reimarus the starting point in a chronicle of the attempts of nineteenth-century scholars to discover Jesus as he really was. (The study of the life of Jesus, he wrote, 'set out in quest of the historical Jesus, believing that when it had found him it could bring him straight into our time as a teacher and saviour. It loosed the bonds by which he had been riveted for centuries to the stony rocks of church doctrine and rejoiced to see life and movement coming into the figure once more, and the historical Jesus advancing, as it seems, to meet it.')[7]

Indeed Schweitzer entitled his book *Von Reimarus zu Wrede* (*From Reimarus to Wrede*: William Wrede was a German New Testament scholar contemporary with Schweitzer himself, who among other things argued that the passages in the synoptic Gospels in which Jesus is made to command certain of those with whom he comes into contact to conceal the fact that they have been cured, and other passages suggesting an element of secrecy, were the creation of the early church to explain why Jesus was not recognized as Messiah, the so-called 'messianic secret').[8] In its English translation, Schweitzer's book was entitled *The Quest of the Historical Jesus*, and it is still indispensable for understanding one of the main problems facing those who study the Gospels, the constant tendency of those who seek to describe Jesus to portray him in their own image.

As Schweitzer pointed out, those who went in search of the historical Jesus found not so much Jesus as themselves. Rather than reading what the Gospels said, they were projecting their own image on to the Gospel texts.

Each individual created him in accordance with his own character. There is no historical task which so reveals a man's true self as the writing of a life of Jesus. No vital force comes into the figure unless a man breathes into it all the hate or all the love of which he is capable. The stronger the love, the stronger the hate, the more life-like is the figure produced.[9]

So true is Schweitzer's diagnosis and so telling his approach that once one has understood the point he is making it is possible to see how not only the books which he surveyed but also virtually all the books written since his time have the same character (and even Schweitzer could not escape his own trap when he came to say what picture of Jesus he himself would paint).[10]

We shall be looking in due course at the different ways in which writers about Jesus have portrayed him. For the moment, all we need to note is how those who set out to write about Jesus tend to end up writing about themselves. The main reason for this is that the Gospel records leave so many gaps; there is so much they do not tell us, and what they do tell us is often so contradictory that anyone attempting to fill out the story has to resort to conjecture and imagination. Subjectivity inevitably creeps in, and that leads to the great variety that can be seen, the result of different interests and concerns, as well as of different arguments from the fragmentary evidence.

Suppose you were to try, nevertheless, to write yet another account of Jesus, how would you have to go about it? Your sources are four Gospels. Using the results of the long researches of others[11] you find that one Gospel, that attributed to John, stands clearly apart. Its Jesus seems to talk in a different way from the Jesus of the other Gospels; the chronology and geography of his ministry differ.

The other three Gospels are so closely related that you can print them in columns side by side. The synopsis is widely used by students, but you would be hard put to find a copy in any parish church or Bible study group, for all their emphasis on the importance of reading the Bible thoroughly. One wonders why.

The similarity between the texts of the three evangelists and in particular the similarity in the basic order in which they present the story of Jesus is so remarkable that there must be some relationship between them. Scholars have argued at length over the precise nature of this relationship, but the accepted explanation is that the Gospel of Mark came first, and that Matthew and Luke each used Mark for their Gospels, together with another source which was made up of sayings of Jesus.[12]

A first decision to be made is how much importance one attaches to John and how much to the Synoptic Gospels. Choices have to be made, because it is impossible completely to harmonize the two traditions. The majority of scholars see John as being later than the other three Gospels,[13] as a meditation on the tradition in which the author and his community[14] have exercised a good deal of their own creativity; so although for a while during the nineteenth century John was a favourite basis for a life of Jesus,[15] scholars nowadays who are concerned to try to get back to Jesus of Nazareth as he was concentrate on the Synoptics.

As one looks carefully at Matthew, Mark and Luke set down in parallel columns, the problems really do begin to multiply. Where all three Gospels have the same episode, quite often Matthew and Luke make significant alterations to the way in which Mark recounts it.[16] Not only do they alter the narrative, but they even change the words attributed to Jesus.[17] It soon becomes clear as one notes the way in which Matthew and Luke do this that the changes are not made because they are concerned to give a more accurate picture. There are theological reasons behind their alterations; in other words, they are altering what they find in front of them to make a point relating to their own beliefs which they feel to be important. Taken together, all these changes begin to add up to a different portrait of Jesus in each Gospel.[18]

The problems intensify when Matthew and Luke leave Mark and produce their own account; because the Gospel of Mark begins with the baptism of Jesus and ends with the women leaving the empty tomb, saying nothing to anyone 'because they were afraid',[19] the points at which Matthew and Luke diverge most are where our curiosity is at its greatest: over the birth of Jesus and over the resurrection. Sorting out the Gospel evidence on the resurrection is one of the most difficult of all problems, because in Matthew and Luke (as indeed also in John) the risen Christ who appears is so much the creation of the evangelist's theology: one couldn't imagine the Matthaean Risen Christ appearing at the end of Luke and vice versa.[20]

Christopher Evans, who has devoted a whole book to the question of the resurrection in the New Testament, has concluded:

However detailed the analysis, it would not diminish the impression that it is not simply difficult to harmonize these traditions, but quite impossible... For what have to be combined are not a number of scattered pieces from an originally single matrix, but separate expressions of the Easter faith. Each of these is complete in itself; each has developed along its own line so as to serve in the end as a proper conclusion for an evangelist of his own particular version of the gospel. Behind and within all the traditions, of course, is the conviction that Jesus of Nazareth continues to be and to operate, and that in him past, present and future are somehow related; but the mode of this continuation is differently conceived in the four Gospels, and in each case is closely related to the theology of the particular Gospel concerned. Each evangelist gives his version as a total version, which was not intended to stand up only if it stood alongside another, or was supplemented by another.[21]

Professor Raymond Brown, a Roman Catholic scholar who has devoted great attention to the two birth narratives in Matthew and Luke, has come to similar conclusions: 'Throughout I have insisted that the two stories are very different, that neither evangelist knew the other's work, and that efforts at harmonizing the narratives into one consecutive story are quite impossible.'[22] Both accounts, he argues, are concerned most to stress the intrinsic connection between the birth of Jesus and what preceded it in Israel, and to develop the continuity of the birth with what is to follow in the subsequent Gospel accounts. In other words, here too we have different theological creations.

There are even problems when the agreements in the material in Matthew and Luke suggest that they resorted to a common source containing sayings of Jesus:[23] such a source would have contained, among other important material, important texts like the Lord's Prayer and much of what we call, on the basis of Matthew's Gospel, the Sermon on the Mount. The text of both the Lord's Prayer and the Beatitudes, those sayings beginning 'Blessed are...', which in Matthew open the 'Sermon on the Mount' and in Luke become the 'Sermon on the Plain', differs quite substantially in the two Gospels[24] – and this difference remains to be explained even if one rejects the theory of some earlier common source and supposes that one evangelist took over material from the other and altered it.

All this will sound very technical, and within the space of a book of this kind I have to keep my account of the problems very brief. So it is worth saying in passing at this point that if all this is unfamiliar to you, and is not a reminder of what you already know, there are three possibilities open to you. You can take my brief and general account of the problems on trust and just note their cumulative effect, without exploring any further; you can pause and look for more detail about the way Gospel criticism works in one of the books to which I refer in the footnotes;[25] or you can dismiss the whole discussion as arid academic hair-splitting. The choice is up to you, but the evidence is all there for the examining – and needs to be explained – and if you take the third possibility, then inevitably you forfeit any right to make your own contribution to the solution of the overall problem of Jesus. After all, at this point we are considering the foundation documents of Christianity themselves, and if you cannot be bothered to join in the explorations of those who have made reading them a lifetime study, you are not really taking the Gospels seriously. Sadly, far too many people pontificate about the Gospels without really knowing what they are talking about.

So, to summarize where we have got to: there is a major difference between the Gospel of John and the Synoptic Gospels, and equally there are differences between the three Synoptic Gospels which need to be explained. One evangelist does not hesitate to change the words of another, and all do this for primarily theological reasons or, to put it crudely, to fit in with their own portrait of Jesus, not to produce a more accurate historical account of him.[26]

It is generally assumed that Mark is the earliest Gospel,[27] and if we accept that, then in looking closely at a synopsis we are seeing how Matthew and Luke have altered his words. But if they have done that, might not Mark in turn have altered whatever material he worked from, to paint *his* theological portrait? Now while we can see reasonably clearly what Matthew and Luke worked from, what did Mark work from?[28] Here the problems become really difficult, because there is no means of solving them: only conjecture. The discussion has been long and complex, but it is now widely assumed that the structure of the Gospel, the sequence of events it describes, is not primarily historical. What the author saw as the beginning of Jesus' ministry, in his case his baptism rather than his birth, had to come at the beginning, and the crucifixion at the end, but there is no guarantee that we can construct from what the Gospel of Mark tells us the motives behind Jesus's ministry or of those who killed him.[29]

For example, the fact that parables are collected together in a sequence in chapter 4 and stories about conflicts with the authorities in a sequence in chapter 12 is the beginning of an argument that the arrangement of material in the Gospels is thematic rather than chronological. And many scholars would also argue that the way in which in the Gospel of Mark Jesus begins to speak of his forthcoming death only after Peter has confessed him as Christ at Caesarea Philippi (Mark 8.29) is also a theological construction by Mark.

The reason why there can be so much argument over the order of events – and the tension between John and the Synoptics is not least because they differ over the order of events[30] – is that the Synoptic Gospels are largely made up of individual units, each with a rounded shape of its own, without very specific details about time and place, linked together 'like pearls on a string'.[31] There would have been plenty of opportunity for rearranging them to create a rather different pattern. What we know about Jesus has come down to us in this form because it seems most likely that when the Gospel of Mark was first written it made use of little stories, or groups of stories, told about Jesus in the earliest churches; these Mark – to limit ourselves to the first evangelist – collected and put in a particular order. The way in which the stories are narrated, the shape that they have assumed (and they make very good stories on their own), suggest that by the time Mark made use of them they had been told and retold many times, taking the most effective shape, just as we may polish a joke or the account of a personal incident that we like retelling.[32]

Precisely how these stories (the technical term for such a story is the Greek word *pericope*) came into being is quite uncertain; confident statements were made in the past, but we just do not have the evidence to come to any firm conclusion. However, we can be reasonably sure that they were not just told to preserve what we would call historical memories of Jesus. Many of the pericopes centre on arguments or points of dispute, convey teaching, give instructions and so on. They will have been needed in the earliest churches in worship, and for guidance as members worked out how to live as Christians in a world from which Jesus had departed.

I called the alterations which Matthew and Luke made to Mark theological, but that is perhaps too difficult a word. What I in fact meant was that Matthew and Luke seem to have written new kinds of Gospel, and to have altered what they found before them in Mark, because they wanted to produce works which were more helpful to their church, truer to their understanding of Christianity, than Mark's Gospel had become for their time and situation.[33] The years went by, new issues came up, the geographical setting was different, and to meet new demands the changes were made.

Because of all this, for a long time scholars have been telling us that we can only see Jesus through the eyes of the early church, since the Gospels are the books of the early church (or churches), produced to meet the church's needs.[34] That would mean that we can only get back towards Jesus through the early church and by taking the activity of that church (or churches) into account. This makes the problem of discovering the historical Jesus even greater, since we have to take account of alteration and indeed invention of material. This should not really surprise us; after all, apocryphal stories and sayings about twentieth-century figures abound. Who is to say that from a very early stage the church did not make up stories about Jesus which it felt to be in character, in order to illustrate who he was?[35]

If we are to try to get back to the historical Jesus, then, we have to seek to distinguish what in all this material we owe directly to Jesus, and what has been influenced or even created by the early church. That means that we need to know more about the early church. But where do we discover that? Here comes the next problem. For most of what we know about the earliest church comes from the letters of Paul, and one of the great puzzles about them is that apart from a reference to the Last Supper in I Corinthians 11 and a brief list of those to whom the Risen Jesus is said to have appeared in I Corinthians 15, Paul says nothing that we can identify with confidence as deriving from Jesus' earthly life and ministry, and certainly gives us no clue as to how that was understood in the communities in which he worked.[36]

The other account of the early church in the New Testament is the Acts of the Apostles, which is also fraught with problems.[37] There are many contradictions and clashes between its portrait of Paul and what we know from Paul's own letters,[38] and although Acts is attributed to Luke, who appears in Paul's letters as one of his companions, there is considerable doubt as to whether this attribution is authentic. Whether it is or not, we know that in his Gospel Luke did not hesitate to paint a new portrait of Jesus, making additions to or changes from Mark, the source that we can clearly identify; and there are indications that he was even more sweeping in his rewriting (or quite simply did not have the information) when it came to writing Acts, in order to give the impression he wanted to give.

That leaves only one other possible source for inferences about the early church: the Synoptic Gospels. But if that is the case, it means that the quest for Jesus is in real trouble. For we find ourselves in a circular argument. Our dilemma is now this: to distinguish authentic information about Jesus and authentic sayings of his in the Gospels from the contribution made to reinterpreting this information by the early church, we need to be able to identify the interests of the early church. Only in that way can we have reliable information about Jesus. But we know nothing about any interests of the early church which may have affected the Gospel tradition other than what we can infer from the Gospels, and such inferences can be made only if we separate that material in the Gospels which reflects the interests of the early church from that which goes back to Jesus. (Paul's letters and the other New Testament documents are not really any help here because of the striking absence of material relating to the 'earthly life' of Jesus of Nazareth and any teaching he may have given, apart from the reference to the Last

Supper, mentioned above, in I Corinthians 11.23-26.)[39] In other words, we have a really vicious circle.[40] That is why, as I said at the beginning, while it may well be that we do know a good deal about Jesus, we cannot always be sure precisely what it is. Certainly our knowledge is not sufficient to provide a basis for much of what Christianity wants to attribute to him.

To many scholars that sounds defeatist, and therefore the struggle continues nevertheless, despite all the problems, to paint some authentic picture of Jesus. There has been, for instance, a constant attempt to discover criteria by which to identify genuine sayings of Jesus. A substantial book on the subject was written in 1967 by the New Testament scholar Norman Perrin entitled *Rediscovering the Teaching of Jesus*.[41] The sort of problem to be faced is easy enough to illustrate. One criterion Perrin produced was the 'criterion of dissimilarity': the earliest form of a saying we can reach may be regarded as authentic if it can be shown to be dissimilar to characteristic emphases both of ancient Judaism and of the early church.[42] But if you use this criterion alone you will by definition end up with a Jesus who is totally dissimilar to his environment, and there is no good reason why that should be the case; i.e. Jesus may very well have taken over elements to be found in the Judaism of his day. Moreover, since new material is still being discovered, what at one point could seem dissimilar might suddenly prove to have parallels in Judaism or elsewhere. It is not difficult to find similar snags with other criteria that have been suggested in an attempt to reach certainty about the authenticity of one saying or another, though it is possible to establish complexes of criteria to achieve some approximate results. So again we run into difficulties.

That is what leads the author of one of the best modern books about Jesus, Professor E.P. Sanders, to say:

> I belong to the school which holds that a saying attributed to Jesus can seldom be proved beyond doubt to be entirely authentic or entirely non-authentic, but that each saying must be tested by appropriate criteria and assigned (tentatively) to an author – either to Jesus or to an anonymous representative of some stratum in the early church.[43]

And some would say that he is being over-optimistic.

But surely, it might be argued, although we may not feel confident about our ability to discover what Jesus actually said (as opposed to what the early church attributed to him), we can feel more confident when we look at the reports of what he did. This is the approach of Professor Sanders, and in his book he leaves the sayings of Jesus out of account in building a basic foundation, relying instead on 'facts'. He produces a number of 'almost indisputable' facts, which he lists more or less in chronological order, and uses them as a basis for his reconstruction. It is interesting to see what they are:

1. Jesus was baptized by John the Baptist.
2. Jesus was a Galilean who preached and healed.
3. Jesus called disciples and spoke of there being twelve.
4. Jesus confined his activity to Israel.
5. Jesus engaged in a controversy about the temple.
6. Jesus was crucified outside Jerusalem by the Roman authorities.
7. After his death Jesus' followers continued as an identifiable movement.
8. At least some Jews persecuted at least parts of the new movement and it appears that this persecution endured at least to a time near the end of Paul's career.[44]

To many Christians that list would seem unacceptably scanty; for example, where is there any mention of virgin birth, resurrection and miracles, to which Christian tradition has attached such importance? To others, such an approach does not get round the problems that we came up against in connection with the sayings.

A representative of the latter view, Gerald Downing, has pointed out that it is impossible to make a neat distinction between sayings and facts:

Quite simply, if Jesus said something, this is a fact (and an event), and as much a fact (and an event), as his supposed entering the temple in Jerusalem on any occasion. And like sayings, 'facts', 'events', 'actions' were always as liable as any saying to be given a different context and a different nuance of meaning, without any sure guarantee that the original 'intentional action' would be left in any way discernible.[45]

In other words, both what Jesus said and what Jesus did, like any other sayings and actions in history, are handed down and taken over by those who receive them in a process of interpretation which gives them a place and a significance in a wider context, and in this process of handing down, changes can take place as a result of which the significance of those sayings and events shifts. Even with 'facts' we are still in the original vicious circle. We still need an account of 'the community or communities that told the tales',[46] and for that the best we can hope for is a hypothetical sketch which is constantly open to the possibility that it needs radical change.

By now some readers may feel that they are in the hands of a hopeless sceptic, and if they have also read the footnotes, will feel that the hopeless sceptic keeps company with others of his ilk, paying scant attention to those who would be much more hopeful. Surely, they may say, the picture is not as gloomy as that? Why can't you be more positive and trusting?

Now it is true, as I said to begin with, that it is my nature and has been my training to ask questions, and I gladly concede that. But the tension between the sceptical and the more trusting is one that can be traced right through New Testament scholarship for almost two centuries and is one which is unlikely ever to disappear, because individuals have different temperaments.

This difference in temperament was the subject of quite a lengthy discussion in another influential book about Jesus.[47] The American scholar John Knox pointed out that critics can be divided into the *a priori* trusting and the *a priori* sceptical not because they refer to different evidence or even interpret it differently but because there is a difference among them in basic conception as to where the burden of proof lies and therefore of what is required of the evidence. Thinking particularly of the famous English Professor C.H.Dodd, he illustrates the contrast. There are those like Professor Dodd who say, 'We have no right to distrust any of the Gospel statements unless there is good cause. There is no reason to doubt the essential accuracy of Jesus in the picture offered by the Gospels, so the burden of proof lies with those who reject it.' And there are those who, like himself (and, obviously, like myself and the scholars to whom I have been referring for support), would rather say: 'The tradition about Jesus has undergone many important changes because of the way in which the Gospels have been so much bound up with the life and faith of the first century. The Gospels tell us more about the early church than they do about Jesus. There is much in them which is more likely to have arisen out of the life and faith of the first Christians than to come directly from Jesus himself.'[48]

This judicious discussion allows the legitimacy of both points of view, but since when Professor Knox was writing, and even more now, the scales so often seem weighted in favour of the trusters and against the questioners, it is important to emphasize that the questioners have quite a legitimate position. Indeed I think that one can go further and say that wherever there is a substantial body of questioners, those who would want to be more positive must accept the existence of those questioners and temper their confidence accordingly. The very existence of people who have doubts over what we can authentically say about Jesus affects the position of those who argue for certainty: the claim of the latter to certain knowledge when there is legitimate reason for doubt is a spurious one. We may choose our option, or our temperament may choose it for us, but where there are two rival options with no universally compelling grounds for choosing one over the other, the only truthful answer anyone can make about what can authoritatively be said about the person, sayings and actions of Jesus of Nazareth must be, 'In the end, we really do not *know*.'

Such a statement is not easy to maintain. There will always be strong pressures against it and those who make it, pressures exercised by the psychological need among many people for answers which will provide security in an insecure world. But that does not make it any the less necessary.

Yet another way of confirming this state of affairs would be to pick up a book on Jesus by a reputable New Testament scholar.[49] Read it through, and all seems reasonable and straightforward, with evidence produced to substantiate the account and usually discussed in some detail: the discussion leads to conclusions and a fairly clear picture. You might at that point wonder what all the rigmarole on the previous pages of this chapter has been about. But then pick up a second book, by an equally reputable New Testament scholar.[50] Though once again, while you are reading it, all may seem reasonable and straightforward, once again with supporting evidence, you will find that the conclusions are rather different. What is taken as assured by the first author may well be put in question by the second, and vice versa. The confusion begins. Take up a third..., and a fourth... Best of all, go back to the Gospels and steep yourselves in them and ask whether any of these authors is doing full justice to the texts. *That* is the problem, and it does not arise because the authors are biassed or incompetent; there just is not enough evidence, temperaments come into play and the result is endless variety.

However, there is a point at which it is possible to draw the line. For all the subtle differences between the Gospels of Matthew, Mark and Luke, it is reasonable to say that there emerges from them a portrait of what might be called the Synoptic Jesus, who is markedly different from the Jesus of the Fourth Gospel and the Christ of Paul's letters (letters which surprisingly enough make virtually no explicit statements about the earthly life of Jesus apart from the fact that he was crucified).[51] That Synoptic Jesus may be an inextricable weaving together in unknown proportions of Jesus as he was and Jesus as he was remembered, interpreted and revered by some early Christian churches,[52] but he is set firmly against an approximate background of first-century Palestinian Judaism and it is in that setting that the portrait belongs.[53]

First-century Palestinian Judaism, with Jesus and his group of disciples active in Galilee and in Jerusalem, represents the first of three stages of the development of Christianity which we can see in the New Testament. (I have highlighted three to keep the discussion simple.[54]) During Jesus' lifetime he and his followers seem to have had an essentially itinerant life-style, and much of what Jesus is reported to have said in the Synoptic Gospels is characteristic of itinerant philosophers; for all Jesus' Jewish background, an illuminating comparison has been made between him and the travelling Cynic philosophers who were such a striking feature of ancient society.[55]

This was followed by a period after Jesus' death when his followers gained new strength as a result of what they called his resurrection, and formed communities which adoped a new life-style, first within Judaism and later in the Gentile world, a life-style with a message that proved so attractive that the new faith spread rapidly round the then civilized world, from the Near East round to Greece and on to Rome. This great expansion was fuelled and motivated not least by the ardent belief that time was short: the world would soon end and Jesus would come again; before that it was vital that the Gospel should be preached to all people.[56]

During that time, in a second stage, Christianity spread from a predominantly rural backwater to the highly urbanized centres of Asia Minor and Greece, from a Semitic setting to the world of Hellenistic culture, with its long-established traditions of religion, literature and philosophy.[57] Itinerant preachers were still in evidence, but in the Christian movement settled communities were growing up as well; we can see tensions between these two types of Christianity in the New Testament and even more clearly in the *Didache*, a short early Christian manual on church practice, which is generally thought to be contemporaneous with the New Testament.[58]

It is not least because of the cultural and sociological shift which took place in the very first decades of Christianity that when we come to the earliest actual documents of the New Testament, the letters of Paul (chronologically they stand roughly midway between the crucifixion of Jesus and the period of the composition of the Gospels), which are our main evidence for this second stage, we are introduced to such a completely different world. Here, indeed, is a Christianity apparently so different that Paul has constantly been accused of betraying the original faith of Jesus.[59]

Though that charge is not tenable in its crude, old-fashioned form, recent sociological studies of these 'first urban Christians'[60] have shown the way in which from this point on a whole variety of factors now have to be taken into account. These begin to shape Christianity in competition with any direct influence from Jesus. For example, it has been argued that the dominant characteristic of Paul's communities was social mobility and that it could well be that powerful symbols of change grounded in tradition and personal or communal transformation, symbols of an evil world now brought under God's judgment and grace, might be particularly attractive to those who had experienced the hopes and fears which went with an ambiguous position in society.[61] By transcending traditional Judaism in the direction of a closer association with Hellenistic and Roman culture perhaps it also proved to be some help towards social mobility and an entry into a new cultural world.[62]

Not long after Paul's death, Jerusalem was obliterated as a result of the failed Jewish rebellion against Rome of AD 66-70, and the Jewish world in which Jesus had lived disappeared from the face of the earth.[63] After AD 70 Judaism changed a good deal, reducing considerably in the process the great diversity of thought previously characteristic of it and for the sake of future survival becoming much more inward-looking: we shall see later how the ways of Jews and Christians parted.[64] At this stage, as we shall see in more detail in the next chapter, Christianity was still developing in a wide variety of contrasting forms.

Thirdly, as the hope for an imminent return of Jesus began to die with the death of those who had known him when he was alive, the churches were faced with the prospect of an indefinite existence in the world, and had to come to terms with the society around them. This led, as we can see from later documents than Paul (the letters to Timothy and Titus, attributed to Paul but almost certainly not written by him),[65] to a quest for ecclesiastical stability, respectability and social assimilation,[66] not least because of the many varieties of Christianity which were now in existence.[67]

As one illustration of the significance of this triple shift for the ethos of the church it is worth looking at the role of women in the communities of the followers of Jesus and the churches to which feminist scholars, above all, have recently drawn our attention.[68] A significant characteristic of the Synoptic Jesus, it is said, is his openness towards women; there are women among his immediate following[69] some of whom are even presented as the first (in Mark the only) witnesses to his resurrection,[70] and prostitutes appear in the Gospel stories alongside the extortionate tax-collectors, who were also regarded as social outcasts, as those who will precede the respectable into the kingdom of God.[71] The story about the forgiveness of the woman taken in adultery, which has somehow found its way into the Fourth Gospel, though it manifestly does not belong there, is perhaps one of the most moving episodes related of Jesus.[72]

Feminist scholars would argue (and there is much evidence to support their view, even if it is perhaps more complex than they acknowledge in stating their case) that in the earliest days of Christianity after the death of Jesus as reflected by Paul, when churches come into being in urban settings, women still have a prominent role. The Christian churches offered their members a place in communities in which men and women were in some respects on an equal footing. Thus we find women mentioned as the leaders of house churches, and they also play a major part in the life and worship of the church. From the letters of Paul we can produce quite a list of prominent women Christians, some of them probably leaders of house churches: Euodia, Julia, Junia, Mary, Nympha, Persis, Phoebe, Prisca, Syntyche and Tryphosa; the Acts of the Apostles adds among others the dynamic Laura Ashley of her day, Lydia of Philippi.[73] All this at the very least puts many question marks against the traditional, male-dominated view of ministry in this period.

But in the third stage, when the church had become concerned to achieve respectability, women sank back to a subordinate and inferior role: they were expected to be very much in the background, not uttering a word. 'Let a woman learn in silence with all submissiveness. I permit no woman to teach or to have authority over men; she is to keep silent... Yet woman will be saved through bearing children, if she continues in faith and love and holiness, with modesty,' says I Timothy.[74]

So within less than a century, the vision of a new way of life as represented in the Synoptic Gospels had been domesticated. There was already a manifest conflict between what the Synoptic Jesus had said and what the church put into practice. The beginnings of a system had been developed and there was no effective room for the Synoptic Jesus in that system. The factors which determined the shape of Christianity were already other than those which were foremost in the message of Jesus.

All this introduces yet another dimension into our problems about Jesus and his ministry. To describe it as simply as possible: even if everything that the Gospels say about Jesus were true, we would still have to cope with a fundamental split. By the end of the first century a church had come into being to which much of what Jesus said was alien. So not only does the New Testament itself provide evidence that his words were altered at one stage; in the later epistles it also provides evidence of a stage at which, had they been cited, they could well have been dismissed as dangerous and irresponsible. Excessively reverential reading of the New Testament, an unhistorical approach to it, and the piecemeal selection of texts, still disguises this problem, as it has been disguised down the centuries, but it is there for all to see.

As I said in the first chapter, it is precisely because of this tension that the Synoptic Jesus has always been a point of reference for discontented individuals or parties within the church who felt that the church was not really being true to Jesus, that its Christ was not Jesus. Because that tension is recorded within the pages of the New Testament, it is one which will always be there to torment us.

However, to return to our starting point in this chapter: it must be stressed one last time that this Jesus is Jesus as particular communities in earliest Christianity saw him and believed in him in the light of the resurrection, not Jesus as he was. And because there is a complex interaction between the figure of Jesus and the life and faith of these communities, there is a sociological dimension as well as a theological dimension to the Synoptic portrait of Jesus. One consequence of this is that while it is natural for people in a complicated technological society like our own to want to go back to the ideals and teachings of Jesus, what they are looking back to is a figure who is part and parcel of a particular kind of society, and the only way of recreating those ideals as a viable option is to recreate that kind of society. That is why when such recreations have been attempted, they have always been a kind of 'opting out' of an existing society and the forming of an alternative one – as for example in the Franciscan ideal. That may indeed be a viable option, but it is always going to be a specialist choice, and has usually been recognized as such. For the majority of Christians the problems of reinterpreting Jesus for a new situation, as these problems present themselves to the second, third and subsequent generations in the early church, remain. And the question then becomes: what are the limits of that reinterpretation, for surely it cannot be the case that 'anything goes'? To that question we now turn.

4 | The Kaleidoscopic Christ

'Jesus Christ is the same yesterday and today and for ever' is another much-quoted saying from the New Testament[1] and is a favourite of many Christians. But is he? That will be our concern in this chapter as we look at the way in which Jesus of Nazareth came to be reinterpreted in so many different ways that at times there might seem to be no obvious connection between the reinterpreted Christ and the Synoptic Jesus. This reinterpretation arose out of changing patterns of Christianity and in turn (again in a complex way) influenced those patterns.

To see the reinterpretation and its background we shall begin by taking two rapid guided tours, each organized by an expert, first of the manifold varieties of Christianity and then of the variegated ways in which Jesus has been depicted. If as a result you feel like someone who has been rushed round all the capitals of Europe in a week, with a confused mass of different images and impressions, then the tours will have succeeded. For it is important that we should be aware of the bewildering number of contrasting types of Christianity and the equally bewildering variety of its Christs, both at the present day and down history, and this is the easiest way of doing that. The guides are relatively neutral and reliable in their provision of evidence because they both adopt a phenomenological approach: in other words they essentially describe what they see and do not attempt to evaluate it in depth and draw any major conclusions from it. Our task, however, will ultimately be rather more than that: we shall not stop at sight-seeing; we shall go on to ask about the significance of what we have surveyed for Christian belief.

Ninian Smart, our guide to the varieties of Christianity, begins his description with the splendour of the Orthodox liturgy in Romania. There the Orthodox Church lives side by side with a

Communist state and on festivals secret police chat affably with abbesses processing into a packed cathedral and the bishop preaches about the need for hard work on the collectivized farm to bring in the harvest. Professor Smart draws attention to this easy relationship with the civil authorities, which can be found in branches of the Orthodox Church in other communist countries. Since faith hinges on the liturgy and the monasteries, it is centred on the community and the church building, rather than being individualistic, and therefore Christians have to work out a *modus vivendi* wherever they are. That does not mean, though, that there is not a deep spirituality; Orthodox faith is comparatively timeless and static, and though it is not untheological, it is dominated above all by icons and music.[2] (Because of developments during the first millennium, including the pressure of cultural differences, an increasing inability of Western Christians to read Greek after the break-up of the Roman empire and the Moslem conquest of much of the Mediterranean world, the Eastern church became isolated and cut off from the expanding Western church. That is why it plays so little role in this book.)[3]

The village of Tremezzo on Lake Como, which provides an introduction to Italian Catholicism, presents a very different picture. Here there are deep roots in folk religion, and the Virgin Mary and the Pope are dominant figures, the former the focal point of a cult of often extravagant dimensions.[4] And if we move south to Rome or Ravenna, we are reminded of a long and complex history in which church and state grew closer together, as well as of a great intellectual and artistic tradition. Assisi reminds us of monastic orders of very different kinds. Here, in Italy, is still the heartland of Catholicism, dominated by the Vatican.[5]

To this, Ethiopian Christianity could hardly be a greater contrast, with the savage climate of its country and an equally savage history. Here is an originally semitic and 'heretical' type of Christianity, in which males are circumcised, as in Judaism, and the sabbath is kept on Saturday. Replicas of the Israelite ark are to be found here, and sacred dances have a decidedly Old Testament flavour – indeed the royal lineage was traced back to the Jewish monarchy.[6]

Swedish Protestantism in the cold north is yet another contrast, arising out of the Lutheran Reformation and closely allied to the state, to the degree that clergy are also bureaucrats and religion has become highly secularized. To outward appearance a Lutheran church may look very like a Roman Catholic church, but the main thrust of Lutheranism is very different: the emphasis lies rather on the Bible, long made available to the people in the vernacular, and on theology, developed by scholars who represent a powerful force in the reconstruction of religious belief. Nowhere is the power of theology more evident than in Germany, which has produced so many intellectual giants over the last four centuries.[7]

A different aspect of the Reformation is represented in the farming country of Pennsylvania by the Amish, conservative in their renunciation of modern technology, which leads them to reject the use of electricity and to travel in horse-drawn buggies, yet going back to a radical tradition of Christian belief, and therefore with a long history of persecution at the hands of their fellow Christians because of their uncompromising approach, which included a rejection of the alliance with the state accepted by Lutheranism.[8]

Already the contrasts have begun to mount up, and we have barely begun. We might feel that the tour was not ambitious enough, and want to set off on our own, say round the African churches, contrasting the Dutch Reformed Church in South Africa with the churches of the independent African nations.[9] We might want to see more of the churches of South-East Asia[10] or Latin America, with their widely differing cultural, social and economic situations.[11] We might want to look at the ethos of black American Christianity, with its history of oppression, discrimination and deprivation in the context of a rich society.[12] And even after that there would many more varieties of Christianity to discover. The 1000 pages of the *World Christian Encyclopedia* published in 1982 are mind-boggling in their complexity and variety, with the 20,800 Christian *denominations* which are listed.[13]

Or we might feel utterly exhausted and just want to stay at home in Britain. But even there we would only have to look at the newspaper, turn on the television, or walk round our own locality to be confronted with the kaleidoscopic variety of local British churches; indeed we could just limit ourselves to one church, the Church of England. Within it, after all, can be found liberals, radicals and conservatives, high and low, Tractarian, Evangelical and Erastian, married clergy and homosexual clergy, those clamouring for the ordination of women and those for whom that prospect is so appalling that they would leave the church rather than countenance it.[14]

As our first guide sums up the phenomenon of Christianity:

It is as if Christianity were a mighty river flowing through a great delta: we begin by tracing the streams as they empty into the sea, and then begin here and there to move upstream, to plot the geography of all the waters, including some of the tributaries that contribute to their volume. We seem to find one river, but even beyond the delta it changes course, divides, twists and is fed by other streams. We hope to reach its source or sources. We begin from the sea, however, which is the present time into which the waters of the delta flow. But unmistakably the streams differ, and this is one of the fascinations of Christian geography. What do the Amish of Pennsylvania have in common with a Zulu Zion? What does Sweden share with the old faith of Ethiopia? What transition is to be made from the Catholicism of Lombardy to the Baptism of Georgia or the Calvinism of the Voortrekkers? And where are the limits of the faith? What a variety Christianity presents, and one is often tempted to drop the singular and speak only of Christianities. One can, it is true, return to the source: or is it sources?[15]

If Christianity is complex, so too are its Christs, and to look at them we follow our second guide, Professor Jaroslav Pelikan, who has described some of the portraits of Jesus through the centuries.[16] These portraits in due course become pictorial ones, but from the early period on word-pictures and theological portraits predominate. The ideas expressed in these verbal interpretations of Jesus are often relevant to Christian art and iconography, since this art often has a symbolism based on the ideas which is not always evident to the untrained eye.[17]

Professor Pelikan begins with the Gospels themselves, and singles out the way in which they portray Jesus as the Jewish rabbi and prophet; but these two categories soon give way to others, Messiah/ Christ and Lord. The Gospels also portray Jesus as preaching the end of the present age and the coming of a future one, but as the expectation of his imminent return began to fade he came to be seen, rather, as the turning point of history, the history of God's chosen people and then of the history of the whole world. This image came to be established in Christian theology above all as a result of St Augustine's great work *The City of God*. At a later stage (much later, in fact, than is usually supposed), this centrality of Christ was given permanent form in the conventional Western system of dating centred on him: BC 'before Christ' and AD 'in the year of the Lord' (it was in fact the Venerable Bede in the eighth century who was a key figure in establishing the dating system from Christ).[18]

The significance of Jesus for the whole world was also represented in the image of him as the light of the Gentiles, illuminating those who had been in the darkness of ignorance and sin; and he brought light not only to the living but also, by his descent into the underworld in the three days before his resurrection, to those who had had the ill fortune to die before his coming. Constantine and St Augustine both saw Virgil's messianic Fourth Eclogue as prophecy of Jesus, and Christians also appropriated the famous Roman Sibylline oracles for their cause: the *Dies irae* of the Latin requiem mass links King David with the Sibyl in prophesying the last judgment, and Michelangelo's frescoes in the Sistine Chapel alternate Sibyls and prophets.[19]

The Jesus of the Gospels preached the kingdom of God, and Christians came to believe that when he came again, he would rule over a millennial kingdom upon earth before the final end. In the kingdom he would be king, and so too he came to be pictured as King of Kings, an image which became particularly prominent once Christianity had reached the imperial throne itself, in the person of the emperor Constantine. As a result of the complex series of historical developments by which the focal point of Christianity shifted to Rome, the papacy increased its power and had to appeal for military support to survive; by the time of Charlemagne the accepted model of political sovereignty was that it had passed from God to Christ, from Christ to Peter, from Peter to his successors and from them to emperors and kings.[20]

Already among the letters which bear Paul's name (even if they may not in fact have been written by him),[21] Jesus is hymned as the firstborn of all creation. This was part of a development in which Jesus came to be identified with the universal Logos, the eternal rational principle of the universe. This was another fateful step, as we shall see in Chapter 5, leading to the idea of the pre-existence of

Jesus.[22] It also provided a title which, when revived by Pierre Teilhard de Chardin in modern times, proved to be particularly evocative: the cosmic Christ.[23]

Another title, Son of Man, has an air of mystery about it in the Gospels. Even now no one is quite sure just what Jesus meant by it, if indeed he did use it: but it looks very much as if it is a reference to some more than human figure.[24] Taking it more literally, though, Christian tradition came to use it as a title to stress the humanity of Jesus, one who has shared in our mortal condition to the full. Jesus was also the second Adam, the one member of the human race who was utterly sinless, thus restoring the image of God which had been lost through the Fall.[25]

The Greek for image is *eikon*, and so the Pauline tradition provides the starting point for the eventual development of Christian graphic art. Christian art has come down to us from the time of the catacombs; in the East icons (as the word is usually Anglicized), representing the Holy Family, saints and other figures came to enjoy great popularity and were the subject of intense devotion. They were thought to have intercessory power, healing power and to serve as a form of defence against the enemy. However, the success of Islam (which prohibited the representation of human figures) and its military victories forced a reconsideration of the role of icons; and a stress on the Old Testament, with the prohibition against 'graven images' in the Second Commandment (Exodus 20.4), led to attacks on the veneration of icons, the long-drawn-out 'iconoclastic controversy'.[26] Here was a tension over the representation of Christ which was to recur later and elsewhere in Christian history.

Interestingly enough, in the earliest representations in the catacombs Jesus tends to be depicted in the form of a Roman citizen. On a famous Sinai icon he was depicted as long-haired and bearded. In the seventh century for the first time the head of the reigning emperor was removed from the front of gold coinage to be replaced with a portrait bust of Christ (one showed the Sinai-type with beard and long hair; an alternative showed him as youthful with short curly hair).[27]

Clearly there were problems in presenting images of the crucifixion. Christ crucified and the sign of the cross do not come in until the fourth century, perhaps when with the official recognition of Christianity a whole new level of society entered the church.[28] Here was a paradoxical image: the cross could be seen as a sign of the identification of God with the depths of human suffering, yet at the same time, over a long period of Christian history after the victory of Constantine following his vision of a cross ('In this sign you will conquer'),[29] the cross was a sign of power. It was thought to provide protection to those going on crusades, defence against witchcraft and the devil, and a cure for diseases.[30]

The nature of Jesus' life as an itinerant preacher with no possessions and nowhere to lay his head resulted in his being seen as the perfect monk, so that he became the ideal and inspiration of monastic orders; and for those who did not marry he became the bridegroom of the soul, so that much language of piety and devotion became steeped in sexual imagery.[31]

Again we could accompany our guide further in this exploration, to Jesus as the model to be followed, the figure who was the inspiration of St Francis, to the later devotions associated with the *Imitation of Christ* and from there through the Reformation to the modern period.[32] Again, however, at this point we might may want to part company with our guide and choose an itinerary of our own.

To see yet more of the kaleidoscope we need only pick up a hymn book and look at the images piled one upon another, until they almost run riot. Many images, often deeply emotional, have been used by hymn writers for personal devotion and the worship of the church, ranging from the classical and sober patristic imagery, through the love songs of the Free Church tradition, to contemporary hymns like Sydney Carter's 'Lord of the Dance' (which some of those who sing it might be surprised to know is of Gnostic origin).[33]

And then there are all the modern attempts to rewrite the life of Jesus on the basis of particular preconceptions or themes, which have produced yet more images of him:[34] Schweitzer's *The Quest of the Historical Jesus* is a nineteenth-century catalogue; the twentieth century has added yet others: the divine propagandist,[35] the Jew from Galilee[36], the proclaimer calling to decision,[37] the eschatological prophet,[38] the man for others,[39] the messianic schemer,[40] the founder of a secret society,[41] the Qumran Essene,[42] the clown,[43] the magician,[44] Jesus Christ Superstar,[45] to mention only some of them.

So after our rapid tours of Christianity and images of Jesus we are confronted with two sets of kaleidoscopic impressions, so varied as to make us almost despair of bringing any more permanent order into them. No wonder, then, that the American Alfred Lovejoy, who with his book *The Great Chain of Being* pioneered the study of the history of ideas, was able to write: 'The term "Christianity" is not the name for any single unit of the type for which the historian of specific ideas looks. Rather, it is a series of facts which, taken as a whole, have almost nothing in common except a name.'[46] No wonder that the Englishman Don Cupitt could write: 'Christianity is a family of monotheistic faiths which in various ways find in Jesus a key to the relation of man with God. It has and will continue to have almost as much internal diversity as Hinduism... God can be believed in and served in as many ways as there are people. In the Christian tradition Jesus is the paradigm of faith, but that paradigm may be re-enacted in a great variety of ways, and we need not labour to reduce their number.'[47]

We have seen something of the evidence for the nature of Christianity down the centuries and the variety of images of Christ which have grown up in it. What are we to make of this evidence? Is it possible to find any coherence in it; is there any way of making it all hang together more closely than it has seemed to so far?

One obvious way of looking for an answer would be to go back to the origins of Christianity and see how it developed from there. Is there really a mainstream of authentic Christianity, a variety of departures from which might be seen as deviations of greater or lesser worth? However, if we begin an investigation of that kind we are immediately confronted with the problem that the multiplicity of Christianity is there from the very beginning. Some years ago Bamber Gascoigne made a television series entitled *The Christians*, also published as a book, in which he, too, portrayed some of the many forms Christianity has taken. Right at the end of the book he referred back to his own personal starting point:

> When planning this book and television series I read the New Testament straight through as if it were the scripture of an unknown religion, or as a Buddhist might read it. I find it impossible to believe that a stranger, coming to the Bible for the first time, would receive from it any clear idea of what Christ or Christianity stood for – so varied and self-contradictory are its messages and parables.[48]

And his verdict is endorsed, in the field of New Testament

scholarship, by Professor James D.G.Dunn, who is hardly regarded as a radical:

> We must conclude that there was no single normative form of Christianity in the first century. When we ask about the Christianity of the New Testament we are not asking about any one entity: rather, we encounter different types of Christianity, each of which viewed the others as too extreme in one respect or another – too conservatively Jewish or too influenced by antinomian or gnostic thought and practice, too enthusiastic or tending towards too much institutionalization. Not only so, but each 'type' of Christianity was itself not monochrome and homogeneous, more like a spectrum. Even when we looked at individual churches the picture was the same – of diversity in expression of faith and lifestyle, the tension between conservative and liberal, old and new, past and present, individual and community.[49]

Don Cupitt goes even further:

> There is not even any such thing as a New Testament doctrine about Christ. As soon as you try to state it you are at once obliged to admit that your statement is interpreted rather differently by different New Testament writers. I doubt if you could write down *any* statement about Christ to which St Mark, St Paul, St John and the writer to the Hebrews would demonstrably have assented in precisely the same sense.[50]

Certainly after a so-called 'tunnel period' at the end of the first and beginning of the second century, so-called because so little information about developments is available, we find a mainstream emerging. But this is a mainstream the breadth of which has already been created at the cost of introducing external constaints into the original tendencies of Christianity. Some of these constraints resulted from completely outside factors. The destruction of Jerusalem by the Romans and the disastrous Jewish War of AD 66-70 wiped out Jewish Christianity and the view it represented – the abolition of this particular option was hardly one which was chosen by Christian leaders; as we shall see in the next chapter, the rejection of everything associated with Gnosticism may not have been an entirely good thing: Gnosticism, like many other 'failed' options, is now being reassessed.[51] So the mainstream was achieved by historical circumstance and a process of blocking off many other courses, not always on the basis of either good arguments or sound evidence. We must therefore take the phenomenon of variety very seriously. But why was it there from the start?

How it developed can be easily imagined, if we go back and think about the stages through which the development of Christianity went that I described in the last chapter. Let us now see how it could have looked from the perspective of individual Christians.[52]

Suppose that in the year AD 35, i.e. five years after the generally accepted date for the crucifixion of Jesus, two men became Christians in Jerusalem. One soon went to Syria to live, the other to Egypt. When they got to their new cities, they told their friends about Jesus and local churches came into being around them. Almost immediately problems would arise. What should we do about the Jewish law? What should we do when we gather together for worship? How are we to understand the meaning of this passage from the Jewish scriptures? How far should we keep our old way of behaving and how far change it?

On some questions a local community would have been able to ask other Christians for advice; there will have been travelling preachers, and other communities in the area. But it would not have been possible to find authoritative answers to every question, and since the traditions everywhere were still embryonic and far from being well defined, questions asked of others might provoke very different answers, depending on the provenance of the person asked. So each church had in many instances to make up its mind in terms of its own situation and its own memories. Don't forget that we are still a long way from the formation of the New Testament as a supreme authority.

Suppose, now, that we move forty years on, to AD 75. During that time, as I described earlier, great changes have taken place including the destruction of Jerusalem. A Christian travels from the church we imagined in Syria, which is now well established, to that in Egypt, also well established, and spends some time there. To his surprise he finds that the two churches have little in common apart from a basic loyalty to Jesus. Fragments of his words have been handed down, but individual sayings no longer have an identical form in both communities; there are differences between the two over keeping the Jewish law, over forms of prayer and worship, and belief in the nature of the resurrection. Indeed, so different have the two churches become that the Christian from Syria is shocked at what he finds in Egypt and a Christian from Egypt going to Syria would be equally so. But which of the two communities is the representative of the original faith?

Complicate the picture further by bringing in communities in Greece and Rome, not to mention the other areas to which earliest Christianity first spread, and it should not be surprising that there should have been variety from the start.[53] But many people do find it surprising, since they have grown up with the idea that Christianity had a clear identity to begin with and that from the foundation of the church by Jesus it moved forward along a well-defined and relatively straight course. How could they have come to imagine that if diversity seems to have been an original Christian characteristic?

We saw in the previous chapter how the Gospels came into being as books for particular churches, and how they reflect the interests of those churches as well as telling their story of who Jesus was. Because the authors of these Gospels were writing in a period after the resurrection, when the churches were already in existence, they cast something of the resurrection light back on to the earthly Jesus in portraying him, and Matthew and Luke, at least, obviously tried to make it seem more natural that what Jesus should have said and done led up to the situation of their own time.[54] 'Luke' in particular (I put him in inverted commas at this point as a reminder that there is considerable doubt as to who precisely he was; a large number of scholars believe from the nature of his work and the problems to be noted in a moment that he cannot have been the companion of Paul) produced a continuous narrative from before the birth of Jesus to the arrival of Paul in Rome by adding a second volume, the Acts of the Apostles, to his Gospel: the first history of early Christianity.[55]

It is this history, above all, that has given the impression that the development of Christianity was well-ordered, divinely inspired, consistent, harmonious, following a particular geographical pattern. The Acts of the Apostles is one of the most readable and enjoyable books in all Christian literature: a good story, entertainingly told, full of action, and ending in triumph. The problem is that New Testament scholars are increasingly recognizing that its literary qualities have been achieved at the expense of good history-writing, and that while (like the Gospels) it may contain some important historical information, as in the parallel case of the tradition of Jesus, we cannot be at all sure what this authentic information was.

Here are three examples. The account of the earliest church in Jerusalem is too sketchy to be of much help and leaves many questions unanswered. Much is made of the need to restore the Twelve to their full complement after the death of Judas, but we hear little of them after the appointment of Matthias;[56] and Acts tells us nothing to explain how James, the brother of Jesus, whom we know from Paul's letters to have achieved a prominent position in that church in the first generation, came to be involved in the Christian movement.[57] There is similarly considerable doubt as to who the 'seven' mentioned in Acts 6 are and why Stephen and his group should have been persecuted whereas other Christians escaped persecution.[58]

Secondly, what Paul says in his letters conflicts quite seriously with what is said about him in Acts.[59] It is impossible to reconcile 'Paul's missionary journeys' as recounted in Acts and to which a map is devoted in every Atlas of the Bible with what we can reconstruct from the letters;[60] the collection which Paul was so concerned to arrange and which seems indirectly to have led to his death indicates a much tenser relationship between Pauline Christianity and that in Jerusalem than Acts indicates.[61]

Thirdly, the straight-line picture of the spread of Christianity as a result of Paul's works distorts what must have been the historical development, which must have involved far more people and have taken place far more diffusely. Acts says nothing, for example about how Christianity got to e.g. Rome and Egypt, which were not Paul's sphere of activity, but it will have done so at a very early stage.[62]

Above all, Acts plays down controversy, variety and lack of success in favour of the triumphant progress of the Gospel, led on by the Holy Spirit (forget all about Acts and read Paul's letters by themselves and a different picture emerges). And because his book is in the New Testament, his propaganda has been taken as history, so that spellbound, generations of Christians have unquestioningly believed that its account describes precisely how it all happened. However, with our greater range of information, our modern historical consciousness and our development of historical criticism, we cannot be so trusting. We have to interrogate Acts if we are not to be open to the charge that Christianity rewrites history to suit itself, and as we interrogate it we discover its shortcomings.

Perhaps the impression of a uniform, mainstream development of Christianity would not have remained so strong had the Acts of the Apostles not later had a successor which continued where it left off. This successor was the *Church History* of Eusebius of Caesarea, writing in the fourth century AD, at the time of the emperor Constantine, with whom Christianity had reached a pinnacle of power. (This was also the time of the Council of Nicaea, to which the creed recited at the Christian eucharist is attributed.)[63] Eusebius was as successful a writer as Luke; so successful that his *History of the Church* became the model for all later writing of church history.[64]

Eusebius, too, is very readable; his story, too, is one of triumph, for he clearly feels that the Constantinian age is one of as great glory for Christianity as the time when it first spread round the Mediterranean world. And like the Acts of the Apostles, his account follows a simple pattern: this time it is the establishment of the apostolic faith against all opposition. Eusebius's *Church History* contains a constant series of battles for the truth between the good and the bad: on the good side are bishops, Christian teachers and martyrs; on the bad side are Jews, evil emperors and heretics. Most important of all, Eusebius was convinced that Christianity was the eternal, unchanging truth, which was accessible to humankind in a veiled form even in the period before Jesus, and before the Christian church began. In his time, he was certain, what Christians believed was the faith that had come down to them intact, despite attacks on it, from the days of the apostles; indeed, heretics were such a danger because they were innovators, bringing in new-fangled ideas. Of course this means that he produces his chosen pictures by making all his characters stereotypes. Here again, we do not have history worthy of the name, but propaganda which needs to be read with a critical eye. And again, it cannot realistically be claimed that Eusebius's work is an objective account of the development of Christianity. It is propaganda, very effective propaganda, which has done its work all too well.

So whether they are aware of it or not, those who have an image of a well-ordered and uniform development of Christianity are under the influence of the Acts of the Apostles and Eusebius and can only retain their impression by refusing to accept the variety which more modern studies make it necessary to accept. Furthermore, as we shall see in the next chapter, the contrast of 'fathers' and 'heretics' is very insidious indeed. So our look at Christian beginnings simply confirms the original impression:

> There is no original Christian faith, no native language, no definitive statement of the meaning of Christ for all times. The dialectic of past and present, tradition and innovation, permanence and change, runs through the whole history of Christianity. What is regarded as novel to one generation becomes authoritative tradition to another. Christians have, in their construction of the past, prized antiquity, stability, and permanence, but the historical record shows us quite another picture. Christians have said one thing while going ahead and doing something else. The apostles spoke several languages, and Christians ever since have done the same. No matter how deeply we probe, how early we extend our search, we will never find an original faith. We can't go home again, not only because the home we once knew has changed beyond recognition. No, there never was a home. From the beginning, Christians have been wanderers and pilgrims whose dream lies not in the past, but before them and all men and women – in the future.[65]

In looking at the variety of Christianity, there is a further dimension that we have to take into account. Christianity has varied not only from region to region at any one time, by taking different forms in different regions as a result of the cultural background, or by giving different answers to key questions in matters of belief and practice. It has also changed as cultures have changed in the long term: as the Roman empire collapsed, eventually leaving the church with a very different role from that which it had had a couple of centuries before: at the time of the Renaissance, the Reformation, the Industrial Revolution and so on. To see the magnitude of these changes we can now follow a third guide, Elizabeth Maclaren, and take cross-sections of Christianity at four different periods in history, beginning with the first-century Syrian Christian whom I chose as an imaginary example earlier in the chapter.[66]

The faith of our Syrian Christian will have been essentially what we would call biblical, governed by the content of the Jewish scriptures which Christianity took over. God had chosen the Jewish people and intervened constantly in their history, most recently in sending Jesus as his Messiah. This Jesus went around healing and teaching, his authority backed up by amazing miracles. Because his work challenged the established authorities, they put him to death on trumped-up charges. But even this death was foretold in the scriptures, and God raised Jesus bodily from the tomb, so that he was seen by eye-witnesses. Although many of the first generation of Christians had died, before all of them died the risen Jesus would come again to judge the world and bring in the kingdom of God on earth.

Now suppose we move to Egypt, not forty years later but four hundred. What would we find? For a Christian living in Alexandria God is the threefold unity of Father, Son, Spirit in eternal communion. Though he never ceased to participate in this Godhead, the second 'person' of the Trinity, sometimes called the Logos of God, had miraculously taken human nature in the man Jesus, living and dying as man. Since, however, his incarnation had inseparably bound mortal human nature to the undying life of God, death could not finally destroy him, and he rose. In this, he anticipated the future of all the universe which, because he had fully belonged to it, could be caught up into the life of Christ's God.

If we go on from there to twelfth-century Italy, the picture has changed all over again. For the typical believer, God has created the world, and humankind has abused its rational freedom by sinning against God in arrogant pride. For this they deserve death, but God is reluctant to undo his creation. So he persuades his Son to become man and pay the penalty of man's sin, taking the guilt and punishment of humanity on himself. This voluntary sacrifice satisfies the demands of justice, and the power of divine love overcomes Satan's evil will to destroy humanity. The merits of the crucified Jesus secure eternal bliss. The faithful can appropriate these merits through the sacraments of the church, confident that through them they will be accepted in heaven.

Finally, let us look at the beliefs of a twentieth-century radical Christian, influenced by existentialist philosophy. He or she believes that 'God' is the word which people have used in the past as a focus for their ultimate concerns of life, death, guilt, hope. Now they must learn to discard the word and the outmoded cosmology that goes with it. Within the cosmological framework of his day Jesus proclaimed a message of liberation and authentic existence which by a process of 'demythologization' can be restated for our own time. Jesus lived with such freedom and openness that not even his death could destroy his impact, and the community inspired by him still finds itself moved to hope that the love he communicated is stronger than death. The world is responsible for its own destiny and there are no divine miraculous interventions. To say that 'Jesus is God' is not to affirm a supernatural incarnation but to accept that the man Jesus clarifies ultimate human concern and gives the clue to the meaning of human existence.[67]

Whether or not these particular cross-sections of the faith of believers are either adequate or completely accurate representations is not the most important thing; they are near-enough as thumb-nail sketches. What is most important is the point that they make yet more insistently, and which could be reiterated time and again by yet more completely different illustrations. Christianity has changed as culture has changed, and this change has produced such variety that the very identity of Christianity becomes problematical. Moreover, because some individuals and groups are more sensitive to changes in cultural background and the questions raised by these changes than are others, and some groups may regard one particular and inevitably culturally conditioned Christianity as an absolute, normative form, the variety becomes even more complex, making urgent the need to find some viable criteria for assessing that variety. Elizabeth Maclaren vividly describes the problems caused for the would-be Christian believer:

> The inquisition which could once be regarded as the organ of divine providence now seems to most Christians a monstrous institution. Today few Christian sensibilities could endorse crusades. Many would be squeamish even about Christian judgments that other religions are false which would have been axiomatic in most earlier times. Ethical standards have shifted. No Christian now would accept slavery as a legitimate social option, whereas many would welcome sexual freedoms deplored by earlier periods. Some Christian groups have been firmly pacifist, while some bishops have blessed battleships and prayed for the destruction of enemies. At times Christianity has manifested itself through Communist practices with regard to property,

while Protestant Christendom has been identified as a main pillar of capitalism.

This variety of doctrine and practice is unnerving. Whether or not believing is choosing, or acting, being struck 'from outside' by something, being conditioned to certain attitudes or having a disposition to respond in certain ways to certain questions, it must have a content. Christian belief (or for that matter, Hindu or Muslim belief) can't be believing just *anything*. But how does one draw lines? How does one say, 'Well, here Christian belief stops and something else starts?'[68]

At this point, of course, the favourite response has been to say that Christianity must always go back to its founder, that Christianity must always be measured by the life and teachings of Christ. This was the note on which a modern survey of religion in Britain ended. In his *Change and the Churches*, David Perman concluded, with a reference to Hans Küng's *On Being a Christian*:

> What is wrong with the churches is that they are not Christian enough; they must strive much more to be like Jesus himself. It is a theme which is taken up by many theologians and church leaders, and it is the best hope for the churches as a whole. It is only by returning to their beginnings that the churches today can be sure of a continuing future.[69]

But who is this Jesus to whom we are to return, and what teachings are we to follow? It is all very well saying that Christianity must be measured by the criterion of Jesus and can find itself again by returning to and following the person of Jesus. But as we saw in the previous chapter, even the New Testament churches had difficulty in following the Synoptic Jesus, and Christianity had to develop its own views of his significance and its own practice in order to become a universal religion. And once the significance of Jesus is developed in terms of the risen Christ, the problem of identifying and defining Jesus Christ is just as difficult as that of identifying and defining Christianity. The images of Christ are, once we look closely and critically at them, too variegated, too contradictory, too much coloured by the varieties of culturally-conditioned Christianity to serve as any guideline that can usefully be adopted.

And so we are led to the last and most perplexing question of this chapter. What is the relationship between the various Christianities and the Christs which they have as their symbols? Are the Christ-ianities a function of a particular kind of belief in Christ, or is belief in a particular kind of Christ a function of a particular kind of Christian culture, society, church or sect? How far are cultures, churches and individuals shaped by a Christ-figure who can legit-imately be shown to be rooted in an authentic understanding of Jesus of Nazareth, and how far is a Christ-figure essentially the projection of the hopes, wishes, dreams, priorities, policies of a particular age – what in view of our discussion in the first chapter we might want to call an ideology?

This is a question which can only be raised; not tackled in detail. The history of the interrelationship between images of Jesus and the societies of particular periods is a vast and fascinating one, so vast that a French publisher has devoted a series of no less than twenty books to it, entitled *Jesus depuis Jesus*, showing how through the figure of Jesus, individuals and groups, communities and insti-tutions, not to mention whole societies, have expressed their identity, their priorities and their hopes.[70] The series sets out to show the interplay between images of Jesus and theological and social traditions and demands, looking not only at mainstream developments but also at the apocryphal and heretical Jesus, the Christ of the barbarian invasions, the Carolingian Christ, the Christ of the conquistadors, the pietistic Christ, the Christ of the French Revolution and so on down to the present day, illustrated with five volumes of pictures! Obviously the collection of more information is important; but the examination of the interaction between a particular image of Christ and a society is a step beyond the stage that we have so far reached. For our question is one of criteria, and that means that it is one of the nature and legitimacy of particular images of Christ, i.e. how far a particular Christ is the product of a particular psychological need or cultural feature, in other words how far Christ-images are projections. Does not the tendency pointed out by Schweitzer, of each writer putting himself into his Christ, go right back through the pre-critical period?

Here, at any rate, are two illustrations to give us pause for thought. The first relates to the area of psychology.

In his fascinating study *The Cult of the Virgin Mary. Psychological Origins*, which has much illuminating material in it indirectly relating to the topics of this chapter, Michael Carroll points to the social change which led to the sudden emergence of the cult of Mary in the fifth century, attributing this to the influx of the Roman proletariat into the church which had begun to take place a hundred years earlier with the recognition of Christianity by Constantine. (He argues that as a result of this, psychologically necessary elements of Roman popular religion found their way into Christianity and that the cult of the Virgin Mary in all probability has its origins in the cult of Cybele.)[71] Now this was the time when the image of Christ crucified first appears:

> Christ is portrayed quite often in, say, the art of the catacombs, but not in connection with his crucifixion or any other aspect of the Passion. Surveys of catacomb art show that the depiction of Christ in this period is symbolic (as in the symbol of a fish), 'allegorical' (under the guise, for example, of the 'good shepherd', a very common motif in early Christian art), or in a New Testament scene unconnected with the Passion... In fact, in all of catacomb art, there is only one depiction of any aspect of the Passion, and that occurs in a single fresco... which seems to depict the crowning with thorns. Even then, the crown of thorns has clearly been transformed into a less painful laurel wreath.[72]

But from the end of the fifth century onwards, there is a relatively sudden development of the depictions of crucifixions which came to be so dominant in the Roman Catholic church.[73]

Carroll sees the simultaneous appearance of the Mary cult and depictions of the crucifixion, both coinciding with the great numerical increase in the Western Christian church by the addition of new social strata, as being characteristic of a widespread social factor at the time, that of the family with the ineffective father. This is a setting in which a strong but strongly repressed desire for the mother is combined with a tendency towards masochism.[74] His argument is worked out in some detail and needs serious consideration. It is important for us as a pointer towards the degree to which psychological forces can plausibly be seen as factors in the creation of Christian imagery.[75]

The second illustration comes from our own day. By it we can see how the cultural priorities of periods which most of us have experienced can be so powerful for particular individuals or groups that they feel that they have discovered the 'authentic' Jesus, his real significance. A generation ago, in his *Letters and Papers from Prison*, Bonhoeffer set down the outline for a book which he planned but never lived to write. In it he noted that ' "Jesus is there only for others". His "being there for others" is the experience of transcendence. It is only this "being there for others", maintained till death, that is the ground of his omnipotence, omniscience, and omnipresence.'[76] Those were words which Bishop John Robinson singled out in his *Honest to God* as being the essential character of Jesus, and so it was that under the widespread influence of his book one could not go far without hearing thoughtful Christians talking about 'the man for others'.[77]

But the 1960s are a different world from that of today, and nowadays you hear little talk about 'the man for others'. Now we are in a more violent, more political world, and the Jesus who has come to the fore is the Jesus who brings liberation, especially from political oppression, the Jesus who takes the side of the poor and is with them in their struggle, so painfully exemplified in Latin America. Liberation theology has no time for the ideals of 'the man for others' under the spell of its very different Jesus: Jesus Christ Liberator[78] and the other related images which have arisen out of the struggle.

Each of these images, the 'man for others' and 'the liberator', has its own power, and no one can deny that each in its own way offers a worthy ideal for human beings to emulate. It is important to be 'there for others', to suppress selfish concerns and be available and open to those who need what this openness can lead to and create. And the poor cry out for liberation from their captivity and for justice in a world whose resources are so unevenly divided and in which freedom is so scarce. But how far can the ideals of either Bonhoeffer or liberation theology truly claim the full support of Jesus of Nazareth? According to what the Gospels tell us he certainly was not readily 'there for others', as the Syro-Phoenician woman found when she attempted to divert his attention from the 'lost sheep' of Israel,[79] and he is reported to have told his disciples not to go among the Gentiles or enter any town of the Samaritans.[80] And as to the poor, the comment of his which is most often remembered is the one he made, to the dismay of Judas, after a woman anointed him with a valuable oil: 'The poor you have with you always.'[81] We shall be looking at this issue more closely in Chapter 6, and in Chapter 8 move on to an even more sinister dimension of it, the way in which images of Jesus can be used in one way or another for manipulation.

So our problems in this area are not solved. Moreover that solution has been complicated by the way in which down Christian history it has been possible for traditional believers to see the images of Jesus as being so to speak presentations, outward appearances, ways of understanding someone whose nature, no matter what the outward form, we know from Christian doctrine: Jesus is God incarnate. So it is to the doctrine of the Incarnation that we now turn.

5 | Problems with the Incarnation

> Following then the holy fathers, we all with one voice teach that it should be confessed that our Lord Jesus Christ is one and the same Son, the same perfect in Godhead, the same perfect in manhood, truly God and truly man, the Same consisting of a rational soul and body: *homouousios* (of the same substance) with the Father as to Godhead and the same *homoousios* with us as to his manhood; in all things like unto us, sin only excepted; begotten of the Father before ages as to his Godhead and in the last days, the Same, for us and for our salvation, of Mary the Virgin Theotokos (mother of God) as to his manhood.[1]

Those words come from the Chalcedonian Definition, a statement made by the bishops of the Christian church, assembled in 451 just across the water from what is now Istanbul. It is a classic statement of the doctrine of the Incarnation, a doctrine which, together with the doctrine of the Trinity, is the foundation stone of the whole theological system of the Christian church. The Council of Chalcedon was called with the aim of bringing peace to a church long racked by disputes over the person of Christ, and marked the culmination of two centuries and more of intensive thought and controversy.[2]

The sort of account that histories of Christian doctrine give to explain what the thinking and discussion during these two centuries were about, and why they had involved the church in so much controversy, adds up, very roughly, to this. The church's centre of gravity had long since moved into the Greek world, and explanation of Jesus in terms of a divinely guided sequence of events, promise and fulfilment, had given way to an understanding of him in relation to a changeless divine realm. This raised major theological and philosophical problems. Initially the main question at issue was the way in which God the Father, Jesus, and the Holy Spirit, could all be said to be God without subordinating either of the latter to God the Father, and without producing three Gods. This question is said to have been resolved at the Council of Nicaea, in 325. In the process the advocate of an alternative approach, Arius, was branded as a heretic.[3]

Attention then shifted to the person of Christ. Given the philosophical climate of the time, the church's interpretation of Christ and his work had to be expressed in terms of two different natures, human and divine, and an explanation had to be given of how immortal divine life could be conjoined with mortal finite life. Thinkers in due course regarded as heretics, like Apollinarius and Nestorius, had arrived at proposed solutions of this problem which introduced an imbalance of the human element over the divine, or vice versa; the significance of the Chalcedonian Definition was that it was accepted as a satisfactory way of explaining, in the conceptuality of Platonist philosophy, how Jesus could at the same time be both God and man, very God incarnate (though it did not put an end to the arguing, which led to yet more controversies in later centuries).[4] I do not propose to go into this development in more detail than that; there are a number of thorough and readable accounts of it at a variety of levels and if you need to know more you can refer to them.[5]

Since that time, for orthodox Christians, both Eastern and Western, the Chalcedonian Definition has remained a yardstick: something not to be gone beyond, the expression of a balance that must not be shifted. More than that, it is an authority: what the Roman Catholic church calls, using a stronger Greek word than the Latin-based 'doctrine', a dogma. It is something that, it has been and still is maintained, Christians *must* believe. To explain what that *must* has signified it is not unfair to cite another doctrinal document from a roughly similar period, the Athanasian Creed (it is in fact neither a creed nor by Athanasius; the precise date of its composition is unknown), still printed in the *Book of Common Prayer*:

Perfect God; perfect Man, of reasoning soul and human flesh subsisting; Equal to the Father as touching his Godhead; less than the Father as touching his Manhood. Who although he be God and Man, yet he is not two, but is one Christ... This is the Catholic

Faith, which except a man do faithfully and steadfastly believe, he cannot be saved.

Believe, or be damned! (And it is worth noting in passing that there was great controversy during the nineteenth century, accompanied by considerable public protest from the clergy, when it was suggested that the official requirement of the Prayer Book for the Athanasian Creed to be recited thirteen times a year should be made voluntary (one bishop threatened to resign if it were touched).[6]

The Chalcedonian Definition came at the end of a long process of theological controversy and had been preceded by a large number of similar creeds and statements, none of which found sufficient favour to become established.[7] Its formulation was a diplomatic as well as a theological exercise; at various points force had to be used to secure the triumph of what eventually became the 'orthodox' party, and historical accident also played a role.[8] However, once established, the Definition took on the authoritative status it has enjoyed since and, like a satellite going into orbit, jettisoned the forces of thrust which had set it in its place. Now it was in the heavens, and Christians came to believe that God himself had put it there – as part of his revelation, in the same way as the Bible was his revelation.

But that option is not open to us. As I have already said, modern scholarship has applied to Christian doctrine the approach which has already been used with great success on the Bible for almost two centuries, and we can look at the doctrinal statements of Christianity as human constructions, negotiated by fallible human beings against the background of the culture of their time as a result of particular developments (which could have been otherwise) and on the basis of particular presuppositions (which are open to critical examination).

Our historical perspective and the knowledge we have gained now makes it possible for us to ask questions which are relatively new to the Christian tradition. Need things really have gone the way they did? Are there not points in the history of the development of Christianity at which, if circumstances had been different, a rather different course might have been followed? Four of these points have been identified in recent studies of early Christian history, and reassessments are being made at all of them: the split between Judaism and Christianity, the rise of Gnosticism, the formation of the New Testament canon and the debate over Arianism. A brief look at the determining factors in these four areas may help as an illustration of just how what are now familiar landmarks actually came to be set up.

Was it really necessary for Christians and Jews to part company in the way they did? That question might seem strange to those who have been steeped in the traditional Christian view that, by crucifying Jesus, the Jews rejected the Messiah whose coming had been clearly foretold to them by the prophets. But such an account of the relationship between Christians and Jews is quite intolerable now. First, we know that what we call the Old Testament, but what the Jews call the Tenach (a term derived from the opening letters of the Hebrew words for Law, Prophets, and Writings, the three parts into which their Bible is divided), cannot reasonably be read as a prophecy of Jesus.[9] Christians may have seen Jesus prophesied in it, but the evidence that they thought they had found in the Jewish Bible is doubtful in the extreme, and the way in which they arrived at their conclusions leaves much to be desired.[10] Moreover, research into the Gospel accounts raises all sorts of questions about the claims which Jesus did in fact make for himself and about precisely who was responsible for his trial and execution.[11] There is plenty of scope for seeing the initial relations between Jesus (and his first followers) and Judaism in a very different light.

The impression given by the New Testament of a dramatic split at a very early stage is probably a most misleading one, not least a result of the fact that the Gospel tradition (and particularly the Fourth Gospel) seems to be influenced by the destruction of Jerusalem in AD 70. Before that time Judaism consisted of a great variety of different groups and, as we saw in the previous chapter, the same was true of the Christian movement. One Jewish expert suggests that on its first appearance Christianity might not have looked all that different from Judaism (he refers to the period of Jesus and the earliest church by its usual Jewish designation, as the Tannaitic period: Hebrew Tannaim means scholars, scribes):[12]

When Christianity began, it must have appeared simply as a group of Jews, otherwise generally conforming to the norms of the Jewish populace of Judaea, who had come to believe that the Messiah had come in the person of Jesus... The Tannaim did not see the earliest Christians as constituting a separate religious community. After all, there was no sin in making the error (as it was to the Tannaim) of believing someone to the Messiah... The Pharisees presumably regarded Jesus as yet another false messiah of a type which was not so unusual in the last days of the Second Temple. Indeed the existence of all kinds of sects and religious leaders was the norm of the day in the Second Temple period as we know from so many sources. Judaism was in what we might call an experimental stage. The biblical tradition was being adapted in many different ways in an unconscious effort to see which approach would best ensure the future of Judaism and of the Jewish people. For this reason, little opposition to the very concept of sectarian divergence existed. Each group argued for its own primacy and superiority, yet no voice called for the unity of the people as a virtue in and of itself.[13]

But that did not last. When there was a revolt against Rome, and Jerusalem was captured and destroyed along with the Temple, Judaism was forced to reorganize itself. From that point on it narrowed the range of diversity that was allowed, excluding on pain of excommunication some views of what it meant to be Jewish and thus making sure that in the long run one particular set of options (which to begin with were only a selection of many) became normative.[14]

Although differences over the Jewish and Christian interpretation of the figure of Jesus are usually seen as the cause for the increasing split between Judaism and Christianity, it may well have been that an even more decisive factor was the Gentile mission, which raised the question of the observance of the Law, and in particular the regulations over 'clean' and 'unclean' food. Neglect of these regulations, as happened when the church moved out into the Gentile world, would have proved deeply offensive, and even within the pages of the New Testament, in the letters of Paul, we can see the controversy which arose among Christians when the food laws were relaxed.[15] But whatever the precise details, the initial disagreements hardened into an irreconcilable parting of the ways. For not long after Judaism began to move towards uniformity and the establishment of rigid norms, Christianity, too, did the same thing.

But it cannot be stressed too often that it was the fall of Jerusalem and the destruction of Jewish Christianity which really opened up the gap between the two faiths. Had Jerusalem not fallen, subsequent events on both sides would have been very different.

If it was the fall of Jerusalem and the need to form a new Jewish community without the holy city that led Judaism to take the course it subsequently did, the first main pressure for the Christian church to exclude certain options and declare them 'heretical' came from the success of Gnosticism. The Gnostic movements were so powerful that, for instance, all the churches in Asia Minor with which Paul had been associated fell victim to them in the generation after his lifetime.[16] To combat them, what was to become the mainstream church felt obliged to insist on strict norms and harden its doctrinal position. Gnosticism is a term used in modern times to describe a variety of religious movements which attached particular importance to knowledge (Greek *gnosis*), hence the name.[17] This knowledge was believed to bring about redemption and to liberate the soul from subjection to cosmic forces. Gnosticism was long regarded as a Christian heresy, but more recent study has come to see it as a movement which in some respects antedates Christianity. For a long time it was known only from quotations of Gnostic works in the writings of its Christian opponents, but the discovery of a Gnostic library at Nag Hammadi in 1945 has proved to be for Gnosticism what the Dead Sea Scrolls are for Judaism between the Testaments, namely source material at first hand.[18]

The availability of this source material has also led to a complete reassessment of Gnosticism. Whereas earlier it was seen as a bizarre and perverse distortion of Christianity, it is now accepted as 'a religion not of despair and hopelessness but of deliverance and release, of light instead of darkness, day instead of night'.[19] What earned it the opposition of Christianity was its rejection of the world of matter as evil; its radical dualism, which included a distinction between a transcendent true God and the creator of the world; and its idea that human beings are essentially akin to the divine by virtue of the spark of heavenly light that they have imprisoned in their earthly bodies. Pressure from Gnosticism established a much narrower view of what it meant to be Christian, thus making sure that in the long run particular favoured options (which to begin with were again only a selection of many) became normative. Again, however, whether this was the only possible response is very much open to dispute. Although feminist scholars may at present be making excessive claims for what they consider to be the positive values of Gnosticism,[20] it seems likely that in cutting itself off from this whole thought-world as abruptly as it did, the Christian movement impoverished itself in many ways.

A third area in which things could have developed differently is that of the canonization of the New Testament, i.e the process of giving it the status of divinely inspired scripture. A long chain of developments led the Jews to form their own canon of sacred scripture, the Law, the Prophets and the Writings, referred to, as we saw, as the Tenach.[21] Because the first Christians were Jews, they continued to use this Bible, but they read it in a different way, and in due course, as Christianity moved into the Hellenistic world, read it exclusively in Greek. Although before the fall of Jerusalem the Jews had used a Greek translation, the Septuagint, in Greek-speaking areas, in their subsequent reorganization they reverted exclusively to Hebrew.

Jewish and Christian Bibles differed not only in language but also in content, since the Jewish Bible still had not reached its final canonical form at the time of the split with Christianity.[22] Moreover, alongside the Bible Jews had previously read a wide range of related religious literature. However, during the consolidation of their religion after AD 70, the Jews did a particularly thorough job of destroying a great many of these books, once in circulation, which they now thought unsuitable.[23] But Christians continued to read them, and what we know about their content comes largely from what was preserved by Christian churches in a variety of languages.[24]

The Christians, then, continued to treasure the Jewish Bible. But in addition to that, again by a gradual process which was not finished for several centuries, the Christians, too, produced their own scriptures and formed them into a normative canon, eventually taking over from the Jews many ideas about its inspiration.[25] The Jewish Bible became the 'Old Testament' (i.e. covenant – the Greek *diatheke*, of which *testamentum* is the Latin translation, means both) and the Christian scriptures, from then on bound up with it in one book, became the 'New Testament' (i.e., again, covenant).

Together, Old and New Testaments became the Christian Bible. But the final decision as to what should be included in the New Testament and what should not led to many disputes and disagreements, and some writings hovered on the edge of the canon for a long time before being either included or excluded.[26]

This was another historical development in which things could have been otherwise.[27] Despite the great importance attached to the Bible within Christianity, Christianity cannot properly be said to be a religion of the Book. It is above all a religion focussed on Jesus, for all the problems that we are at present exploring. It could have treasured its foundation documents (and those others which hovered on the edges of the New Testament, for in fact the line between what is actually in the New Testament and what is not is very blurred. Indeed some of what is in the New Testament has been included under false pretences and some of what was omitted has undeservedly been left out) without elevating them to the status of holy Scripture. As Christopher Evans asked in a telling comment:

> Would it not have been better, and would it now be better, for the church to be content with saying, 'Here are these books; we believe them to be profitable books from experience; they have come out of the lives of some of us and they express something of our faith; they are all we have, let us get on with it'? Is it, after all, so obvious that the Christian faith was meant to have a holy Scripture in the sense of the Old Testament, which it suceeded in demoting but fatally took as its model? Granted that the written text is strong precisely where tradition is weak, that as a fixed text it is less prone to corruption and more capable of acting as a purge, are these more than debating points, as good in their way as the debating points from the other side that it is the church which decides the canon and that Scripture does not interpret itself? Do they have to be blown up into a doctrine of holy authoritative Scripture? Granted also that such a Scripture has affected reform in the church, notably at the Reformation, did it do so without grave distortion, and except as achieving its immediate and necessary aim was not the Reformation something of a disaster, and nowhere more so than in its belief that it had achieved a fixed doctrine of the position of Scripture in the church? ... Has not reform in our own time come from other sources, and

included not only reform by the word of God but reform of the word of God?[28]

These comments take on even greater force when we consider them against the background of the questions raised in Chapters 9 and 10 below.

And fourthly, there was Arius. Branded by the church tradition as an arch-heretic, Arius lived at the end of the third and beginning of the fourth century AD. No one suffered more abuse than he did, and it was to combat what was thought to be his pernicious teaching that the great Council of Nicaea was held in AD 325. Even more than with the Gnostics, it is not easy to tell precisely what Arius did to incur his notoriety, since we know of his writings only through fragments preserved in the works of his opponents: no spectacular new source material has come to our assistance. The briefest of summaries of his teaching would quote his famous saying 'There was when he was not'; in other words, Arius denied that Jesus Christ was the divine Logos, God from all eternity, and claimed that the Son was a creature, not one with the Creator.

But beyond question Arius is now undergoing a rehabilitation,[29] so that the older view that his teaching was 'a mass of presumptuous theorizing… a lifeless system of unspiritual pride and hard unloving-ness',[30] crypto-pagan, polytheistic, illogical, unspiritual and a hindrance to true salvation has given way to the feeling that if one tries to see the problems with which Arius was coping from his perspective, there is a good deal to be said in his favour. He may have been inadequate in much of what he taught, but that can equally well be said of others with a more orthodox reputation. The line of his opponents which won the day at Nicaea is also not without its problems, and Arius was at the very least a gifted theologian trapped by his presuppositions. But heretics are made only after the event and sometimes it is politics which determines who comes out on top. In the process of controversy, initially they are an essential part of the exploration, though they end up as being those who happen to come out on the losing side.

So there are ways in which Christianity might have developed differently. The reason why I have stressed this is because it is important to see that the results with which we have been left are not miraculously safeguarded absolutes but what ultimately emerged from a complicated historical process. It may be that the alternatives they replaced could have proved utterly disastrous, but since the alternatives did not prevail, it is impossible to tell what would have happened (and we must never forget that what we have been left with is always the version propagated by the winning side). Even then, it is clear – and will become clearer when we proceed – that those developments like the formation of the canon of the Bible and the endorsement of particular statements of Christian doctrine – are very much 'in earthen vessels', rather than in the divine splendour in which they are sometimes decked. The way in which stress on the content of the Bible as the Word of God has led to a disastrously bigoted form of fundamentalism and the stress on the incarnation of God in Jesus has led to a Jesus who is often not recognizable as a human figure are just two of the penalties which have had to be paid.

But things did not in fact develop differently; they developed as they did. So the next stage is for us to look at the course the understanding of the person of Jesus did take.

When we considered the nature of the Gospel evidence about Jesus, there was one important aspect of it that we only touched on in passing and did not investigate in any detail, namely how Jesus understood his own person and how the evangelists understood him. This whole area is one of great complexity, and many books have been written about it, and about other ways of understanding the person of Christ which can be found elsewhere in the New Testament. For all the details, you will have to refer to them.[31] What concerns us here is the conclusion that can be drawn from these detailed studies. Once again, Professor James Dunn provides what would be regarded as a moderate and balanced assessment; others would be more doubtful about his positive assertions:

Did the doctrine of the incarnation begin with Jesus? If we accept the possibility of penetrating some way into Jesus' own self-consciousness, self-understanding, self-estimate, or whatever is the appropriate phrase, what do we find? We find one who was conscious of being God's son, a sense of intimate sonship, an implication that Jesus believed or experienced this sonship to be something distinctive and unique; but the evidence does not allow us to penetrate further or to be more explicit... We find one who claimed to be inspired by the Spirit of God, to be a prophet in the tradition of the prophets, but more than that, to be the eschatological prophet, the one anointed by God to announce and enact the good news of God's final rule and intervention. We find one who may well have claimed to speak as the final envoy of Wisdom, with an immediacy of revelatory authority that transcended anything that had gone before. But there is no indication that Jesus thought or spoke of himself as having pre-existed with God prior to his birth or appearance on earth. Such self-assertions appear only in the latest form of the canonical Gospel tradition, and presuppose substantial developments in christological thinking which cannot be traced back to Jesus himself.[32]

In other words, the Gospel evidence suggests that Jesus did not say that he was Son of God or even Christ; these were titles given to him later by his followers, who elaborated them, developed them and added to them as time went on. The most crucial stage in this development was that of the assertion of the 'pre-existence' of Christ, which took place at a very early stage. Jesus as the Christ was identified with a number of the characteristics of God which in the Old Testament seem almost to take on a life of their own: God's wisdom, God's word and so on. Now in the Graeco-Roman world, where Logos, the Greek for word, was also used in philosophy to denote the principle of universal reason, Word had a whole series of other connotations which then came to be attached to the person of Jesus as the Christ. Since God's wisdom and God's word and the Logos were all so to speak eternal, it followed from the association of them with the person of Jesus that Christ had to be eternal too, and therefore that he existed before Jesus of Nazareth.[33]

But this approach had another even more far-reaching effect. It brought together two completely different spheres of thought so that they were combined around one focal point: the sphere of mythology and cosmic drama characteristic of the world of first-century Judaism, and the more sophisticated world of Greek meta-physical philosophy. These two very different spheres thereafter remained intertwined and in fact cannot be separated without tearing apart the fabric of Christian doctrine. As Professor Houlden, who has explored this issue at much greater length, has pointed out, the doctrine of the pre-existence of Christ 'began (for example, in Philippians 2.6-11) as frankly mythological, in the sense of giving a description of supernatural realities as wholly continuous with the observable world. But later, when it received metaphysical statement, it could never abandon its mythological side, simply because it was, after all, a statement about the previous life of one who had actually lived in the world and was known from the pages of the Gospels. It could never become pure philosophy.'[34]

The power of the idea of the pre-existent Christ can be seen from the fact that it made its way against two factors which pushed in the opposite direction: first the fact that the Gospels presented a Jesus who for all the miracles associated with him had lived a fully human life and died a human death, and second the strictly monotheistic faith which was a characteristic both of the Judaism out of which Christianity came and of philosophical reasoning. The history of Christian doctrine is a history of a constant struggle against these pressures. But the power of the pre-existent Christ is not without its disadvantages. As has been pointed out, once a pre-existent divine person is taken as the model for christology, it becomes extremely difficult to maintain convincingly that the earthly Jesus had a human will alongside his divine will. 'For the divine being who assumes human nature is conceptualized as "Jesus Christ who came down from heaven and was incarnate". It is natural, then, that he should be pictured as a wholly divine Jesus; he acts, speaks, thinks and wills like a man, but with a consciousness, a purpose, and a will that are divine.'[35] As a result, as I have said, throughout the history of the early church and even today, in much of the Christian tradition, popular understanding as well as academic theology finds great difficulty in seeing Jesus as *truly* human.

The development of Christian doctrine was also a battleground over the interpretation of the Bible. This interpretation was often bizarre and arbitrary in a most disturbing way. Professor Wiles, another doctrinal critic, has given a telling example. One of the main concerns of the theologians of the second and third centuries was to demonstrate the distinct existence of three persons in the Godhead against those who denied their reality (they are referred to as modalists and monarchians). Tertullian, one of these theologians, appealed to the Fourth Gospel with all its texts which speak of the Son as being sent by the Father, and so on, and went on to ridicule Praxeas, his monarchian opponent, by saying that he ended up by having the Father crucified. Scripture, and particularly the last taunt, won the day for Tertullian.[36] However, what was a winning argument for him could prove embarrassing at the next stage of the doctrinal debate. Now the opponent was Arius, and Arius, it will be recalled, had no problem over the distinction of the three persons in the Godhead. It was his argument, rather, that they were a hierarchy, not co-equal. So the Arians could use the Johannine texts against the 'orthodox', and the only way in which the latter could cope was by explaining away their earlier interpretation of them.[37]

Here are two examples of reasoning within the development of doctrine; others could be quoted, but it is time to ask some questions of what we have already seen. How acceptable is such an approach today?[38] What do we make of the pattern of argument which led to the assertion of the pre-existent Christ? What do we make of an approach to scripture which could not possibly gain acceptance in the modern world? Does not the character of both these approaches raise serious questions about the ultimate validity of the conclusions reached by them? Granted, more than argument went into the making of the doctrines of Trinity and Incarnation: worship and the experience of salvation were equally important factors. But here too, if we had the time, questions could be asked.[39] What can be said of the role of worship in connection with the development of the major Christian doctrines can also be said in connection with the development of Roman Catholic Mariology leading up to the doctrines of the Immaculate Conception and the Bodily Assumption, and here the evidence has very strange features.[40] Nor is it easy to see why the salvation of humanity need necessarily depend on the two principles which played such an important part in the doctrinal debates over the nature of salvation, that a saviour must be fully divine and, to put it in the traditional terminology, that 'what is not assumed is not healed'.[41]

Professor Wiles has also made another important point in connection with the development of Christian doctrine.[42] It is evident that belief in the incarnation arose within a certain complex of other beliefs – creation, fall, redemption – which are all closely connected in Christian thought: God created the world, but Adam sinned and

Jesus, the second Adam, remedied that sin and brought redemption. For a long time it was thought that each doctrine (creation, fall and redemption) could be affirmed meaningfully only if it was based on one specific event in history. So it was felt that the doctrine of the creation of the world by God and particularly of humankind in his own image was threatened by the theory of evolution, and denial of the historicity of Adam as first man endangered the doctrine of original sin (as is indicated by the papal encyclical *Humani Generis*). However, it can in fact be argued that neither doctrine intrinsically needs to be associated with a specific historical event and that detaching the doctrines from historical events in fact makes them more meaningful. There can still be a doctrine of creation even if the Genesis account is not literally true, and there can still be a doctrine of the fall and of sin without a historical Adam. It is clear where Professor Wiles's argument takes us: if that is true of creation and redemption, cannot there also be a meaningful doctrine of redemption without it being so firmly based on the person of Christ as the traditional one is? And might not the whole edifice of doctrines surrounding the person of Christ, technically known as christology, be mistaken and misleading?

> Christology arose because it was not unnaturally, yet none the less mistakenly, felt that the full divine character of redemption in Christ could only be maintained if the person and act of the redeemer were understood to be divine in a direct and special sense. In the parallel cases of creation and fall our forefathers had to learn – and it was a painful process – that what they thought was a logically necessary link between the theological assertion and particular occurrences in history was not as logically necessary as they thought it to be. Are we perhaps at the equivalent – and even more painful – moment of learning the same truth about the doctrine of redemption?[43]

Of course, Professor Wiles's argument has provoked criticisms and counter-arguments, even from some of his sympathizers, but though there may be quibbles about some of the details, the question he asks is clearly a legitimate one.

Here we have moved from making a critical examination of the way in which christological doctrine came into being to asking whether the concerns which led to the formation of that doctrine really had to end up where they did, thus making this clearly a fifth instance in the series that we have been considering. That question was taken a good deal further by Professor G.W.H.Lampe's book *God as Spirit*.[44] The basic purpose of his argument was to replace the model of incarnation as a way of understanding the presence of God in Jesus with that of inspiration. The concept of God as Spirit seemed to him to provide a more satisfactory theological model than that of God the Son, 'for the latter almost inevitably tends to suggest either that deity revealed in human terms in Jesus is somehow other than God whom we conceive of as Father, or that God whom we acknowledge in Jesus was united in him with something less than a fully human personality. The history of the ancient controversies shows that the one defect can be remedied only at the cost of making the other worse.'[45] In his first chapter he took up the argument of Professor Wiles that we have already looked at, and developed it further, going on, for example, to argue that the abandonment of the notion of a historical fall removed the necessity of seeing redemption as the remedying of a catastrophic reverse in human evolution. He wanted to understand creation and redemption as part of the same continuing process, a view which incarnational theology can distort. He also questioned the traditional idea of a once-for-all act of God, for 'we are not saved by an event as such, not even the event of Good Friday, but by its effect upon us when it is interpreted in a certain way'.[46] Myth, too, may have saving efficacy.

On the positive side, Professor Lampe was keen to stress the positive value of models like Spirit and inspiration. He saw salvation coming through the creative interaction of God's Spirit with the spirit of humankind, making men and women whole in a process of creation out of recalcitrant material.[47] Such a process, he argued, causes suffering to God, a mystery which we can see as it is incarnated in human love (not just in Christ) and in the suffering which that entails. Professor Lampe did not refer to what is known as 'process' theology,[48] which has gained a wide following for its similar line of argument, but his argument was very much along that line. In this continuous incarnation of God as Spirit in the spirits of men, he went on, the Jesus presented to us by the Gospels holds his unique place:

In Jesus the incarnate presence of God evoked a full and constant response of the human spirit. This was not a different divine presence, but the same God the Spirit who moved and inspired other men, such as the prophets. It was not a different kind of human response, but it was total instead of partial... We can speak of the life of Jesus as God's self-revelation, no longer dimmed and distorted, as in other men, by the opaqueness of sin in the mirror which reflects and communicates it.[49]

(At this point perhaps it ought to pointed out in passing that both Professor Wiles and Professor Lampe represent the best of British patristic scholarship; what they say is not a superficial judgment but one based on and drawn out of years of study of the theology of the early church. Professor Lampe, who died in 1981, was also editor of the *Patristic Greek Lexicon*.[50])

Professor Lampe's arguments might have attracted much more attention had they not been overshadowed by the publication that same year of a book which gave notice to the world at large that some theologians now felt the doctrine of the Incarnation to be so inadequate that it was time for it to be abandoned. Even before the day in 1977 on which it was published, *The Myth of God Incarnate* was already attracting newspaper headlines. John Hick, the editor, was joined for the volume by six other British scholars (soon to be known as the 'Seven against Christ', echoing a taunt made against the seven contributors to the collection *Essays and Reviews*, published in 1860, which caused a famous controversy in the Church of England. This was a manifest 'own goal', since time showed those who challenged *Essays and Reviews*, which argued, for example, that the books of the Bible could be read in the same way as any other books, to have little more than fear of modern knowledge to be said for them.[51]) John Hick described the purpose of the book in the preface:

The writers of this book are convinced that another major theological development is called for in this last part of the twentieth century. The need arises from growing knowledge of Christian origins, and involves a recognition that Jesus was (as he is presented in Acts 2.21) 'a man approved by God' for a special role within the divine purpose, and that the later conception of him as God incarnate, the Second Person of the Holy Trinity living a human life, is a mythological or poetic way of expressing his significance for us. This recognition is called for in the interests of truth; but it also has increasingly important practical implications for our relationship to the peoples of the other great world religions.[52]

Or, as John Hick was to explain elsewhere, to call Jesus God, Son of God or God incarnate is to use language which is an expression of love and commitment, and is therefore misused as a set of propositions understood literally as the foundation for further argument. Talking about Jesus as Lord and Saviour is very much the same as saying one's beloved is the most beautiful woman in the world. Logically there can be only one most beautiful woman in the world, but to take that phrase literally and infer that every other woman is less beautiful than the beloved in question is to misunderstand the kind of language being used. Similarly, to infer from statements that Jesus is Lord and Son of God that the only way to God is through Jesus is to turn commitment and love into dogmatic exclusiveness.[53]

Here we can see how criticism of the doctrine of the Incarnation is bound up with the questioning of the uniqueness and finality of Christianity, an issue that we shall look at in detail in Chapter 11. That also explains why in addition to those Christians who were shocked by *The Myth of God Incarnate* as a threat to their faith there were many others, Christians and those of other religions, particularly Moslems, who welcomed it as a positive contribution to the dialogue between religions.[54]

I do not propose to go into the arguments put forward in the text of *The Myth of God Incarnate* here; we have been able to see during this chapter the various discussions and objections which led to its composition, and the contributors included several of the writers to whom I have already referred, who in the book developed arguments which they had already begun elsewhere. And despite all the storm over the book, it seems in fact to have done little more than state, perhaps in a rather more radical form, views which were quite widely held. For by the early 1980s, when a call for restatements of Christian belief was increasingly heard and the Church of England Doctrine Commission and other groups attempted to provide them, it was widely noted that since 1977 the Church of England had assimilated most of the arguments of *The Myth of God Incarnate*, and that, the extremist wings apart, its position had virtually become accepted belief (in this respect, too, it resembled *Essays and Reviews*).

However, the Epilogue by Professor Nineham, perhaps the least noted part of the book, does need our further attention. Other contributors, like Professor Lampe before them, had not only presented serious criticisms of the doctrine of the Incarnation but had offered a positive alternative interpretation of the person of Christ. It was this positive alternative that Professor Nineham challenged. Earlier drafts of some of the papers, he remarked, including one by Professor Hick, had claimed that Jesus was 'intensely, *totally*, and overwhelmingly conscious of the reality of God', with his spirit '*wholly* open to God' (and in the quotation from Professor Lampe on p.87 we can see a similar use of the word 'total' in connection with the inspiration of Jesus by the Spirit). This use of words like *totally* and *wholly* reflected a tendency in modern theological writing to suppose that although some of the imagery by which traditional theology had sought to express the uniqueness of Christ might no longer be possible, it was possible to be sure about the reality of at least some of the unique facts to which the traditional models were intended to do justice, and therefore to express them again in a way that would be appropriate in the present day.

What Professor Nineham had in mind, he went on to say, was the view that 'Jesus' life was at every stage and every level centred entirely upon the being, grace and demands of God, and so introduced into history a new humanity, a new way and possibility of being human'. And he went on to quote some words of John Robinson from *Honest to God*:

> It is in *Jesus*, and Jesus alone, that there is nothing of self to be seen, but *solely* the *ultimate, unconditional* love of God. It is as he emptied himself *utterly* of himself that he became the carrier of the 'name which is above every name'.[55]

But how do we know this? How can we be sure? It is all very well to use the language of finality and absoluteness when speaking about Jesus if you have first accepted the doctrine of the Incarnation; but reject the doctrine of the Incarnation, and begin from Jesus the man and what we know of him, and such language cannot be validated. Negatives cannot be proved. Given the evidence we have, indeed given all possible evidence, how can one demonstrate utter purity, absolute selflessness or whatever from historical records?[56]

To put the matter in a different way: having rejected the arguments for the metaphysical uniqueness of Jesus, i.e. that by virtue of the doctrine of the Incarnation Jesus may be believed in as both God and man, theologians cannot fall back on arguments, say, for the moral uniqueness of Jesus, the man for others, the best man who ever lived. There is no rational way in which such arguments can be defended. So we cannot escape from the problems of the church's formidable and archaic doctrines into the simplicity of a Jesus who was demonstrably the paragon of all virtues and a supreme example of human nature. Even if we had far, far more evidence – which we do not – that would be impossible to demonstrate.

Professor Nineham's argument shows that the doctrine of the Incarnation, then, is not something to be discarded lightly, and theologians fighting something of a rearguard action in favour of it have proved to be very well aware of this. But the doctrine of the incarnation cannot be maintained, either, as a revealed truth which has dropped down from heaven and is above all historical and rational criticism. Even if the positive alternative to it does not prove viable, the criticisms made of it still remain. Indeed, we shall be examining further problems connected with the nature of Christian doctrine in Chapter 10. Before that, however, we must look at other claims and problems associated with Jesus, first at more images and then at Jesus' ethical teaching.

6 | Can Jesus be Everyman?

As most people have come to know it, Christianity means putting Christ at the centre of life. This is a thought to be found not only in simple piety but also in scholarly christologies. In Jesus, it is often said, a Christian is to see the perfect exemplar of humanity, and therefore the normative model of ethical Christian life. By implication, this norm extends to all life, and the church has long taught that Christ Jesus is the true centre of the temporal world.[1]

This sense of Christ at the centre, of Christ as model, of Christ as representative humanity, indeed pervades Christianity, but it does so in a diffuse – and confusing – way and is one of the most difficult aspects of Christianity to discuss rationally or to make sense of in any ordered fashion.

The whole area is complicated by the fact that it borders on another area, equally important for Christians: that of the manner in which Christ brings salvation, of his 'saving work', at the heart of which lies the doctrine (or more properly doctrines) of the atonement.[2]

The first area of imagery, discussion and Christian teaching is confusing because it is so often unclear precisely what figure is being used as a norm or an exemplar, and the use of 'Christ Jesus' in the quotation with which I began the chapter highlights this. For example, if we are supposed to have Jesus of Nazareth in mind as a norm or exemplar, then the Gospel tradition gives us at least the outline of a life-style – one which has inspired monastic orders down the centuries. But that is an option which has always seemed to be open only to a minority, and even then those who have developed the pattern have had to work out much for themselves: Jesus did not leave behind any form of 'rule' or community which handed on a distinctive life-style. We have already seen that when Christianity reached the cities of the first-century Roman empire its ethos changed substantially.[3] And in fact Paul, as we have also seen, has little occasion in his letters to refer to the earthly Jesus. We have already seen that his most-quoted and admired passage in this connection, that in Philippians 2.5ff., 'Have this mind among yourselves, which you have in Christ Jesus...' has to be described as mythological,[4] in that it is about a divine figure who sheds his divinity, is obedient even to death, and as a result of that obedience is given by God an even higher place than he had before.[5] Though we may be deeply moved by its poetry, if we apply our minds to it we have to reflect that we are not divine beings who have shed our divinity, and that the question 'obedient to what?' is not answered.

And this brings us to the problems of the second area. For not only is Jesus a norm or exemplar; he is also saviour, the one who (according to traditional Christian doctrine), being Son of God in human form and without sin, has achieved that which sinful humankind was unable to achieve. That being the case, is there in his human life that which we cannot expect to achieve, or even imitate? Does he as it were have a 'head-start' in his human career along with innate qualities which enable him to live in a manner which would be disastrous were we to attempt it in precisely the same way? Ought we not, given our limitations and his uniqueness, in principle to try for a less demanding aim and life-style? But if that is the case, what happens to any use of Jesus as norm or exemplar?

Such would seem to be the confusion here that it would take an entire book to analyse all the issues and even raise the questions in a systematic way. So I shall limit the discussion to three areas: first that of the atonement, and then of the problems felt by two groups marginalized by the emphasis on Jesus as norm or exemplar.

The New Testament uses a great variety of imagery to describe the saving significance of what had happened in Jesus Christ,[6] and in the patristic period, the Middle Ages and at the Reformation this was supplemented with a further variety of worked-out theories.[7] These ranged from the view that Jesus had worked through and reversed all the errors of humankind[8] to ideas of a ransom paid to the devil,[9] a victory won over the devil,[10] to satisfaction[11] and substitution.[12] However, because such views are so heavily conditioned by the cultures in which they were held they have been found quite inadequate by many Christians from the nineteenth century on.

This complexity is reflected in more recent studies of the doctrine. For example, Russell Barry, one of the great twentieth-century bishops and also one of the few leading Anglicans to come out of the Church of England's involvement in the First World War with any credit, was convinced that any viable doctrine of the atonement could only be a psychological one and wrote a book along those lines.[13] And in perhaps the most comprehensive and best book on the atonement, F.W.Dillistone bases his whole treatment on the assertion that reconciliation between God and man, man and God, cannot be expressed through any single shape or pattern.[14] Though he himself wrote from a committed Christian position, the range of material that he introduced and the tone of his argument did not produce any sharp division between Christianity and other world faiths:

> The persistence of the story of redemption achieved does not necessarily depend upon commitment to its Christian formulation. We are convinced that whenever, in limited and imperfect fashion, man submits himself to the pressure and the onslaught of powers obviously greater than his own, with the object of achieving a fuller freedom, somehow, somewhere, this action is of superlative value, even if on the plane of history it ends in apparent disaster. In our own imperfect and limited fashion we are prepared to commit ourselves to this pattern of action as alone worthy of emulation and praise.[15]

And he goes on to refer to beliefs such as that the assassination of an Abraham Lincoln was not the extinction of the fire which he had kindled and that the crushing of the 1956 Hungarian rising (a decade before he wrote) was not the last word in human affairs. To other Christians that may seem a reduction of what the doctrine originally set out to state, and they will find this kind of approach unsatisfactory. But we shall see that there are many problems associated with accusations of reductionism:[16] can there be 'reductionism' from a doctrine, i.e. a theory, which is demonstrably no longer adequate?

It may also be the case that all doctrines of the atonement have difficulties because, as with the doctrines of creation, fall and Incarnation which we considered in Chapter 5, they are concerned to associate the 'atonement' too narrowly with one particular point in time (and with one particular person).[17] But if that is the case, here again, with the doctrine of the Incarnation, we see pressure building up from various perspectives about the idea of Christ the centre. And that brings us to those for whom the presentation of Jesus, or the Christ, at the centre causes acute problems.

As Rosemary Ruether points out, christology has been the doctrine of the Christian tradition that has been most frequently used against women.[18] She refers to the argument put forward by Thomas Aquinas that the male is the normative or generic sex of the human species, that only the male represents the fullness of human potential, while women are by nature physically, morally and mentally defective. That makes the incarnation of the Logos in the male an absolute necessity, with the consequent argument that Christian priests must be male. And all this is bound up with an alleged sacramental 'mystery':

> Behind this christological argument of the necessary maleness of Christ and his representative, the priest, lies, it seems to me, a theological assumption; namely the maleness of God. Not just Jesus' historical humanity, but the divine Logos, the disclosure of the 'Father', is necessarily male. In a remarkable forgetfulness of their own traditions of analogy and the *via negativa*, images such as 'Father' and 'Son' for God are not regarded as partial images drawn from limited (male) human experience, but are taken literally. 'Daughter' or 'mother' are not regarded as equally acceptable analogies.[19]

Those who have been following the debates over the ordination of women will have noted the way opponents of such ordination seem to presume that at least in God's dealings with humankind, God is male, even if in a context in which theology had less of a direct application they would protest that they believed God to transcend gender.

The whole debate is also bedevilled in its approach on the human side by the constant difficulty Christianity has had from the start in integrating human sexuality into its thought and living. If, as is so patently obvious – and as Woody Allen has brought home to us so vividly – the two dominant features in all human life are death and sex, why does Christianity say so much about death and so little about sex? Of course there is an awareness that it *ought* to, but all attempts somehow seem doomed to failure from the start. One only has to compare the joyful association of sexual intercourse with the sabbath in the Jewish tradition[20] with the idea of a similar combination of 'sex and Sunday' in the Christian to see something of what Christianity lacks.

If Jesus is highlighted as being a norm or exemplar for Christians the fact of his maleness is complicated by our virtually complete ignorance of the nature of his maleness in this important respect. That has not prevented theologians from speculations, some of which might seem quite outrageous, but given the way in which Jesus is presented as an example, the questions raised are not unnatural ones to ask. However, here as elsewhere the sheer paucity of the evidence allows virtually anything to be asserted.

For example, in the late 1960s Canon Hugh Montefiore, later to become Bishop of Birmingham, suggested that Jesus might have had homosexual inclinations:

> Why did he not marry? After all he was fully a man. Of course there is no evidence, and we can only speculate, and speculation can be done with reverence. But having raised the question we must look it in the face – why did he not marry? Could the answer be that Jesus was not by nature the marrying sort?[21]

And he went on to say: 'Women were his friends, but it is men he is said to have loved. The homosexual explanation is one we cannot ignore.'[22]

By contrast, the American theologian William E.Phipps wrote a book with the title *Was Jesus Married?*[23] and a sequel *The Sexuality of Jesus,*[24] in which he concluded that Jesus was probably married to a Galilean woman before he was twenty. Since ancient Judaism, he argued, valued married life and disdained celibacy, it was likely that Jesus shared these views. It was Hellenistic sexual asceticism that was responsible for the view that Jesus was perpetually virginal.[25] And *Jesus Christ Superstar* has not been the only work to suggest a degree of sexuality in the friendship between Jesus and Mary Magdalene. In his novel *The Last Temptation,*[26] Nikos Kazantzakis leads up to a marriage between Jesus and Mary, and the German theologian Elisabeth Moltmann-Wendel reads out of the Gospel record 'a special and personal relationship' between Mary Magdalene and Jesus, a 'special love' of Jesus for her. In their brief dialogue in the garden on Easter day, 'there seem to be a delight, a happiness, an eroticism which transcend the teacher-pupil relationship'.[27]

To all this, the only thing to be said is the usual 'We just cannot know.' But it is that which raised the problems from the beginning. Combine the somewhat tantalizing tradition about Jesus and women in the Synoptic Gospels with the extremist teaching on sexual matters governed by the expectation of the imminent coming of the kingdom (including 'there are eunuchs who have made themselves eunuchs for the kingdom of heaven', a statement which Origen in the third century imitated literally),[28] with the strict emphasis on the subordination of women in marital respectability put under pressure by the influence of the Gnostic sects, and one hardly has source material which will be of much help in sexual counselling down the ages.

As Elisabeth Moltmann-Wendel goes on to point out:

> In sexual questions the early church remained profoundly uncertain, because of the practice of Jesus. The adulteress whom Jesus did not condemn, the woman of Samaria whom he makes the first apostle to the Samaritans, despite the blemishes in her married life – all these were facts which it was difficult to cope with in the solid development of Christian morality. Augustine sighed over them and regretted that the story of the adulteress was ever included in the Gospel of John.[29]

Nor was the uncertainty limited to the early church. Uncertainty, and worse, has been a characteristic of Christian attitudes to sexual love, and this has not been helped by the fact that so much has been written about it by celibate clergy and members of religious orders living in a highly artificial atmosphere, or by those who cannot cope with the emotions unleashed by the sexual dimensions of friendship and marriage.

The failing of the Christian tradition in the whole area of sexuality (and by that I mean a much wider sphere than that of physical sexual relations or sexual emotions; we move on to the obvious fact that half the human race is female, not male) is now having repercussions which are being felt in the churches with some force. For after two millennia of male-dominated theology, feminist theologians are now insisting that proper account be taken of their perspective, and of the problems caused for them by the inevitable stress on maleness because the tradition has the male Jesus at the centre.

Nowhere has the problem of the predominance of the masculine in religion, the imaging of God in the male Christ, been more evident than in Roman Catholicism with its celibate clergy. And so in reaction there has come into being the understandable, but utterly fantastic, cult of the Virgin Mary to compensate for the lack of femininity in the saviour. One of the factors which makes one suspicious of the wealth of images that have developed around the person of Jesus is the almost equal wealth of images that have developed around his mother Mary, with far less justification.[30]

Does this not indicate a very high degree of projection of human needs, fears, longings and hopes of believers on to Jesus and Mary rather than an interpretation of the persons of Jesus and Mary as they once were? Mary Daly is surely right in arguing with some anger that 'the psychological acrobatics of Christians surrounding the symbolizations of Christ and Mary have little to do with the historical Jesus. They have even less to do with the historical person Mary, the mother of Jesus, and are devastating to the fifty per cent of the human race whose lot she shared.'[31]

And again it is Rosemary Ruether who spells out the problem for women of a religion which has a male saviour:

> Precisely because it is the central symbol in Christianity, the saviour figure is also the symbol most distorted by patriarchy. All efforts to marginalize women in the Church and Christian society, to deprive them of voice, leadership, and authority, take the form of proclaiming that Christ was a male and so only the male can 'image' Christ. Woman, while the passive object of his redeeming work, can never actively represent him as mediator of God's word and deed. If feminist theology and spirituality decide that Christianity is irredeemable for women, its primary reason is likely to be this insurmountable block of a male Christ who fails to represent women.[32]

And the page opposite which these words are printed carries a photograph of a sculpture, 'The Crucified Woman', by Almuth Luckenhaus.

The book in which Rosemary Ruether's comments occur is an anthology of material aimed at creating a theology which expresses the full personhood of women, and the comments themselves are part of an introduction to passages about male and female saviours. She ends her introduction with a long series of questions:

> Do we need a saviour? Is the Christ simply an objectification of our own ideal self, which we project on the heavens and then 'encounter' as something beyond our own capacities that we need to receive from beyond? Would this process work better or not work at all if we recognized that what we were about was our own self-redemption rather than a 'work' of redemption done outside our own capacities?
>
> If the redeemer manifests for us the gracious, liberating face of God/ess and our own true human potential, won't an exclusively male Christ ever alienate women from claiming their humanity as women? Is it enough to claim that Jesus represents 'generic humanity' or even was an antipatriarchal male, if he alone remains the exclusive face of the redeeming God and of our authentic humanity?
>
> Can Christology remain encapsulated in a single, 'once for all' figure of the past who 'completed' the work of salvation, even though we and our history remain obviously unredeemed? Must not the Christ image be ever projected on the new horizon of history that appears before us, leading us on to our yet unrealized potential? As our perception of our incompleteness changes with new sensitivities to racism, sexism and European chauvinism, must not the image of Christ take ever new forms: as woman, as Black and Brown woman, as impoverished and despised woman of those peoples who are the underside of Christian imperialism?[33]

I have quoted Rosemary Ruether at some length because this particular passage has so many important features. First, rather than being assertive, it consists almost entirely of questions. Second, it maintains a tension not always to be found in feminist writings, which are produced under so much pressure: it is all too tempting for feminist writers either to abandon Christianity altogether, writing it off as having betrayed and wronged women, or at the other pole to pull their punches and not raise enough questions out of a desire to remain within the Christian fold. And thirdly, it shows how the area with which we are at present concerned leads on to other areas: we shall be considering later in this chapter the relationship of Christ to those with skins of another colour than white, and in Chapter 11 we shall be discussing the claim of Christianity – and its Christ – to be unique and once for all.

But what is the logic of a sentence which suggests that the image of Christ must also take a new form, as woman? Is that not pushing the tension beyond breaking point? It is parallel to the practice of some continental feminist writers of talking of a female *Jesa Christa* alongside their male *Jesus Christus*.[34]

In fact the association of feminine imagery with Jesus goes right back to mediaeval times, if not before. A well-known representation of Jesus as mother is to be found in the *Revelations of Divine Love* by Julian of Norwich, the fourteenth-century anchoress. However, it goes back further than that. The most recent study of Julian, by Grace Jantzen, quotes a passage in Anselm's 'Prayer to St Paul' in which he combines Jesus as mother with biblical allusions to the feminine qualities of God: 'Mother Jesus, know again your dead son (Anselm is referring to himself), both by the sign of your cross and the voice of his confession. Warm your chicken, give life to your dead man, justify your sinner.'[35] And Dr Jantzen refers to other passages, including one from the writings of the Carthusian prioress Marguerite of Oingt, who exclaimed: 'Ah! Sweet Lord Jesus Christ, who ever saw a mother suffer such a birth! For when the hour of your delivery came you were placed on the hard bed of the cross... and your nerves and all your veins were broken.'[36]

In connection with the fourteenth 'shewing' Julian, too, links the motherhood of Jesus with the crucifixion and the crucifixion with child-bearing: it is the moment of cosmic travail when the creation struggles towards transformation. And on the fifteenth 'shewing' she wrote:

> The Mother may lay the child tenderly to her breast, but our tender Mother, Jesus, He may homely lead us into His blessed breast, by His sweet open side, and shew therein part of the Godhead and the joys of heaven, with spiritual sureness of eternal bliss... This fair lovely word Mother, it is so sweet and so close in

Nature of itself that it may not verily be said of none but of Him; and to her that is very Mother of Him and of all... He is our Mother in Nature by the working of Grace in the lower part for love of the higher part.[37]

From more recent times, Don Cupitt has drawn attention to an unpublished work by Florence Nightingale in which she saw herself as 'Cassandra', the prophetess of 'a female Christ, who will resume in her own soul the sufferings of her race'. To such a degree, he goes on to comment, was the full humanity of women denied with the apparent approval of the church, and to such a degree were the feelings provoked by this denial incomprehensible to males, that Florence Nightingale separated 'Jesus' from 'Christ' in her mind and became one of the first Christians of the modern period to formulate the idea of a female Christ.[38]

But is this kind of imagery justified? Is it viable for the future? Is the way forward, as Rosemary Ruether suggested, that the image of Christ should take 'ever new forms', including that of woman? Or is the combination of male Christ and mother image not rather an indication of a deep-rooted problem in this whole area, caused by the fixation of divine activity to a historical male individual who is then elevated to the status of God, who indeed often in Christian language, thought and practice seems to have wholly taken over the place of God? And is not Mary Daly more correct here in taking a much more radical stance, and saying forthrightly that the problem lies in 'the exclusive identification of the person of Jesus with God, in such a manner that Christian conceptions of divinity and of the "image of God" are all objectified in Jesus'.[39] For her the Christ-olatry (idolatry, with Christ as the idol) which consists in this excessive reverence for Jesus has to end, and indeed will end, as a logical consequence of the liberation of women. She speaks of the need for the coming of Antichrist (an image which, she argues, need not necessarily be a negative one) as a step in the movement towards bringing freedom from the oppression which comes from the idea of redemptive incarnation being effected uniquely in the form of a male saviour.

What if the idea has arisen out of the male's unconscious dread that women will rise up and assert the power robbed from us? What if it in fact points to a mode of being and presence that is beyond patriarchy's definitions of good and evil? The Antichrist dreaded by the patriarchs may be the surge of consciousness, the spiritual awakening, that can bring us beyond Christolatry into a fuller stage of conscious participation in the *living* God.[40]

This particular discussion is still in its early days and a great many issues in it need to be clarified much further; obviously they are far from being resolved. The worst thing one can do is treat them lightly or dismiss them as extremism, because their subject-matter is of crucial importance, and one thing is quite certain: that discussion of the whole nature of Christianity and the person of Jesus will be much healthier when it is shared in by both women and men on much more equal terms. But it is hard to see how, if the discussion is to be a contribution to the quest for truth, it can allow the persons of either Jesus or Mary to continue to play some of the roles that they at present have in Christianity. The element of projection in the imagery attached to them needs to be taken much more seriously.[41]

As obvious as the fact that humankind is divided into two different sexes is the fact that it is divided into men and women of very different cultures and different coloured skins – various shades of white, black, brown, red, yellow. Nor are these differences cosmetic ones; with them go very deep differences of climate, living conditions and experiences, which for much of our history has included those of being treated as sub-human, of enduring slavery and of being victims of racism. What is the relationship between the historical Jesus of Nazareth and representations of him as having been of another culture, colour or race?

This is a question which has been raised in a particularly acute form by the 'black' theology which has been developed in the United States of America and, to a lesser degree because of the circumstances, in South Africa. In many accounts and indeed in many statements by its spokesmen, black theology can be made to seem an extremist ideology and an utter distortion of Christianity, with a substitution of violence for the gospel of love. But we need to reflect that in this respect it is doing no more than holding up a mirror to what white Christianity has done over various periods of its history, that it is showing us – literally – the dark underside of that history. Starting from there, if one is prepared to give black theology a reasonable and unbiassed hearing, it is evident that it has many important things to teach us about images of Christ. Here I shall be singling out just one of them: the stress on Jesus as *black*.

Manas Buthelezi, writing from South Africa, has given a powerful account of what it is to be black:

> Blackness is an anthropological fact which utterly governs my whole existence day by day: it determines where I live, whom I meet and with whom I can share my daily life. Everyday life unfolds before me within the limits and range of possibilities inherent in the black situation. The word of God speaks to me where I in fact am, in my blackness. I can only go to a black church, and usually the service can only be taken by someone who is black, as I am.[42]

So it is argued that if Christ is to speak to someone in such a situation, he must be black. The position of black people who feel that only a black Christ can speak to them is as desperate as that of Florence Nightingale, whom I mentioned earlier, so badly hurt that she could think of no salvation coming from the male sex and therefore dreamed of a female saviour. As James Cone, one of the leading advocates of black theology, puts it: 'Christ is black, not because of some cultural or psychological need of black people, but because and only because Christ *really* enters into our world where the poor, the despised and the black are, disclosing that he is with them, enduring their humiliation and pain, and transforming oppressed slaves into liberating servants.'[43] And if it is objected that this stress on the blackness of Christ seriously endangers his universal significance, Cone retorts:

> Indeed their insistence upon the universal note of the gospel arises out of their own particular political and social interests. As long as they can be sure that the gospel is for everybody, ignoring that God liberated a particular people from Egypt, came into a particular man called Jesus, and for the particular purpose of liberating the oppressed, then they can continue to talk in theological abstractions, failing to recognize that such talk is not the gospel unless it is related to the concrete freedom of the little ones.[44]

In the black community, then, it is believed that the Christian gospel can make sense only if Christ is black, because only by presenting him in that way can the realities behind the words be given proper expression. And if white Christians dislike, attack, criticize, dismiss this approach, it is because they are blind to the racist dimension in their own Christianity. Their picture of the *white* Christ – how often does one ever hear that expression among those theologians who are critical of a black Christ? – is just as restrictive. White is just as much a colour as is black, brown, red or yellow; it is not a neutral expression of being human.

So black theology is most effective at pointing out the hidden presuppositions of white theology, of making us as it were attempt to step out of our skins and look at our Christianity from a very different perspective. It also begins to open our eyes to the way in which the figure of Jesus can be used either to reinforce the domination of those in power or as a symbol of liberation by those who opposed them, depending on the circumstances. This is an issue which we shall be returning to in much more detail in Chapter 8.

But while there is much that we do not know about Jesus, we can be certain that he was neither an Aryan white nor an African black. He came of Semitic stock and he was a Jew. Moreover, he is not a contemporary but a figure from the historical past. He did not live in South America or East Africa or Japan but in the Roman province of Syria. We are back to the questions with which this chapter began and find in black theology the same symptoms of discomfort as in feminist theology, tackled by making statements behind which lies a deep existential truth, but which raise a whole series of historical and theological problems.

We have touched on just two areas in which people feel marginalized as a result of Christian teaching as they understand it. The list could be extended considerably, as it is by Tom Driver, who concludes: 'The Christ who has *already* come provides little hope for "outsiders". I maintain that what does not liberate them for the world of God does not liberate anyone of conscience.'[45] And it is for them, not us, to tell us that they are liberated: 'free at last'.

All this should give food for thought to those who, in pastoral work or preaching sermons, so easily say something like: 'No matter how deep the suffering, no matter how great the pain, no matter how shattering the bereavement, Jesus has been there before you. For in him God took on the whole of human experience, even to the point of dying the most agonizing death imaginable.' The impression is given that Jesus suffered the utmost physical pain, in his crucifixion, and the utmost psychological pain, in his sense of being abandoned by the Father with whom he had had the most intimate personal relationship; and that by reason of his life and suffering he 'knows what it is like' to be in any human condition. No matter how desolate, oppressed, persecuted, agonized, despairing, bereft, humiliated, a person may be, for him or her, for all of humanity Jesus is the companion, support, helper or inspiration, because 'he was there too'.

Now it is obviously important that those who believe in a loving God – and indeed those who do not – should offer all help, support and comfort possible to the 'wretched of the earth'[46] (above all by attempting to change their condition), but whether an approach like this, in terms of the person of Jesus, is a legitimate way of going about it is quite another matter.

Let Stevie Smith have the last word:

Was he married, did he try
   To support as he grew less fond of them
   Wife and family?

Did he feel pointless, feeble and distrait,
   unwanted by everyone and in the way?

Did he love people very much
   yet find them die one day?

Did he ask how long it would go on,
   Wonder if Death could be counted on for an end?

Did he never feel strong
   pain for being in the wrong?

He knew then that power corrupts but some must govern?

Did he lack friends? Worse,
   Think it was for his fault, not theirs?[47]

It is her heartfelt puzzlement that led me to put the beginning of another poem as the heading to the whole of this book:

O Christianity, Christianity,
   Why do you not answer our difficulties?[48]

7 | Jesus and Ethics

As we saw earlier, even without the support of a doctrine of the Incarnation, modern Christian theologians have wanted to claim that in one way or another Jesus was the supreme and unique instance of humanity. Yet those who have found it impossible to accept Christianity have put forward cogent reasons for finding Jesus and his ethical teaching less than perfect.

When in Chapter 3 we looked at the way in which John Baker began his consideration of the conflicts between the Christ of doctrine and the Jesus of the Gospels, we saw that the first point that he took up was the sinlessness of Jesus.[1] Straight away he quoted a saying by the great Jewish scholar C.G.Montefiore, that 'Jesus was not good enough to be God',[2] and went on to point out that it was not hard for any reader to find incidents or passages in the Gospels which, 'if read without the presuppositions of faith',[3] give colour to this charge. If John Baker's reaction is that of someone firmly within the Christian church, it is not surprising that many voices outside have been much more outspoken.

A number of perceptive writers, from Bertrand Russell to Philip Toynbee, have pointed to Jesus' excessive emotionalism, as recorded in the Gospels, and particularly to his anger – again a feature to which John Baker points. As Bertrand Russell put it:

> One does find repeatedly a vindictive fury against those people who would not listen to his preaching – an attitude which is not uncommon with preachers, but which does somewhat detract from superlative excellence. You do not, for instance, find that attitude in Socrates. You find him quite bland and urbane towards the people who would not listen to him, and it is, to my mind, far more worthy of a sage to take that line than to take the line of indignation.[4]

And like so many others, he referred especially to Jesus' apparent belief in hell.

A substantial development of criticisms of Jesus and his teaching is to be found in one of the great books of modern British philosophical humanism, Richard Robinson's *An Atheist's Values*. He takes up the objection to the element of harshness in Jesus' teaching, and points to its paradoxical character and its obscurity because so many of the texts are fragmentary. He, too, notes the contradictions. For example, it is difficult, Robinson remarks, to see what Jesus' law of love can amount to in view of his overwhelming insistence on the priority of the law of piety:

> We cannot give material help to our neighbours because the law of piety demands improvidence and poverty. We cannot take family love very seriously because it may interfere with our devotions. Any two rules of conduct will conflict in some cases, and it seems quite clear that Jesus' first two rules must conflict very often. But, in accordance with the unsystematic character of Jesus' teaching, there is no recognition of this in the Gospels. There is hardly a recognition of any possibility of conflict between any two rules.[5]

Robinson goes on to point to human ideals wholly absent from Jesus' teaching, later indeed adopted into Christianity but in fact illegitimately labelled Christian. The ideal of truth and knowledge is wholly absent. On the contrary, Jesus poured contempt on the professors of knowledge and declared that the kingdom of heaven is hidden from the wise and prudent. There is no place for beauty or justice. Above all, Robinson points out, Jesus says nothing on any social question except divorce, and all ascriptions of any political doctrine to him are false. He does not pronounce about war, capital punishment, gambling, justice, the administration of law, the distribution of goods, socialism, equality of income, equality of sex, equality of colour, equality of opportunity, tyranny, freedom, slavery, self-determination. 'There is nothing Christian about being for any of these things, nor about being against them, if we mean by Christian what Jesus taught according to the synoptic gospels.'[6]

But these are the comments of writers standing outside Christianity. Does not Jesus fare rather better at the hands of those within the tradition?

It has often been commented that Jesus' teaching really does only relate to personal ethics. By his chosen pattern of life Jesus was a stranger to the issues, the complexities and the tensions which arise in communal living, in the context of marriage, the family or a fairly close-knit social group. We need only think back to the complaint of Stevie Smith in the previous chapter. Jesus' style of life, his teaching, centres essentially on one-to-one relationships without complications. 'Leave the dead to bury their dead.'[7]

And even here there is a serious problem, which was highlighted by the American Professor John Knox. Jesus' teaching puts us under a moral responsibility which even the best effort of even the best person is utterly unable to discharge. And this means that that teaching, as recorded in the Gospels, does not give us the practical guidance we often seek when confronted with a dilemma.

> Does it help us to be told the perfect thing to do, when we are not in a position to do the perfect thing, whether because the external situation does not allow of its being done or because we ourselves are morally incapable of doing it? We are told that on one occasion a man whose brother apparently had stolen his inheritance came to Jesus with his problem. Jesus refused even to discuss it, but instead said to the complainant in effect, 'Renounce covetousness, and you won't care whether you get your inheritance or not; indeed, you will be glad to let your brother keep it.' But actually the man was unable to renounce covetousness; besides, he probably felt that a matter of justice and equity was involved. To this particular man in his particular situation, it may be held, Jesus said nothing really useful. Nor, it is further contended, does he (or the New Testament) still have anything really useful to say to those who come with questions as to what one should do in situations where the perfect thing, for one reason or another, cannot be done.[8]

C.G.Montefiore, who has already been quoted, complained that Jesus' ethical teaching is 'strung too high',[9] that it does not produce such good results as less imaginative and less ambitious codes tend to produce. To start from an impossible ethic can, in the field of conduct, whether personal or social, actually discourage ethical action and fail to provide any incentive for it. If an impossible perfection is the command which has to be obeyed, and that perfection is totally out of reach, why bother at all, especially if God is there to forgive and to welcome?

There are also problems with the motivation (and the rewards and sanctions) which the Synoptic Jesus gives in connection with his ethical teaching. Sometimes no motive is given for a particular action at all, but simply the demand for a self-sacrifice that does not count the cost nor ask for anything in return. At other times there is an appeal to his hearers' sense of what is right. Sometimes there is an appeal to a religious motive, or the motive is dedication to a person or a cause. And quite often the only apparent motive is one of sheer self-interest. Nowhere, though, as Professor H.J.Cadbury was not slow to point out, is there a clear appeal to the rights or needs of another party or to the interests of society in general.[10]

And that brings us to the sphere of social ethics, the lack of which in Jesus' teaching was so criticized by Richard Robinson. There were many social institutions in Jesus' day and most of them are mentioned in his parables or elsewhere in the Gospels; moreover Jesus is specifically said to have consorted with people in a wide range of callings, including soldiers and tax-collectors. There is one exception to this, the institution of marriage, on which a saying of Jesus is recorded; the difficulty here, though, is that it has come down in two contradictory versions, which at the very least indicates that whatever Jesus said was found to be problematical.[11]

Jesus was also indifferent to the solidarity of society and social groupings. This is all the more remarkable given the degree to which such groupings were prominent in the concerns of the Jewish people from whom he was descended, and again his words – and his life – are full of encounters with some of them: Pharisees, Sadducees and so on. But even where he refers to these groups and points out their faults, his aim is personal repentance, not structural reform.

None of these comments is particularly new. Indeed the comments on social morality which I have drawn from Professor H.J.Cadbury date from more than fifty years ago. He also remarked:

The incompleteness of our records, the uncertainness of their transmission, the original inchoateness of their presentation are all admitted. Jesus laid down no rules to be universally applied; his teaching was casual and illustrative, *ad hoc* and particular. Nevertheless we are told that there is enough clear evidence to assert that he had an intense interest in human society and gave utterance to fundamental social principles which accord with the best findings of modern sociology and were intended as guidance for the revision of human relationships.[12]

No wonder, then, that Jews, for example, are so quick to point out the weakness of Christian ethical systems in comparison to their own, above all because in so many areas virtually no accepted casuistry, i.e. working out procedures for particular situations, has been developed. We are so familiar with the chaos of Christian moral teaching, in the past and today, that it often seems to be taken for granted on all sides. It is surprising, though, that the detrimental effect of the degree of chaos in Christian ethical teaching is not emphasized more widely. Over the last century the scandal of divided, conflicting and mutually exclusive churches has been widely noted, and largely unavailing efforts have been made to remedy it. Is not the scandal of moral division and conflict (on issues as varied as the observance of Sunday, contraception and abortion, the consumption of alcohol and pacifism) just as great – and one which has its ultimate origin in the enigmatic nature of the earliest ethical teaching of Christianity, that attributed to Jesus, and the church's extremely arbitrary use of it over the centuries?

We now move on to yet another indication of the chaotic nature of Christian ethics, the remarkable fact that while it is unthinkable that a Jew or a Moslem should write a book on ethics without referring to Moses or Mohammed respectively, it is quite possible to write a book on 'Christian' ethics which does not refer to Jesus at all. An old friend of mine, Michael Langford, a philosophy professor in Newfoundland and author of an excellent simple introduction to Christianity, went on to write an equally good introduction to Christian ethics. When the typescript arrived to be prepared for publication, there was virtually no mention of Jesus in it from beginning to end. I pointed this out and suggested that at the very least he should add a section which explained what some people might find this strange omission. His subsequent justification was as follows:

> If it is the case that the content of ethics is essentially the same for Christians and for all other people of good will, then any attempt

to explore the content of ethics must not rely on authority, but rather on tests or criteria for what is right of a kind that can appeal to people of all faiths or of none. This is particularly evident when the moral issues under discussion are controversial. In such cases appeals to the teaching of Jesus, while they may be of great power to the committed Christian, are not appropriate within the general debate concerning these issues. Even if the debate is between Christians, appeals to authority are not satisfactory when controversial questions of interpretation arise. Moreover... Christians within the catholic tradition (with a small 'c') have always held that while God always commands what is good, it is not his mere commanding of an action that makes that action good. Essentially God commands x because it is good, x is not good just because God commands it. Therefore, in principle, there must be some grounds on account of which x is good, apart from the commands of God or the teaching of Jesus.[13]

There are points in this paragraph to which we shall be returning when we come to discuss criteria of theological truth in Chapter 12. But its content should be noted, and it is interesting that Michael Langford chose as the title of his book not something recognizably Christian; it uses some words in a combination from the classical tradition, which did not originate with Jesus but were taken over by Christianity when it moved into the Graeco-Roman world: *The Good and the True*.[14]

The same absence of the teaching of Jesus can be noted in another book, this time actually on early Christian morality. Professor Wayne Meeks points out:

Those who are familiar with other books on the New Testament or early Christian ethics will miss in this one several familiar items. I do not have a chapter on 'the ethics of Jesus'. Interesting as that topic might be, it is both elusive – we probably do not have enough firm information to write anything like a rounded account of either Jesus' moral behaviour or his moral teaching – and beside the point.[15]

So far, the whole discussion has been going on as though all the ethical teachings attributed to Jesus in the Gospels go back to him and can be treated as being on the same level as 'the teaching of

Jesus'. But that, of course, is not the case, as we saw in Chapter 3. What was said in that chapter about the difficulty of knowing what Jesus was or did or taught; about the contribution of the early church, to the point of even attributing to Jesus remarks that he did not make; about the theological portraiture of the evangelists, also applies here. And that means that as well as having problems in evaluating the ethical teaching of Jesus, we also have considerable difficulty in discovering just what it was. I have already mentioned one example, which can be seen very clearly if you use a synopsis: Mark and Matthew differ over Jesus' teaching on divorce. In Mark Jesus categorically forbids divorce; in Matthew it is allowed in cases of adultery (the so-called 'Matthaean exception'). The most likely explanation here is that Matthew's version is reflecting needs within his church, and that the exception does not go back to Jesus, but once we see that at least one evangelist (or the tradition before him) must have been ready to change what Jesus said, the possibility that Jesus' ethical teaching has been adjusted must always be taken into consideration.[16]

Discovering the complex way in which the Gospels came into being does remove some of the problems over Jesus' ethical teaching which arise from treating all the Gospel material as authentic on the same level; recognition of hostility to the Jews in the early church which has been reflected by the evangelists and is often projected back on to the time of Jesus (most notably, of course, in the Gospel of John) also slightly relieves the dimensions of, say, Jesus' anger. But it does not remove these problems altogether, and indeed introduces a possibility which goes beyond the mere alteration of words of Jesus. Since we do not know for certain what Jesus said and what he did not, it is by no means unlikely that some ethical teachings attributed to him and treasured as being his by the church ever since were not his at all, but are the creation of some anonymous early Christian or Christians.[17]

Given the precedents in Jewish literature, it would in fact be surprising had that never happened. For certainly not all the law attributed to Moses goes back to his time – indeed it is hard to see precisely what does, since the Ten Commandments, supposedly given on Mount Sinai, presuppose that the Israelites are already settled in the Promised Land – and it was a common practice to attribute one's words to an authoritative figure, from the distant and in some cases the not so distant past.[18]

And there is a much deeper problem still, when we look at the ethical teaching of Jesus in the Gospels in the light of modern biblical criticism, a problem which adds a new dimension to the whole of our discussion so far. It seems almost certain that in his teaching, as in all his life and action, Jesus was dominated by the thought that the existing world would change very soon, to be replaced by another, brought in by God, and that the early church took over this belief.[19] What significance does that have for his ethical teaching?

When at the end of the last century it became possible to read the Gospels without quite so many preconceptions governed by tradition or overt prior concern, perhaps the most disconcerting feature of the teaching of Jesus to emerge was that he and the early church seemed to expect an imminent end to the existing order and the beginning of a new one. This was the discovery which provided the main features of the life of Jesus that Albert Schweitzer himself produced at the end of his survey of lives of Jesus written by others. Summarizing its consequences elsewhere, he described them like this:

> The ideal would be that Jesus should have preached religious truth in a form independent of any connexion with any particular period and such that it could be taken over simply and easily by each succeeding generation of men. That, however, he did not do, and there is no doubt a reason for it. We have, therefore, to reconcile ourselves to the fact that his religion of love appeared as part of a world-view which expected a speedy end of the world. Clothed in the ideas in which he announced it, we cannot make it our own...[20]

And that is, of course, also true of his ethics.

Schweitzer's view – and its implications – did not find widespread acceptance, for obvious reasons, but that does not mean that it was misguided, and it is interesting to note that perhaps the best study of Jesus to have been written since his, that by E.P. Sanders, takes very much the same line.[21]

The Gospel tradition preserves sayings like 'There are some standing here who will not taste of death until they see the kingdom of God coming with power.' The choice by Jesus of twelve disciples is obviously related in some way to the twelve tribes of Israel, and in another passage the disciples are told that they will 'sit on thrones judging the twelve tribes of Israel'. They are sent out on mission, and told that 'you will not have gone through all the cities of Israel before the Son of man comes'.[22] These are only a few of the more obvious passages: once accept the perspective and there are many more which can be seen to fit in with it.

That expectation was also present in the early church. Paul, for instance, told the Thessalonians, worried because some of the members of their church had died before this change had taken place, that 'we who are alive, who are left until the coming of the Lord, shall not precede those who have fallen asleep. For the Lord himself will descend from heaven with a cry of command, with the archangel's call, and with the sound of the trumpet of God. And the dead in Christ will rise first; then we who are alive, who are left, shall be caught up together with them in the clouds to meet the Lord in the air; and so we shall always be with the Lord.'[23] Paul repeats the same sort of view to the Corinthians, in that passage which has been read at so many Christian funerals: 'We shall not all sleep, but we shall all be changed, in a moment, in the twinkling of an eye, at the sound of the last trumpet.'[24] What he means here is that not everyone will die (= sleep), though some will. However, everyone, whether dead or still alive, will be changed from their mortal form into an immortal form. As we have seen,[25] it is also seems likely that Paul's haste to preach the gospel round the known world (he had hoped to go west to Spain) was prompted by the same motive of an imminent coming.[26]

Although there is no disputing the existence of the evidence I have cited, there is considerable argument as to how it should be interpreted. Attempts at a complete reinterpretation to eliminate any future expectation of this kind have not unnaturally failed, and even John Robinson, not unknown for his ingenuity when it came to offering new slants on old problems, did not convince others of his view that the idea of the second coming of Jesus does not go back to Jesus himself but was a misunderstanding of Jesus on the part of the early church.[27] However, though it seems as certain as anything of which we can be certain in connection with Jesus and the early church that neither expected the present world order to continue for very long, here too there is considerable doubt as to how much of the Gospel material on this theme goes back to Jesus and how much is the creation of the early church.[28]

Still, the indications that Jesus expected an imminent divine intervention are enough to give substance to the problem with which we shall now be concerned. If the expectation of an imminent end to the present age conditions the whole of Jesus' ethical teaching, what becomes of that teaching since he proved to be mistaken? Of course the suggestion that Jesus can be demonstrated to have been mistaken sends seismic tremors through many forms of christology, particularly most of the incarnational ones that we were concerned with in Chapter 5, and that explains why the controversy here has been so fierce. But it is hard to dispute that on this central issue Jesus' expectations were not fulfilled.

That Jesus did not expect the present age to last very much longer means that he did not envisage a church, and therefore that all subsequent church structures, however time-hallowed, however elaborate and appealing to divine authority for their existence, ethos and hierarchical order are *in the last resort* no more than improvisation to cope with a situation over which initially Jesus left no guidance.[29] (There will always be argument over Matthew 16.18, 'You are Peter, and on this rock I will build my church', but before jumping to any conclusions everyone should at least look at the passage in a synopsis and ask where it comes from – it is not in the two parallel passages – in the light of Matthew's overall portrait and then trace the development of the way in which it came to be used.)[30]

As I indicated in Chapter 4, the Acts of the Apostles has cast its spell on most Christians when they come to consider the rise of the earliest church, and its confident portrayal of the Spirit-led progress of the gospel from Jerusalem to Rome and the way in which eschatology is played down in both the Gospel of Luke and Acts leaves no room for an account of the problems that manifestly arose. But the last chapter of the Fourth Gospel, usually regarded as an appendix, is evidence of an expectation that the 'beloved disciple' would not die (before the second coming),[31] and the second letter attributed to Peter, almost universally thought to be not by him and by reason of its content to be virtually the latest document in the New Testament,[32] refers to scoffers who say: 'Where is the promise of his coming? For ever since the fathers fell asleep, all things have continued as they were from the beginning.'[33] Consequently it resorts to an expedient used earlier in Judaism in connection with similar unfulfilled prophecies: 'With the Lord one day is as a thousand years and a thousand years as one day. The Lord is not slow about his promise as some count slowness.'[34]

So in addition to the pressures of the development within the early church which we surveyed briefly in Chapter 3, from Jesus the itinerant preacher to the communities established in the major cities of the Mediterranean world (a development in which Christians had to work out a good deal for themselves as they went along), we have to take into account the influence of the steadily receding 'second coming'. This delay will have left its mark on the churches during the first century, not least in their ethical teaching.

Moreover because some of the varieties of Christianity were getting out of hand, leading to extremes of asceticism or, more dangerously, to libertinism and what by any conventional standards amounted to immorality,[35] more solid and more detailed moral teaching became imperative. We can already see Paul coping with such deviations in his first letter to the Corinthians, and the history and practices of Gnosticism over the next century or so indicates how attractive they were.[36] Such deviations had to be combatted by what was later to become the mainstream church, which sought to secure a measure of stability and in addition now had to prepare for a long existence in Graeco-Roman society and make it quite clear that Christians were also responsible citizens. Respectability was the name of the game, and to attempt to stand out by deviant behaviour or to shock was to court trouble. So in the last stratum of the New Testament we find that Christian teaching has taken over almost word for word stock catalogues of virtues and vices, good behaviour and bad behaviour.[37]

Here, for example, are some instructions from the letter to the Colossians:

Wives, be subject to your husbands, as is fitting in the Lord. Husbands, love your wives, and do not be harsh with them. Children, obey your parents in everything, for this pleases the Lord. Fathers, do not provoke your children, lest they become discouraged. Slaves, obey in everything those who are your earthly masters, not with eyeservice, as men pleasers, but in singleness of heart, fearing the Lord. Whatever your task, work heartily, as serving the Lord and not men.[38]

All very respectable, but how 'Christian' could it be said to be? One wonders what Jesus of Nazareth would have made of it, at a period at which, had he lived the life-span achieved by some of his contemporaries, he could have still been alive to see it.

No wonder that one commentator can write on this passage: 'We cannot fail to be struck by the meagreness of the instruction given to the different family groups, and by the entire lack of appeal to any specifically Christian motive in the exhortation to husbands and to fathers, and the indefiniteness and generality of the Christian motivation adduced in the address to wives and to children.'[39] Similar passages can be found in many other of the later letters in the New Testament. Granted, they often have a much more markedly Christian colouring, but this is essentially cosmetic. It is not that Christians have a distinctive ethical code to offer the world; they have simply taken over the code of contemporary respectability and expressed it in the terms of their own communities.[40]

So it is that the author of a book on ethics in the New Testament could say:

> To put the matter now most sharply, Jesus does not provide a valid ethics for today. His ethical teaching is interwoven with his imminent eschatology to such a degree that every attempt to separate the two and to draw out only the ethical thread invariably and inevitably draws out also strands of the eschatology, so that both yarns lie only in a heap. Better to leave the tapestry intact, to let Jesus be... a Jew of Palestine of nearly two thousand years ago; let him have his eschatological hopes that were crushed, as Schweitzer said, on the wheel of fate that was his cross; let him believe in the imminent end of the world and God's imminent judgment and, in prospect of that, call his hearers to a radical surrender to God.[41]

Professor Jack T. Sanders wrote those words in 1975. When his book was reissued with a new preface just over ten years later, he commented on the hostile reception that his views had received in many quarters. He suggested that, to judge from their reactions, many reviewers felt that they had to reject it before they even read it, and its denial that the New Testament was relevant to ethical decisions today had provoked an automatic negative reaction from Christians who believed that their day-to-day conduct should be largely governed by New Testament principles. But, he went on to say, he did not invent his findings – the material to support them was there in the New Testament. 'The wonderful ethics that challenges the imagination is formulated under the mantle of imminent eschatology.' 'It is the main thesis of the book,' he concluded, 'that imminent eschatology was the necessary framework for the selfless ethics of Jesus and of Paul, and that when the imminence faded Christian ethics became little more than bourgeois propriety.'[42]

It is hard to see how any work on Christian ethics based on an appeal which does not take that finding into account can command respect. And we have one more set of problems to add to our list.

8 | Jesus, Power and Politics

So far we have amassed a substantial number of questions about Jesus relating to Christian thought and life: relating to the New Testament, to the interpretation of Jesus down history and the images of the Christ that have been developed; to worship, doctrine and ethics, to personal devotion, pastoral counselling and cultural differences. The impression that the accumulation of these questions gives might rightly seem to be a very negative one, amounting to a devastating attack on Christianity, rather than an attempt at clarification.

At this point, therefore, before we go on to asking questions in two areas relating to history and historical consciousness, it is worth while pausing to remind ourselves of my initial argument that as well as being negative, the questions being raised here have two positive consequences. One of these positive consequences is that a properly questioning attitude to one's own tradition and to the problems that it raises can be an important asset to dialogue aimed at a greater understanding of those of different faiths. Christians who are narrow-minded and dogmatic about Christianity can hardly be expected to be really open to believers from other traditions when they are regarding them from an attitude of either tacit or explicit superiority,[1] whereas those who are used to looking at their own beliefs from a variety of perspectives and asking questions about them can take on questions asked by others. That is a positive aspect to which we shall be returning in Chapter 11.

The other positive consequence of the questions that have been raised, and the one with which we shall be concerned here, is that they are capable of bringing liberation from half-truths which have been used to dominate and control, to instil fear and endorse the acceptance of social injustice, inequality of the treatment of the sexes and the perpetuation of institutions which have outlived their day: in short, half-truths which have tended illegitimately to postpone change. That capacity for questioning is one which is particularly in need of consideration in the more conservative and authoritative atmosphere of our day, and is much less obvious than it was, say, twenty years ago.

Now we turn in the light of this questioning to a difficult and under-discussed area of belief in Jesus in the context of the church: the use of Jesus (or the Christ) in the context of power and of politics – not just secular politics, but also the politics of church government and authority.

I begin by recalling what has almost proved to be a sub-theme of some of the earlier chapters: although biblical and doctrinal criticism and the results which it has had are so often regarded as abstruse, academic, boring and of little point by many clergy and laity, they have come into being as a result of a great deal of heart-searching, hard thinking, personal dedication, sacrifice and indeed suffering by scholars and others, many of whom have felt themselves to be engaged in an enterprise worth dedicating their whole lives to, regardless of the personal cost. One has only to read the lives of, and attacks on, some of these figures, to see just what a battle scholarship has been. That tends to be disguised by the way in which the previous year's (or decade's, or century's) battles tend to be far less exciting (except perhaps to those who fought in them) than those going on in the present – but while they are being fought it is a very different matter.

I use the term battle deliberately, because it is all too easy to imagine study and discussion of the person of Jesus going on within relatively stable and tranquil groups: school RE lessons and university tutorials and seminars, church discussion groups and further education classes, or in scholarly papers and books written by experts in their particular field. But the possibility for that more tranquil discussion to continue, where it does, is one that has only been achieved after a good deal of struggle and is by no means secure. 'Battle' is an appropriate word for the majority of earlier discussions of Jesus down the centuries because the figure of Jesus – or the Christ (and I said at the beginning that these were two distinct representations around which different groups of Christians have polarized at different times in Christian history) – is such an evocative one and is a source of such power for those who use it –

indeed, in some cases control it. One might recall the fighting connected with the Arian controversy, not least after Nicaea; the iconoclastic controversy, the Monothelete controversy and the Reformation, to mention just a few major conflicts.[2] The power of the symbol of Christ can be turned to the use of religious or secular, political or psychological manipulation, and has been and is used for such manipulation by certain parties within churches, religious movements and indeed states to further their aims or endorse certain patterns of behaviour.

Statements about the supposed attitudes of Jesus on one or other issue have been used by church authorities to endorse particular claims to power (e.g. Matt.16.19 to defend the claims of the papacy);[3] questions raised about these statements by biblical scholars can in turn be used to set up those scholars as the new authorities: during the nineteenth century it was not infrequently argued that they had become the new 'popes'.[4] Nor is the dissimilarity between these two groups in terms of potential power as great as might seem at first sight; indeed the power of theologians has even been described as 'formidable':

> How else are we to interpret the activities of presiding over, or addressing large congresses of experts, or writing large works which figure on theological reading lists, of compiling reading lists, of framing syllabuses, of recommending students for appointments, including and especially appointments at theological seminaries, and of participating (or not participating) in church commissions? All these activities, especially those connected with the theological education of the ministry of the Church, embody interventions both in the Church's power and in the Church's participation in the external power conflicts.[5]

And if that sounds somewhat far-fetched in Britain, where theology has such a low profile, one only has to think of the enormous influence exercised until very recently by the German theological 'schools' with their internationally famed heads,[6] or of the great power of 'the guild' in contemporary American theological scholarship. And that against an essentially 'liberal' background; I leave out of account the more closed theological groupings with their manifest or *de facto* censorship.

Then on the world political scene we now have the picture of

President Reagan impressed by prophecies of the end of the world in the Gospels, prophecies which among the right-wing Moral Majority certainly lead to a great readiness to contemplate nuclear war ('What does it matter, we shall get caught up to Jesus in "the rapture"?') and to disregard conservation and ecological issues (after all, the world does not have long to go anyway, so why not use its resources up while we're here).[7] In Britain we have Mrs Thatcher arguing that 'The central theme of Christianity is freedom of choice', and along the same lines Norman Tebbit invoking the parable of the Good Samaritan to justify tax cuts. In a far more sinister way the Church Struggle in Germany during the 1930s was above all a struggle over the use of the symbol of Jesus. The Synoptic Jesus was too powerful and – with his Jewish origins – too unacceptable a symbol to be left available for unrestricted use, so attempts were made by the 'German Christians' to produce a Jesus more compatible with the aims of the Third Reich: a blonde, Nordic, Aryan Jesus preaching purity of race and of the German people, who was a complete caricature of Jesus of Nazareth. And this was combatted with an alternative symbol; one which was a rallying point (clearly more authentic, albeit inevitably ineffective, given the opposition) against the immediate danger but which was to have damaging consequences for the post-war period (as we shall see in Chapter 10).[8]

In more narrowly ecclesiastical circles the symbol of Jesus is one that is being fought over in connection with the division in both Roman Catholic and Anglican churches, and a factor which plays a crucial role in the battle is the degree to which control can be maintained of a particular interpretation of the work of Jesus to be used as an endorsement for the validity of often dubious arguments. The Pope completely refuses to contemplate women priests, because Jesus chose male disciples; so does the Bishop of London, because for him it is as *man*, i.e. male, that Jesus is the incarnation of God and celebrates the eucharist. So the discussion of the symbolization of Jesus as a woman in Chapter 6 and the problems associated with having a male at the centre of Christianity which we shall be considering in Chapter 11 are no abstract matters; like many of the other questions raised in this book, they have their context in a quite specific setting, a controversy over the use of power.

The roots of controversy within Christianity and of constant

disputes over the use and control of power which have been
characteristic of it over the centuries go right back to its beginnings
and are a direct consequence of some of the ways in which the
Christian movement came into being. As we have seen, 'What is
Christianity?' has always been an almost unanswerable question,
and the lack of an established direct relationship between the
teaching of Jesus and the life and practice of the churches before
the end of the first century, coupled with the great creative freedom
which these churches seem to have exercised from the start, led to
the great variety of interpretation and life-style on which I have
already touched. But that has never prevented individuals from
getting up and saying 'Christianity is this', putting forward their own
particular version of it, and then finding themselves confronted by
others who say 'No, Christianity is that'. Paul's letters already refer
to an argument between Peter and Paul over essentials of Christian
practice,[9] and as we shall see, these letters are a particularly vivid
illustration of the use of power and authority in Christianity.

We have already considered the diversity of earliest Christianity
at some length. The point to be added here, developed at more
length in the important study by Professor Stephen Sykes from
which I have already quoted, is that this diversity is no accident but
is inherent in the very nature of Christian tradition.

I have shown that a faith which is spread by appeal to the teaching
and example of Jesus has certain inherent ambiguities which will
give rise to different interpretations. I have also shown that the
way in which the faith claims the allegiance of human beings,
heart, mind and soul, creates an inescapable problem for the
terms on which intellectual and cultural discoveries and achievements are accommodated to discipleship; of this problem the
relation with philosophy provides the most acute example. This
is by no means a modern phenomenon. But at the Enlightenment
two further features emerge to exacerbate the situation. New
political conditions enable the controversy implicit in the very
profession of Christian discipleship to be conducted more openly;
and critical historical enquiry finally destroys the always unrealistic
hope that appeal to the scriptures would end controversy. The
truth was, and has always been, that the Christian faith is
unprotected from the eruption of disputes both about its content

and about the practice of Christian discipleship. The only question was to what extent did these disputes matter, and if they mattered how were they to be contained.[10]

That, he goes on to say, leads to the need for guidance. But since human beings are what they are, and institutions are what they are, the dividing line between guidance and manipulation is a very narrow one indeed.

The whole problem is complicated even further by the way in which the symbol of Jesus, at the heart of Christianity, has drawn to itself and retained, by a literally magnetic force of attraction, other areas of symbolism some of which we have already looked at. Those symbols of themselves have – or had – not inconsiderable power, but in their Christian use tend simply to intensify the all-embracing power of the central symbol. We saw in the previous chapter, by way of an accusation from the atheist Richard Robinson, the way in which Christianity took over the ideals of truth, beauty and knowledge.[11] In Chapter 4 we saw the kaleidoscopic variety of imagery which became associated with Jesus. What we did not consider at that point, though, was the darker side of the adoption of all that imagery, and one which is far more rarely noted. As is often said, it is impossible to understand the New Testament without a considerable knowledge of the Old, because so much Old Testament imagery is included in it. But that inclusion is also appropriation, appropriation of the territory of a rival which is then used for attacks on that rival. And that process continued in the centuries to come. For example, from a very early stage the imagery of the exodus of the Israelites from Egypt was applied to the interpretation of the resurrection, and is a striking feature of many Easter hymns.[12] This gave Christianity a very powerful image of liberation, associated with Jesus, but it was also used as an image of liberation from Judaism, as a liberation from the law, interpreted in a way which would now be argued by Jews to be a caricature of the actual role of the law in Judaism.[13]

It is known, too, well enough, how by a process of Christianization the church took over pagan festivals and customs and incorporated them into Christianity, from major feasts like Christmas to a wealth of minor local practices.[14] And even if the argument put forward by Michael Carroll that the rise of the cult of the Virgin Mary in the fifth century AD may well be connected with the influx into the Western church of a new stratum of the populace who had previously been devotees of Cybele and now brought with them features of their old allegiance is thought too bold, it does indicate a trend which is likely to have taken place on numerous occasions and in numerous areas during the rapid and extensive spread of Christianity.[15]

So by a process of snowballing Christian imagery has taken on its vast, 'catholic' range of imagery clustering round its centre, Jesus. That process, too, cannot be seen in a purely neutral perspective. It is also the accumulation of a kind of power. Now the accumulation of that kind of power went almost unquestioned during the period when the Christian church had great public authority and influence within society, the period now often referred to as Christendom.[16] Indeed this widespread Christianization was regarded in a positive light, as 'the extension of Christ's rule to all the corners of the earth'. But in a more pluralistic, less confident period like our own, with the proportion of practising Christians in society a tiny percentage, along with the internalization and privatization of so much of Christian belief, the motives behind 'extending Christ's rule to all the corners of the earth' are analysed much more closely; and in that analysis they can all too often (though not always) be seen as a thinly veiled form of commercial and economic exploitation and empire-building.[17]

Our age is one which has seen demands for recognition by minorities of many kinds, the disintegration of empires and spheres of influence; the disintegration, too, of those institutions which once so symbolized the claims of Christ to the whole of the life of an individual, the religious communities.[18] Christianity has lost an enormous amount of its power or has been forced to transfer it to other, inward areas if it wants to retain it. But in that context, what happens to the 'empire' that it built up over the best part of two millennia? What happens when the Jews are in a better position to stress their perspective on that part of the Christian scriptures which is their own Bible and not just an 'Old' Testament, and can share, through their own contribution to international and inter-faith biblical scholarship, in casting doubts on much of traditional Christian argumentation like the argument from prophecy and the New Testament verdict on the Jewish law? What happens when biblical and doctrinal scholars working with standards widely accepted throughout the rest of the academic community raise far-reaching questions about the truth of Christian claims which undermine many of the traditional practices of the churches and invalidate long-traditional arguments? These are problems of the painful period in which we are living, and unless we realize that the issues also relate to power and prestige, we shall find it difficult to understand why reason so often not only does not prevail but does not even succeed in making its voice heard.

As I have indicated, it is often argued that these tensions arise as a result of the collapse of Christendom, that period when Christianity had so close an identification with the instruments of earthly power. New Testament Christianity, this argument goes, was very different, and if only we would get back to that our problems would be solved. Unfortunately, however, things are not quite so simple. We saw above in passing that there is evidence of power struggles even in the New Testament period, and the use of authority based on Jesus for the purposes of manipulation, and a close examination of the letters of Paul in this connection, does not make encouraging reading. Professor Sykes, in the book quoted above, drew attention to Paul's ministry as an exercise of power, pointing out that it is a common misunderstanding to suppose that to be powerful one has to be self-assertive. Great power, he argued, can be exercised by those who locate the origin of their authority outside themselves, in God, however humbly they may refer to themselves as earthen vessels.[19] And that his comments could be substantiated at very great length was demonstrated by Graham Shaw, in his disturbing book *The Cost of Authority*.[20]

Shaw's book is a letter-by-letter survey of the Pauline epistles which demonstrates a good deal about the role of power and manipulation in the New Testament that tends to escape more traditional, complacent readings. As a result of this detailed investigation he came to the conclusion that:

> The Pauline prayers, for instance, are not simply an early chapter in the history of Christian spirituality: in their context they have a blatantly manipulative function. The eschatological fantasies of the early believers are consistently exploited to inculcate an anxiety which only membership of the apostle's privileged

community can allay. A rationale of persecution is put forward which makes Paul's position unassailable and provides him with fertile means of projecting his image. Accounts are given of hostility and dissent which enable them to be easily discounted. Repeatedly in writing to communities which he has founded, the privileges he accords to his readers compel them to assent to his own privileged position. His approach involves the pervasive inculcation of bitterly divisive attitudes which he needs to provide the sanctions which protect his authority and the privileges which make it palatable.[21]

And all this from one who claims to know 'the mind of Christ'! Of course this is not the whole story: but it is an important part of it, and those who have had their eyes opened to this dimension in the earliest documents of the New Testament will also be alert when they come to read the Gospels themselves, so that they pause to think carefully about the way in which they can be seen to contain 'the manipulation of eschatological anxiety and the offer of privilege in another world; the divisive emphasis on divine judgment to provide sanctions to control behaviour; the stress on secrecy which gives to the initiates a special status; the prestige derived from persecution, and explanations of dissent which render it harmless; accounts of the relation to secular power which are both dismissive yet aquiescent; a stress on internal unity at the cost of external antagonism',[22] and so on.

But if the New Testament church is not a haven from power and manipulation, there is no doubt that the problems of the use of Christ as a symbol of power increase dramatically as soon as we get to the age of Constantine. For with Constantine the figure of Christ becomes caught up in the Roman imperial ideology.

The story of how Constantine saw in a dream a sign capable of a Christian interpretation and then, against all the odds, defeated his rival Maxentius at the Battle of Milvian Bridge in AD 312 to become Emperor of Rome is a famous high point in Christian history.[23] How far Constantine was a Christian and what the sign symbolized for him are matters of historical dispute and need not concern us here;[24] the changes which these events brought about, however, are important. For Constantine's subsequent recognition and toleration of Christianity not only brought in new features from the Emperor's own ideology, as we shall see in a moment, but also favoured elements in the tradition, many of them taken over in a Christian interpretation of Old Testament/Jewish narrative and ideology which were connected with the exercise of power by those in positions of leadership, whether in church or state.

This, it should be remembered, is the time in which Eusebius of Caesarea wrote the *Church History* that we looked at in Chapter 4.[25] It is to him that we also owe an oration 'In Praise of Constantine', delivered in the presence of the Emperor himself in 336 and therefore by any standard first-hand evidence of the outlook of Constantine's empire. The historian Norman Baynes described the oration as the first clear statement of the imperial political philosophy:

> The basis of that political philosophy is to be found in the conception of the imperial government as a terrestrial copy of the rule of God in Heaven; there is one God and one divine law, therefore there must be on earth but one ruler and a single law. That ruler, the Roman emperor, is the Vicegerent of the Christian God.[26]

Thanks to this kind of presentation, which lost none of its attractions over later centuries, the emperor thus became a kind of messianic figure and it did not seem out of the question to regard him in the same perspective and even assign him the same stature as the Christ. (This process was helped by the way in which Eusebius went so far as to call him the representative on earth of the all-pervasive Logos of God,[27] that principle by which God orders the world.)[28] In this way the foundation was laid for a Christianization of imperial values or, to put it even more bluntly, for the creation of a picture of Christ in heaven which in effect amounted to a projection of Constantine himself.

These were the values which were to dominate institutional Christianity for the next millennium, and this development was to be further encouraged by the role which bishops found themselves playing in default of any other competent and effective administrative structure. The history of the second half of the first Christian millennium is full of instances of the exercising of a wide range of secular powers by bishops,[29] and of course in the West this period was the prelude to the rise of feudalism with its prince-bishops.

At the end of the eleventh century, Roman law, too enjoyed a renaissance within the Western church.[30] However, because the links between images of Christ and the use of power are so obvious over this period, there is no need for us to dwell on them here in any detail. Since that period is now coming to an end, what is more significant, and also more problematical than it might seem at first sight, is the movement which has arisen as a reaction to this type of Christianity, referred to most often as 'liberation theology' or 'political theology'.[31]

To some degree, in this context 'political theology' is a misnomer. This chapter should already have made clear the extent to which theology has almost always had a political function, and that also emerged from our brief survey in Chapter 2.[32] What differs, of course, is the degree to which theology is *perceived* as political. It is easy enough to see when one's opponents are using theology for political ends; less easy to see when one is doing it oneself, for example in support of establishment or *status quo*; and the reason why the theology which we shall be looking at briefly next is felt in some quarters to be so illegitimately 'political' is that it is essentially a theology of the opposition to them.

As a prelude to that theology, and not entirely unconnected with it, came a discussion among New Testament scholars of an aspect of Jesus' ministry which we have barely touched on so far. Was he, after all, a political figure? Here is yet another instance of the battle over Jesus as a symbol. Traditional biblical interpretation, singling out a few specific recorded sayings of Jesus in support, had stressed that Jesus had an impartial and apolitical attitude to civil society and was always above political realities, rejecting the expectations bound up with Jewish messianism.

It should not be thought that this particular battle involved the politicizing of an area of theology which had previously been unpolitical. For in a less obvious way, as I have suggested above, the Christ of the church had long been a political figure, or at least a symbol used in a political way. This has vividly been pointed out by one Catholic critic:

The biographical apoliticism of Jesus has not prevented the politicization of christological dogma. Indeed, even within the Catholic orbit, there has arisen a curious dissociation between the

Jesus of history and the Christ of faith. On the one hand every effort has been made to erase from the biography of Jesus not only any desire for kingship (an effort well founded exegetically) but also every trace of political messianism and political interest in general. On the other hand, however, the Christ of faith was simultaneously exalted as a king. To be sure, he was regarded as a king in some transcendent sense. Yet this King Christ of dogma gave rise to political effects: emperors and kings governed in his name. Thus the apoliticism of the historical Jesus has been linked with a political christology, and the image of this political Christ has obstructed our efforts to comprehend the political messianism of the historical Jesus.[33]

So in a reappraisal of the Gospel tradition which was not without ulterior motives studies appeared in the late 1960s and early 1970s which on the basis of interpretation of a different set of New Testament texts brought out the political dimension of Jesus' activity.[34] Some studies argued that Jesus' messianism was in many respects political and related to the Zealot movement,[35] a fact which was later disguised to some extent by the tradition; others that while Jesus was not a political messiah, his activity appeared to those in power to have that character,[36] so that it was as a political rebel that he was crucified. Here again, however, the whole debate is inevitably bedevilled by the way in which making decisions in any direction is complicated by the problems of dealing with the Gospel material that we considered in Chapter 3. Moreover, the significance of the whole discussion is diminished by the difficulty which applies to all areas of the Bible, of deducing political maxims from biblical statements. In the particular case of Jesus, even if he were shown to be wholly and completely apolitical, it would not necessarily follow that armed resistance or guerrilla warfare were to be rejected: we are back in the problems of the previous chapter.

These studies are referred to, and many of the discussions and conclusions in them have been taken up, not uncritically, within Latin-American liberation theology. But if we look more closely at that liberation theology, we see that in contrast to the 'black theology' of North America that we examined in Chapter 6, the figure of Jesus plays a surprisingly minor part.[37] A look at the indexes of the major works of liberation theology[38] will immediately show how little discussion there is of him, and what discussion there is is almost always limited to a polemical contrast between the Jesus of history and the Christ of the church, always of course attributing some political role to the latter. No wonder, then, that one recent critic can argue, echoing the Brazilian Hugo Assmann, that christ-ology is one of the most dramatic of the gaps in the theology of liberation in Latin America.[39] This situation is not altered by the existence of books with promising titles like Leonardo Boff's *Jesus Christ Liberator*,[40] which is not really about liberation theology, and Jon Sobrino's *Christology at the Crossroads*,[41] which is more a critical dialogue with traditional Chalcedonian orthodoxy concerned to replace it with a greater focus on Jesus of Nazareth. Perhaps because of its very character as 'theology starting from the praxis of liberation',[42] neither Jesus or the Christ in fact seems to be the driving force here, though the communities from which liberation theology comes cannot in any way be denied the character of Christian communities. The fact gives pause for thought.[43]

What seems to be the case here is that the *symbol* of Jesus is of the utmost importance for political, liberation theologies. It would not be the same if they were to take as their symbol Socrates or Spartacus instead. And surely the reason why the symbol is important in liberation theology is that it has been the motive force behind a rival tradition, and that combatting that tradition involves in one way or another taking over that symbol, even if liberation theology has not been very convincing so far in its attempts to do so.[44]

The discussion in this chapter has been one of constant conflict, and as I pointed out at the beginning that is inevitable not least because we find from any reading of the Gospel material that the stories which the Christian communities chose to tell of Jesus as a reflection of his public activity are essentially stories of conflict. We hear how Jesus was in conflict with the authorities of his day, who were inevitably political as well as religious – and this was conflict over the nature of power. Christians and churches who are blind to this fact and wish to restrict Christianity to some form of inwardness totally misunderstand their tradition: conflict will always be there.[45] But that is no legitimation for the manipulative, dogmatic and authoritarian tones which we can find in the so-called 'theologies of liberation'; and however justified they may seem to their proponents, they too are just as much in need of questioning as some of the abuses to which they seek to be the answer.

9 | Problems with History

It will soon be two thousand years since the traditional date of the birth of Jesus and his historical figure is steadily retreating further back into the past. If we are to understand *him*, and not turn him into a creation of our own who cannot even claim to be a 'risen Christ', because he is our reconstruction or interpretation of a person who once lived, then we have to try to see him as clearly as possible against the background of the world in which he lived. But a great gulf separates the first Christian century from our own, and there are a great many obstacles that we have to overcome if we are to make the journey back from our time to that of Jesus. If we fail to take due account of those obstacles we shall end up with a historical fiction, and even if we do note them, our difficulties are not yet over. These are the problems that we shall examine in this chapter, which focusses on our tendency to 'modernize' Jesus.

We begin with the matter of translation. All the sayings of Jesus that we possess have come down to us in an indirect way, because we have no writing of his, nor is there any indication in the Gospel that he ever wrote any of his sayings down. Moreover, unless we have been trained to read the Greek in which the New Testament was written, any words attributed to him come to us through what were in all probability two stages of translation, from Aramaic to Greek and from Greek to English. Among the many gaps in our knowledge of Jesus, we have no idea whatsoever of his linguistic range or ability.[1] We are also fairly ignorant of what languages were spoken in his environment during his lifetime: since Alexander the Great had conquered the area in the fourth century BC, hastening a Hellenization which had already begun as a result of trading, Greek will have been widely spoken, particularly in Jerusalem,[2] and it is not out of the question that Jesus knew some. However, it seems likely that he regularly spoke Aramaic (it is impossible to tell whether from synagogue worship he could also understand Hebrew, the language of the Jewish Bible).

The first collections of sayings of Jesus that were made will have been in a Semitic language (one would expect it to have been in Aramaic).[3] However, the Gospels we now have were clearly written in Greek.

Now translating from one language to another always raises a great many problems. Translation from Semitic languages like Hebrew and Aramaic is particularly difficult, because the very structure of the language is so different from those to which we are accustomed. This means that even if one translates Hebrew or Aramaic literally, it is possible to give a misleading impression of what the speaker intends. To take just one example, Hebrew and Aramaic have no comparative to express relative degrees ('better than', 'more than')[4] and the nearest they can get is by using opposites ('I love that and hate that'). So it can be argued that when Jesus was saying 'No man can serve two masters, for if he does he must love one and hate the other',[5] he was in fact conveying what a Greek would express by saying 'he has to make a choice between them, prefer one to the other'.

That is true as far as it goes, but there is rather more to the issue than that. For it is not the case – as seems to be being implied – that Jesus was thinking as a Greek (or as we) would do and trying to express himself through the obstacle of the Aramaic language. He was not struggling to say 'he will prefer one to another' through the imperfect medium of Aramaic. He was saying 'love one and hate the other', and because that is the way in which he spoke, the way in which he thought would be controlled by it.

The kind of language that is available to us dictates the concepts that we are able to form and the way in which we think, and therefore – first – there will have been a wide range of concepts, second nature to someone speaking in Greek, which Jesus would have been unable to entertain, simply on linguistic grounds. But vice versa, his conceptuality could not be expressed precisely in a language other than his own. This factor needs to be added to the others associated with the sayings of Jesus that we have already considered.[6]

In some cases, with a good deal of difficulty the translation can be traced backwards to illuminate this transition, and many attempts have been made to reconstruct Aramaic sayings of Jesus.[7] But such attempts prove impossible when the evangelist (or a Greek-speaking church before him) has played too active a part in the transmission of material (this seems to have been the case with much of the material peculiar to Luke), and there are instances where it is impossible even to be sure of the meaning of a word used in the Greek translation. Perhaps the most striking example of this problem is the Greek *epiousios*, which occurs in the Lord's Prayer. It is customarily translated 'daily' ('daily' bread), but the standard New Testament Greek lexicon devotes nearly a page to discussing it, referring to more than a dozen scholarly articles and listing as alternatives e.g. 'necessary for existence', 'for the following day' and 'for the future'.[8] Origen in the third century thought the evangelists invented the word – but that hardly elucidates its meaning.[9]

Translation from Aramaic to Greek was only the first stage in the handing down of the words of Jesus and the earliest stories about him. After a long period during which it was predominantly read in Latin, the New Testament was translated into a number of vernacular languages, including English. For several centuries, the unchallenged domination of the Authorized/King James Version tacitly conveyed the impression that Jesus spoke the language of Shakespeare, and the feeling that this is the only 'right' version of his sayings is still hard to dispel in some quarters. Now, of course, we are swamped with a plethora of translations into modern English.

This kind of translation raises even more problems. For now it is not just a matter of translating from one language into another but translating an ancient document nearly two thousand years old into a modern language. Some of the problems are indicated in the Introduction to the New Testament in the *New English Bible* by Professor C.H.Dodd, who was Director of the project. He concluded by commenting that 'Only those who have meditated long upon the Greek original are aware of the richness and subtlety of meaning that may lie even within the most apparently simple sentence, or know the despair that attends all efforts to bring it out through the medium of a different language.'[10]

According to Professor Dodd, the *New English Bible* claimed to be 'a translation in the strict sense, and not a paraphrase',[11] but such a thing is harder to achieve than it sounds. In contrast to the older translators who considered that 'fidelity to the original demanded that they should reproduce, as far as possible, characteristic features of the language in which it was written, such as the syntactical order of words and the structure and division of sentences', Professor Dodd said that the members of the committee of which he was head 'were enjoined to replace Greek constructions and idioms by those of contemporary English'.[12]

But if one takes these steps, it is not much further to the approach of the modern 'popular' translations of the Bible like the *Good News Bible/Today's English Version*, in which translation has really turned into interpretation.[13] The basic philosophy here and in even freer versions seems to be something like this. The Bible is the good news for everyone and therefore everyone must understand it; therefore the translation must put things in the simplest possible terms in such a way that a modern audience can understand it. There is even the impressive sounding term 'dynamic equivalence'[14] used by the *Good News Bible/Today's English Version* to describe its approach; it often does not attempt a literal rendering of the original but substitutes what the translator feels to be an equivalent modern idiomatic phrase. The result, however, is that the readers of these translations are even further away from what Jesus said: separated from it not just by a third party and two translations made with the intention of reproducing the text in another language as faithfully as possible, but by a third party, a translation and an interpretation. And in this way Jesus is 'modernized' into saying things which he never did.

Moreover, since scholars are only human, it is manifestly difficult for them to prevent their own idiosyncratic theological views creeping in so that their translation is already a one-sided interpretation of the text. The *New English Bible* contains a particularly notorious example from Professor Dodd himself. You will recall that when we were considering the passages in the Gospels which seemed to indicate that Jesus talked of an imminent divine intervention and the problems they cause, I mentioned that some scholars had tried to dispute this imminent expectation. Professor Dodd was one of these and in an influential book written in the 1930s he argued that in a saying usually taken to refer to the future Jesus was in fact referring to a divine intervention which had already taken place – in his own coming.[15] This position came to be known as 'realized eschatology'. One of the most difficult sayings to reconcile with Dodd's position is Mark 9.1, which we have already come across.[16] In the literal and accurate translation in the *Revised Standard Version* it reads 'There are some standing here who will not taste death before they *see* the kingdom of God come with power', but in the *New English Bible* it has become 'There are some of those standing here who will not taste death before *they have seen* the kingdom of God *already* come with power'. The addition of the 'already' and the change to 'have seen' helps considerably to bend the text in the direction of Dodd's view of this verse that 'The meaning appears to be that some of those who heard Jesus speak would before their death awake to the fact that the Kingdom of God had come.'[17] But, as they say, 'It's not in the Greek.'

Thus unfortunately virtually none of the modern translations can be trusted to bear the weight that is put on them. As one survey of them puts it: 'In the nature of the case no single translation of the New Testament can be recommended as a completely clear and accurate reading.'[18] In particular, 'The desire to achieve idiomatic English style may result in a translation which is misleading, no matter what context it is read in.'[19] It is not that these translations are utterly bad or incompetent, but in one way or another they are attempting the impossible and give no indication that that is what they are in fact doing. Moreover we have to take into account a further point.

Modern translations are dangerous because they modernize much of the text but not all. Above all they do not modernize the conceptuality and thought-world of the New Testament. By giving the reader so many familiar words, tailored to his or her understanding, they gloss over the inevitable strangeness of the world of the first century AD and give it the semblance of familiarity.

The theologian who drew attention to this most strikingly was the German Rudolf Bultmann, significantly as a result of his work with wartime pastors of the Confessing Church in Frankfurt. In a famous paper entitled 'New Testament and Mythology' he argued that it was impossible to use electric lights and radios and go to the doctor when ill and at the same time to believe in the demons and spirits of the New Testament world. The stars, he went on, are physical bodies whose motion is regulated by cosmic law; they are not demonic beings who can enslave men and women.[20] The outlook of the New Testament is, in his view, mythological – and he defined mythology as a way of representing the other-worldly in terms of this world, the divine in terms of human life.[21] What was necessary was to reinterpret the whole of the New Testament – miracles, demons, expectation of an imminent end to the world, and all – in a consistent way;[22] and Bultmann did this by using the existentialist theology of Martin Heidegger.[23]

Everything about this argument and proposed solution by Bultmann was subsequently criticized: his analysis of the New Testament world, his analysis of the modern world, his definition of mythology, his use of existentialist philosophy – to mention only the most obvious points. But however much one may differ from Bultmann's approach, it is hard to deny that he had a point and that there are problems in our relating to the New Testament world, as we shall go on to see.

There is another, more subtle, form of translation which takes place in the move from Aramaic to Greek, from Jesus to the evangelists, more difficult to identify but which we know to be there. It seems almost certain that none of the Gospels was actually written in Palestine and that they were written at least a generation after the time of Jesus, if not later (Mark is usually dated to AD 69, just before the fall of Jerusalem; Matthew and Luke twenty years or so later). This means that some of the details of the surroundings in which the Gospels set Jesus and his activities may have been changed, because the way in which the evangelists imagined those surroundings was coloured by their own experience and restricted by the limitations in their knowledge of Palestine.[24] This was a development which was to have its head completely, not so much in written works, since the Christ of the church was predominantly a supernatural figure, a creation of its doctrine, and lives of Jesus are a post-eighteenth century phenomenon, as in paintings. Careful reading of the Gospels can catch the evangelists out in anachronisms and incongruities in setting.

And then there is the problem that the Gospels are not historical accounts of what Jesus said and did, descriptive works, but are full of theological symbolism, inspired by the Old Testament and other imagery current at the time.[25] Sometimes this symbolism is obvious and arises out of what we would call historical words and actions; sometimes it is far less obvious and totally unhistorical. Because our minds work so differently from those of ancient authors and readers it is very easy to get their intentions wrong and completely to misunderstand what they have written and described. This will happen above all if we treat symbol literally. I shall be saying more about theological symbolism and miracle in the next chapter. However, it is worth pausing over a couple of astronomical details to illustrate the point in passing.

A great deal of time has been spent discussing what might have been the nature of the star which led the wise men to Jesus.[26] But that is not at all the question which we are meant to ask or the way in which we should approach this detail. That is clear if we look at the account of the crucifixion. Here again there has been a great deal of discussion of detail, and in many circles the darkness which took place at the sixth hour[27] is assumed to have been an eclipse. But that is quite impossible. No matter what the exact date and year may have been in which Jesus was crucified, we know that it was near the passover, that the passover always takes place around the time of the full moon and that solar eclipses can occur only at the time of the new moon.[28] The darkness is symbolic, and symbolic only; in the same way, of course, as are the details added to Mark about the rending of the veil of the temple and the opening of the tombs of the saints.

This observation on the darkness at the crucifixion comes from a classic work by H.J.Cadbury, to whom I have already referred in a previous chapter, entitled *The Peril of Modernizing Jesus*. It is particularly relevant here, since the problem of translation from ancient documents inevitably brings with it that of unconscious modernization.

Professor Cadbury especially warns against this unconscious tendency to modernize not just in connection with the setting in which Jesus lived but also in connection with his personality: his beliefs, his thoughts, his purposes.

Not even the use of Jesus' own terms prevents an almost complete modernizing of him. In fact to use them in a modern sense only deceives ourselves and others into thinking that we are accurately representing his ideas. It is doubtful, of course, whether Jesus used a word 'gospel' at all, but if he did its content was almost certainly very different from most that goes under its name in any sort of pulpit. We are doubtless correct in supposing that Jesus called God 'Father', but that the word was for him pregnant with meanings such as we give it, is not so probable. Terms for God are peculiarly conventional, and human fatherhood, neither then nor today, carries even ideally such concepts as we often read into Jesus' use of it, – of unity of will, and mutual understanding; of loving care on one side and filial dependence on the other. The modern Christian speaks too, after Jesus, of 'the Kingdom of God'. In how many directions our view of the Kingdom is unlike Jesus' view it would be tedious to enumerate. One difference, however, is particularly clear. For Jesus the Kingdom was nothing that men themselves build or create as for the average modernist. If these frequent and familiar terms of Jesus are used by us to describe our modern humanitarian ideals, our sense of creating a better world, our longing for fellowship and mystical communion with God, how much more likely are we to miss his meaning in other passages.[29]

This argument is very much that of Rudolf Bultmann, but considerably antedates his demythologizing.

As I pointed out at the beginning of this chapter, the danger of modernizing becomes most acute at the very point when people are seduced by the resources of modern historical scholarship into thinking that they are on the way to recovering the 'real Jesus', rather than the Christ of traditional doctrine. What is happening is all too likely to be something else, the beginnings of the creation of what might be called a monster, a creature who never existed, a subtle idol created by human beings. For Jesus cannot be reclaimed from the past for the present in that way.

It is only if we are aware of the reality of the past as past that we can feel it as alive and present. If, for example, we try to make Shakespeare literally contemporaneous, we make him monstrous. He is contemporaneous only if we know how much a man of his own age he was; he is relevant to us only if we see his distance from us. Or, to take a poet closer to us in actual time, Wordsworth's *Immortality Ode* is acceptable to us only when it is understood to have been written at a certain past moment; if it had appeared much later than it did, if it were offered to us now as a contemporary work, we would not admire it; and the same is true of *The*

Prelude, which of all works of the Romantic Movement is closest to our present interest. In the pastness of these works lies the assurance of their validity and relevance.[30]

That this point is made in a different context, by a writer on English literature, gives it added weight. And if that can be said of Shakespeare and Wordsworth and their works, is it not even more true of Jesus and the Gospels, where the pressure to modernize is so much greater?

Yet such is the power and attraction of the symbol of Jesus that attempts continue nevertheless, and we shall never escape coming across them. It is therefore worth our while going yet further into why they happen and what other pitfalls they present to us.

Professor Cadbury points out that because we are not just seeking to recreate Jesus out of idle curiosity but to relate him to values that we can make our own, one important factor here is that we tacitly assume that our outlook is correct and that Jesus inevitably shared it; we are looking for his endorsement.[31] We rarely consider the possibility of a completely different view of the world from our own and forget, as I have stressed before, how many of our categories of thought, almost as taken for granted as the air we breathe, are consequences of that scientific revolution in a wide range of disciplines which separates us from Jesus.[32]

The most striking chapter in Cadbury's book is that on 'Purpose, Aim and Motive in Jesus'.[33] We assume, he says, that it is a mark of a great man that he has a clear purpose in life. We therefore assume that Jesus had an aim, even if there is dispute as to what it may have been. But did he? Is not this yet another modernization? When did self-consciously making a career fully develop in human history? Cadbury suspects it to be of Puritan origin. Did Jesus consciously plan his life at all? Might he not have led a basically unreflective vagabond life, with much of the purpose in it being projected on to it later from the Gospels onwards?

Here once again things are complicated by the possibility that so much in the Gospels may be the product of the early church reflecting on Jesus. Certainly he may well have felt himself to be under pressure from the urgency of the crisis with which he believed himself and the world to be faced (one saying attributed to him is 'I came to cast fire on the earth and would that it were already kindled;

I have a baptism to be baptized with and would that it were already accomplished!',[34] though even that may be the product of later reflection; we cannot be *sure*). But if he was impelled by this pressure, did he also have a direction, 'a Purpose with a capital P – unwavering, conscious, absorbing, glorifying'?[35]

When it comes to purpose, aim and motive in Jesus we therefore have to be very careful to understand our own presuppositions and to think ourselves back into his time.

The sense of purpose, objective, etc., as necessary for every good life is more modern than we commonly imagine. Some men in antiquity lived under it – a sense of calling, mission, etc. Paul may be an example... My impression is that Jesus was largely casual. He reacted in situations as they arose but probably he had hardly a programme or plan. His martyrdom is not in conflict with such a view, for one form of martyrdom at least is that of men who, without planning or scheming, submit to adversity as it comes. The religious man in particular leaves planning to God and simply submits to the inevitable. He may foresee it, but that is not the same as courting it or planning it or incorporating it into his self-justification. As Jesus says, 'I go on my way today and tomorrow and the third day I am perfected.' A large part of Jesus' sayings, interpreted as indicating an intelligent and chosen aim, may be understood in this sense of passive fatalism. Submission to the will of God does indeed give life a kind of unity, yet it lacks all that creative planning, intelligent selection, singleness of purpose and the like that we usually mean in our efforts to preach the integration of life. There is nothing irreverent or improbable in such a view of Jesus. Modern purposiveness has no guarantee of divinity about it, though we naturally attribute it to God and to Jesus, making them in our own image.[36]

If this seems strange to those familiar with the text of the Synoptic Gospels, with their reiterated stress on the fulfilment of the scriptures[37] and the picture of Jesus setting his face to go up to Jerusalem,[38] I would remind them of the whole discussion in Chapter 3, which is particularly relevant here. We just cannot tell how much of the structure of the Gospel narratives is the creation of the evangelists, but it looks as though a great deal is. As I said in the opening pages of this book, one of the early essays I had to write was 'Did Jesus foresee his death and if so, what significance did he attach to it?' It is in looking at problems like the extent to which the framework of Mark's Gospel is the creation of the evangelist rather than being historical reminiscence, or the degree to which the early church has altered the Gospel material,[39] that the question of Jesus' intentions really become acute. And that is above all because between the life of Jesus and those Gospels comes 'the resurrection', something of which we only have conflicting theological portraits.[40]

The question of what Jesus actually planned or foresaw becomes even more acute if one extends the question and asks whether Jesus foresaw his resurrection as well. The Synoptic Gospels certainly say that he did. But that raises the question, at a theological level, whether to go to the cross in confidence of resurrection does not devalue the significance which many Christians attach to the death of Jesus.[41] Can facing death be the same if one *knows* that three days later one is going to be raised up to share the glory of the Father?[42]

There are complex questions here which are all too rarely tackled and which we have few resources for answering. However, no matter what our final conclusion – or perplexity – may be, one clear conclusion follows from the discussion in this chapter. If we are to discover as much as is humanly possible about who Jesus of Nazareth was, we have to adopt the methods of the critical historian, and do the utmost we can with them to recreate the world in which he lived, *all the time steeping ourselves in that world and not attempting to relate it over-hastily to the present.* To join Jesus as he was – or as near as we shall ever be able to get to him as he was – we have to attempt as best we can to go to live with him in the past. And even a lifetime's study of Jesus in his world will only produce the most blurred reflection of what it was like because we are attempting the impossible, because of the distorting spectacles our conditioning gives us, the lack of information and the erroneous presuppositions with which we approach it. And our perception of that past, as of any past, will constantly be changing. It will be changing because we ourselves will change as we come to grips with the task, as we become aware of points at which our perspective is wrong and learn to allow for them and try to correct them; and it will be changing because the evidence at our disposal is changing. Not, as I said earlier, the basic evidence about Jesus, which barring some almost miraculous discovery will remain the Gospels, but the evidence about the world in which Jesus lived.

Compared with a generation ago, for example, our knowledge of Judaism at the time of Jesus has been transformed. This is not just as a consequence of new discoveries, like the Dead Sea Scrolls, though discoveries have been made. It is not least because of social and international changes in our modern world following from the holocaust and the new attitude to Jews and to the state of Israel that old Christian presuppositions about first-century Judaism have been challenged, both by the considerable contributions made by Jewish scholars who have become interested in the background to Jesus and his person and by a first hand re-examination by Christians of assumptions and evidence that was all too often taken for granted, leading to verdicts and illustrations that had been passed from one writer to another at second or even at third hand. A series of important Jewish writers on the New Testament has come into prominence since Joseph Klausner wrote his *Jesus of Nazareth* in 1925,[43] of whom the best known is Geza Vermes;[44] and in his *Paul and Palestinian Judaism*, E.P.Sanders showed how first-century Judaism has to be seen from a much more favourable perspective than that of most nineteenth- and earlier twentieth-century Christian scholars.[45] As a result it is now taken for granted that the starting point of enquiry into Jesus must be how someone who lived totally within Judaism was the origin of a movement which separated from it.

But perhaps this interest in first-century Judaism and the desire to show Jesus' place in it as a Jew is leading to yet another distortion. It could be argued that 'Jesus the Jew' is yet another image of Jesus like those we looked at in Chapter 4; more sophisticated and with more substance than most, but nevertheless with a considerable degree of projection in it. For this perspective may lead us to fail to see other possible parallels which exerted influence.[46] Yet the gains in this new approach have been great.

Every new attempt at even a fragmentary portrait of Jesus will be controversial because it will be wide open to criticism from those who do not share its assumptions or its assessment of the evidence. As I have said so often, there is too much room for difference of opinion and there will always be too many gaps in the evidence for any widely agreed picture to become established. So if in present circumstances such a picture does become established or achieve widespread currency we may assume that there is a serious distortion in it, or that those who take it over are doing so unthinkingly as the course of least resistance.

We have, then, to look for Jesus of Nazareth in his own time, the past, among the approximations and relativities and contingencies of history. Therefore almost a century after it was written, Albert Schweitzer's comment is still true:

> The historical Jesus will be to our time a stranger and an enigma. The study of the Life of Jesus has had a curious history. It set out in quest of the historical Jesus believing that when it had found Him it could bring Him straight into our time as a Teacher and Saviour. It loosed the bands by which He had been riveted for centuries to the stony rocks of ecclesiastical doctrine, and rejoiced to see life and movement coming into the figure once more, and the historical Jesus advancing, as it seemed, to meet it. But He does not stay; He passes by our time and returns to His own.[47]

But if Jesus of Nazareth can only be himself if he belongs to the past, that raises yet more problems. First, how many people have the time, the training, the resources and indeed the inclination to embark on their own quest of Jesus? Are not the majority condemned to be the spectators of, receivers of the discussions and findings of the constantly changing and never unanimous findings of the particular New Testament scholars of their day, having indeed to accept their domination as the new popes?

And if that is the case, does not the question also arise whether, given our realization of the complexity of the task of discovering who Jesus was, it is worth while any longer trying to trace our understanding of the nature of our relationship with God, redemption and forgiveness, exclusively back to some identifiable element in the life, character and activity of Jesus of Nazareth? Is it worth the risk of ending up with a 'monster' of our own making? Is not the reality in fact that we should be saying 'I do not know?'

So it is easy to see why during the last century the *enfant terrible* of New Testament scholarship, the brilliant David Friedrich Strauss, at one time professor of theology in Tübingen and hounded for his views, should have written:

It is impossible that the happiness of man, or to speak more intelligibly, the possibility of fulfilling his destiny, can depend on his recognition of facts into which scarcely one man in a thousand is in a position to institute a thorough investigation and, supposing him to have done so, then to arrive at a satisfactory result.[48]

Surely there must be a better alternative for belief? But if it is connected with Jesus, what can it possibly be? We have seen the problems associated with traditional Christian doctrine, and we have seen how it is inevitable that any attempt to link Jesus with our own day by seeking to give a portrait of him which has not been checked with all the rigour at our disposal and is not set against the context in which he lived almost inevitably produces that 'monster', something that never was and has no real life, something which, if it nevertheless has popular appeal, is all too likely to become the breeding ground for ideologies. Since the difficulties in getting back to 'Jesus as he was' are so great, is it not overwhelmingly probable that we shall end up, through his person, in creating God in our own image? And what is that, if not idolatry?

It is certainly the case that over the past generation there has been a substantial improvement in our knowledge of first-century Palestine and of Judaism and indeed of how the Gospels have to be used if the best historical portrait of Jesus possible is to be produced. But it seems all too likely that nevertheless the begetting of 'monsters' and the construction of ideologies is on the increase. The commercialization of popular translations of the Bible each vying to be the most up-to-date is bad enough. But in addition we have reached the point where versions of the New Testament are regarded as an entertainment industry as well (think of *The Gospels in Scouse*, *The Gospels in Geordie* and their folksy American equivalents).[49] This has trivialized the whole business of translation. Furthermore the portrayals of Jesus on television with their powerful impact (unavoidably anachronistic, even though they may be filmed in Israel) are steadily making it impossible to argue for a more critical, more selective, more refined approach. That is particularly the case where the assumption still persists that the Man of Nazareth must be understandable to everyone and those who argue otherwise are dismissed as academic or élitist.

It is all too likely, in the present climate, where the institutional

churches are fighting for their survival and cannot afford to have
'fifth columnists' in their midst, that the situation will get even worse.
So if the world continues to be able to support a human population
for further millennia and there are still Christians upon it, the Jesus
of two thousand years ago will become the Jesus of a still more
distant past and the Palestine of his day will become even more
unimaginable, because the agricultural, pre-technological society
which was familiar to our forefathers will be so far beyond living
memory. It is difficult enough now for those living in the urban
centres of the technological Western world to begin to realize the
nature of life in an agricultural community even at the beginning of
this century; and that task of thinking oneself back into such a setting will become more and more difficult as technology develops
even further and hard manual work and the pressure of the rhythms
of the seasons become even more alien. Professor Nineham once
asked in connection with the Bible, putting himself into the very
distant future: 'What will be the case with the Christ of 2,000,000,000
years ago? That is a question theologians should not ignore, for
we are quite credibly informed that the human race may yet have
2,000,000,000 years to go. When the Lord then comes will he find
"the faith" on the earth? Do we really expect him to?'[50]

Remarkably enough, his line of thinking was anticipated almost
three hundred years by a certain John Craig, writing in 1699 at the
dawn of the age of reason. He argued that Christ would have to
return by AD 3150 because after that the historical facts of his life
would no longer be believed. Craig's presuppositions and arguments
may seem somewhat alien, but he had a point.[51]

10 | History, Doctrine and Miracle

The very nature of historical investigation and the uncertainties of its findings, along with our historical consciousness of which it is a part, brings us up against yet another series of problems, this time of a more theoretical nature. If the findings of historians are so tentative, changing and basically uncertain, how is it possible to find any basis or justification for the claims of Christian doctrine within them? What is the basis of Christian doctrine? On what grounds can it be regarded as an absolute when everything in history is relative? The problem was formulated during the Enlightenment, at the end of the eighteenth century, in now famous terms by the German philosopher G.E.Lessing. One particular sentence of his is often quoted: 'Accidental truths of history can never become the proof of necessary truths of reason.'[1] Lessing added that this was the 'ugly, broad ditch' that he could not get across, however he tried.[2] Put in that form the question is not framed very satisfactorily, though one can see what Lessing was getting at. There was a problem, and by the end of the nineteenth century it had come to be posed in a more sophisticated and more threatening way.

As a result of that historical consciousness which conditions all our thinking,[3] we have now become aware (or can be made aware) how societies over a period of time actually change their values, morals and basic mental concepts. This happens as a result of historical, cultural, social and structural changes and means that the values of a particular society begin to appear relative to those of other societies. Given this historical relativity, it is difficult to see how any one set of beliefs, any one figure, can have *absolute* value. However, the Christian church has claimed precisely this for its belief in Christ: Christ is the absolute alongside which everything else is relative. What can possibly be the basis for such an assertion?

The classic discussion of this question is in an article by the

German philosopher Ernst Troeltsch, written right at the beginning
of this century and never, so far as I am aware, translated into
English: 'On Historical and Dogmatic Method in Theology'.[4]
Because this article states the issues so clearly and so uncompromis-
ingly, it is well worth looking at in some detail. But before that, we
also need to look at the background against which it was written.
An understanding of this background will help to explain why we
have to go back as far as Troeltsch for problems which are so high
on the theological agenda.

The end of the last century, the time of the composition of the
article, was preceded (and followed) by a period of intense academic
activity in connection with Jesus, the Bible and the Christian religion,
particularly in Germany. Explorations of archaeological sites,
discoveries of texts and researches into specialist topics were beginning to be consolidated, and a detailed picture was being built up of
the ancient Near East, its history and its culture. For the first time
ever it was possible to set Judaism and Christianity alongside the
other religions of their time and to see the wide variety of cultural
and religious life over the biblical period.[5] Not unnaturally, in this
sudden flood of new material scholars often leaped to hasty and
unjustified conclusions, and all kinds of theories were proposed
which have later proved to be rash and unjustified.[6] But the
discoveries kept being added to.

All this raised a series of philosophical questions about Christianity and its claims which few were prepared to tackle. Seeking an
answer to them became the life-work of Ernst Troeltsch, and four
enormous volumes of collected writings bear witness to his efforts.[7]
However, Troeltsch could hardly have been writing at a worse time,
for his activity in this area fell in the period immediately preceding
the outbreak of the First World War. That event radically changed
the interests of theologians, along with everything else. One factor
in this change was a letter written by the liberal scholars and
theologians with whom Troeltsch sympathized and the consequences of whose work he was exploring, which was a declaration
of support for the Kaiser's war policy.[8] From that point on, liberal
theology and the research to which it had contributed were in
eclipse, not least because the letter was to be one of the stimuli to
the new 'dialectical', 'kerygmatic' theology of Karl Barth.[9]

Hostility to liberal theology was fuelled by the way in which until the rise of Hitler and the creation of the Third Reich, the Christianity from which that liberal theology had not sufficiently distinguished itself proved to be increasingly infected by nationalism and 'folk' elements. These elements, along with growing antisemitism, turned Christianity into a caricature of itself with the complete repudiation of Judaism and a Germanic, Aryan Jesus that we noted earlier.[10] Only radical, narrowly focussed concentration on 'preaching the pure gospel of Jesus Christ and him alone' could counter this perversion;[11] and since any compromise in the direction of the old liberal approach was seen as the first slippery step to the corruption of Christianity, in Germany liberalism and the academic study of the history of religions faded into the background. At the same time, war and adverse economic conditions greatly reduced the process of archaeological exploration and assessment.

Karl Barth's position came to be more and more influential because it, and 'biblical theological' approaches not dissimilar to it,[12] were the only ones in Germany to come out of the Third Reich and the Second World War with any credit and integrity. This is not the point at which to go at length into Barth's theology and life, of which there are many accounts, or to stress his positive achievements. But we should note that as a result of the development I have outlined, this theology was firmly centred on Christ, it completely rejected any possibility of pointers towards God anywhere in the natural world, and it saw Christianity as quite distinct from any other religion: Christian faith was not a religion but 'the end of all religion'.[13] The negative side of Barth's theology was to deal a savage blow to thinking on the lines along which Troeltsch and the great liberal scholars had preceded him and to brand the questions asked by them as illegitimate.

Karl Barth is said to have become more mellow in his old age. If that is an apt description of the following statement from that period, made in his last lectures, those unfamiliar with his early writings may imagine the kind of fire and single-mindedness there was at the beginning of his career.

The post-biblical theologian may, no doubt, possess a better astronomy, geography, zoology, psychology and so on than the biblical witnesses possessed: but as for the Word of God, he is not justified in comporting himself in relationship to those witnesses as though he knew more about the Word than they. He is neither president of a seminary, nor the Chairman of the Board of some Christian Institute of Advanced Theological Studies, who might claim some authority over the prophets and apostles. He cannot grant or refuse them a hearing as though they were colleagues on the faculty. Still less is he a high-school teacher authorized to look over their shoulder benevolently or crossly, to correct their notebooks, or to give them good, average or bad marks. Even the smallest, strangest, simplest or obscurest among the biblical witnesses has an incomparable advantage over even the most pious, scholarly, and sagacious latter-day theologian.[14]

No wonder, then, that at around the same period Barth could write scornfully of the 'authoritative New Testament men, who to my amazement have armed themselves with swords and staves and once again undertaken the search for the "historical Jesus" – a search in which I now as before prefer not to participate'.[15] To many people nowadays, including myself, this blissful detachment, ignoring one of the most crucial questions facing Christianity, carries little conviction (though as I said, it had a very different and important impact against the background of Nazi Germany and its distortions of Christianity). But the fact is that it reflects an attitude that dominated continental theology, and more importantly the thought of the World Council of Churches, for a generation.

In this respect Barth found support from his Marburg contemporary Rudolf Bultmann, though Bultmann differed from Barth by being as impressive as any liberal in the range of his knowledge of the ancient sources.[16] Nevertheless Bultmann, too, could put questions of Christian faith in another dimension altogether and argue not only that we know virtually nothing about Jesus but also that even to enquire after the historical Jesus is illegitimate: 'We do not enquire about Jesus, but he puts the decisive question, that of faith, to us.'[17] What really mattered was the Word as proclamation, referred to by the Greek word for proclamation, *kerygma*. This was the context of the programme of 'demythologizing' which I mentioned in the previous chapter, in which Bultmann set out to reinterpret the whole message of the New Testament in terms of the existentialist philosophy of Martin Heidegger.[18]

Had I been writing this book twenty years or so ago, when the spell of kerygmatic theology was fading and reaction to it was gathering force, in addition to describing the quest of the historical Jesus I should have had to write a good deal about Bultmann and about his approach. (The fact that I am passing over him so quickly here implies no disrespect, since I personally learned a great deal from him; the questions he asked were very important, even if the answers he gave were fatally flawed. In addition to critics who questioned the accuracy of his analysis of the New Testament world and the modern world, his definition of mythology and the appropriateness of his use of existentialist philosophy, even those sympathetic to him pointed out that he never really convincingly explained how talk about God and Christ in his theology could be said to escape the need for demythologizing,[19] and as the years went on and the kerygmatic theology[20] with which his whole approach had been associated was also criticized, he increasingly came to look more like an old-fashioned Lutheran than anything else.)

I should also have had devote a chapter to what was known as the 'new quest of the historical Jesus', which was a rebellion against Bultmann's insistence that it was illegitimate for Christian faith to enquire who Jesus was. This 'new quest' sought to create yet another portrait of Jesus which was not open to the objections levelled against the old quest, one that was to be based on the 'selfhood' of Jesus.[21] However, the 'new quest' has not withstood the passage of time any more than the old one did, and has come to seem very much a case of withdrawal symptoms from addiction to Bultmann; its approach and findings were questioned from the start. Nevertheless, it did mark the beginning of a return in Germany to the sort of questions which were being asked at the beginning of the century by people like Troeltsch, and were never answered.

Admittedly, much of this discussion was limited to the German-speaking world and to the areas of American theology much under its influence;[22] it generally by-passed the Anglo-Saxon theological world. But the atmosphere there was just as inimical to Troeltsch's questions, focussed so closely as it was on 'biblical theology', the view that Christians could find a viable restatement for their beliefs by reverting to authentic, biblical categories and modes of thought. The rise and fall of biblical theology has been adequately documented elsewhere,[23] so it need not concern us here, though we have yet to hear the last of it. With the vast growth of Roman Catholic biblical scholarship after Vatican II, the idea of a 'biblical theology' is again proving attractive in the Roman Catholic church, which has yet to encounter its drawbacks.

All this, then, explains why Troeltsch's voice has gone so long unheard. However, it is now becoming increasingly clear that the questions that he asks have become the questions of our time, particularly in theology. They are raised as soon as biblical scholars or doctrinal theologians using modern techniques try to fit their findings into a wider picture, and they are raised as soon as those attempting to do systematic theology by traditional methods attempt to make use of the findings of other scholars who fully accept the application of historical criticism.

Troeltsch's greatest achievement is that more clearly than anyone else he demonstrated the nature and consequences of historical consciousness and the use of the historical method. In his article, which the sub-title states to have been written as comments on articles by a fellow German theologian on the 'absoluteness' of Christianity,[24] Troeltsch seeks to correct misconceptions about earlier comments of his. His concern is to demonstrate what has led to the shattering of the whole Christian perspective, namely 'the historical world-view as such', in other words the effect that the modern historical method has had on the understanding of Christianity generally. The historical method, he says in a famous image, 'once it is applied to biblical scholarship and church history, is a leaven which transforms everything and which finally causes the form of all previous theological methods to disintegrate'.[25] There is no point in trying to remedy the situation by tinkering with individual problems; this is a matter of principle.

What is this 'historical world-view' and 'historical method' that has brought about such a change? Troeltsch begins by reminding his readers of the nature of modern historical method. He does so by identifying its three most characteristic features: *probability*, *analogy* and *correlation*, which we should look at in a little more detail.

First, at best all that historians can arrive at in their historical approach is a degree of probability, greater or lesser, depending upon the instance. That should be evident enough: it is never possible for us to have all the evidence about a past event, however well documented, and one only has to read the books of any historian in any historical field to see this principle in action.

But, secondly, how does the historian know whether something is probable or not? He assesses the degree of probability by the use of analogy, measuring the unknown by the known. Perhaps one of the most dogged users of analogy to dispute probability was Archbishop John William Colenso, a notorious nineteenth-century Old Testament critic who had the time of his life with the implications of the Old Testament statement that six hundred thousand able-bodied men left Egypt at the Exodus. He worked out that this implied a total population of at least two million, from which he produced his analogies. This was equivalent to the population of London, in which there were 264 births a day, one every five minutes; the congregation on the march would have been twenty miles long and six yards wide; the 22,000 levites would have had to travel six miles 'for the common necessities of nature', and so on.[26] It is a far cry from that to the reconstructions of ancient cultures by modern historians, but the same principle, in a vastly more sophisticated form, is still at work. A decision is made as to whether or not events are likely to have taken place by seeing how they match up to developments and conditions which are normal, customary, or attested on a number of occasions. And that means, for example, that the history of Judaism and Christianity (including that narrated in the Bible) must be studied in the same way as any other history.

All history is interrelated, so:

Biblical scholarship has been compelled, bit by bit, of its own accord, to illuminate the beginnings of the religion of Israel by analogies from the religions of other Semitic peoples; to connect the deep original transformation brought about by Yahwistic religion with the general situation in the world of the Near East, its great catastrophes and its general cultural and religious horizon; to explain Judaism in terms of the conditions during the exile and the reorganization of the community together with its markedly changed attitude in terms of ideas developed in the exile; to connect the origin of Christianity with the disintegration of Judaism and political movements and apocalyptic ideas; and to illuminate the rise of the Christian church by the interaction between earliest Christianity and its setting within the Roman empire.[27]

And that brings us to Troeltsch's third feature of the historical method: correlation. All historical happening is bound together in a permanent correlation, and any one event is related to all the others. This means that all events are relative to one another, and that by the principle of analogy all take place within one and the same arena. Within that arena what happens at any one point affects the overall pattern in some way. And events happen – once – and do not recur, so that there is no permanence in them. Moreover this 'individuality and relativity attach not only to the object of historical studies, but also to the subject, the historian. All these principles (probability, analogy, correlation) must take into account the unceasing development – the dynamics, the novelty, the freedom, the unpredictability – of the historical process. In this respect Troeltsch is the Heraclitus of historiography.'[28]

Troeltsch stresses that the historical method is not dependent on *a priori* philosophical considerations. The important thing about it is that it works, and that it provides an amazing degree of illumination. However, it does so at a price; and here he makes the remark I quoted in Chapter 1 to the effect that anyone who has given it his little finger must go on to give it his whole hand.[29] It is certainly a revolution in our way of thinking and changes everything.

This historical method has two important consequences, which are inherent in it. First, it makes it impossible to use any individual fact as a basis on which to construct a system, since each historical fact is relative to all others. Therefore, secondly, each individual fact must be judged in the light of the whole. So it is not the case, as many theologians would want to argue, that one can pass judgment on Christianity on the basis of its own claims about itself. Christianity must be judged in terms of the wider context of the history of human development. The historical method relativizes everything; historical theology has penetrated into every pore, so that even Christianity can only be regarded as an entity which has its setting in the overall context and needs to be explained and evaluated in that context. Moreover only investigations inspired by this view have produced truly historical results, while all opposition to and restriction of the method have been effective only in individual instances; they have not amounted to an independent principle. Therefore the dogmatic method is no longer viable for anyone who realizes the degree to which historical consciousness has established itself.[30]

And so we come to the dogmatic method, with which Troeltsch is comparing the historical method. The dogmatic method, i.e. that of traditional Christian doctrine, starts from a fixed point which is totally removed from history and its relativities. Its pronouncements are absolute and independent of the contingencies of history. So from the start, this method is totally opposed to the historical method.

By nature it has an authority which carries conviction because it is completely detached from the overall context of history, analogy with other events, and thus from all historical criticism with its essentially provisional results.[31]

It seeks to bind men to individual facts of history, to facts which display their authority by being removed from all historical analogy. For its facts are different from ordinary history and therefore can neither be established nor demolished by criticsm; they are substantiated by a miraculous tradition and are confirmed by an inner seal of substantiation in the heart.[32]

Thus the dogmatic method lacks any of the three characteristics of historical method – criticism leading to mere probability, analogy and correlation – and indeed is extremely hostile to them. It cannot tolerate criticism because it cannot cope with the uncertain results which are inevitably a consequence of criticism. It cannot concede that it has analogies because if it did so it would surrender its very being and put Christianity on a level with other religions. And it cannot take the plunge and occupy its place in the overall context of events because its claim to be the sole truth is diametrically opposed to such a conception. Of course dogma wants to appeal to history, but its history is not ordinary secular history but 'salvation history', a sequence of saving events which are evident as such only to the eyes of faith and which have precisely the opposite characteristics to those of secular history.

For Troeltsch, then, the decisive thing about the dogmatic method is its appeal to miracle, and it is the argument from miracle that gives it its force:

> The crucial metaphysical basis for the dogmatic method, without which it is like a knife without either handle or blade, lies in its claims for the supernatural character of its authority or for miracle. The division of historical life into a sphere without miracle, subject to the usual method of historical criticism, and a sphere permeated by miracles and to be researched by special methods based on inward experiences to which reason is subjected in humility, is the basic foundation on which it works. The construction of such a concept of history and the establishment of dogmatic-historical or salvation-historical methods with their quite independent special conditions is the basic presupposition of the dogmatic method of theology. The theological investigations of the last centuries are full of these special salvation-historical methods and the transcending and avoiding of secular historical method which takes place in them, and of special Christian epistemological theories which are to be grounded on either the principle of obedience to the church or on being born again and inner experience; and only excessive weariness of such barren apologetic can excuse the amazing habit of present-day dogmatic theologians of thinking they can pluck the fruit without having the tree or cut a tiny drying-up branch from the old tree and expect that it will provide them with fruit.[33]

What Troeltsch is arguing is that an essential element in the dogmatic approach is the concept of a God who intervenes in the ongoing process of history from time in an extraordinary way which interrupts the regular course of historical events. Such a view, he claims, is the indispensable presupposition to dogmatic method. But it creates what, if one reflects on it, is a remarkable situation. Nothing, Troeltsch says, is more amazing to the young student beginning theological studies than the way in which it is assumed without further ado that one can take for granted a basis for theology in concepts of God, the primal human state, original sin or miracle without taking account of the ongoing process of world history as it must now be understood. But, he wryly comments, it is amazing what one can get used to, and it is easy to make a virtue out of any necessity. However, it is not a virtue for anyone concerned for clarity, consistency and integrity.[34]

It is worth remembering that Troeltsch was writing half a century before the doctrinal criticism which we looked at in Chapter 5. But his remarks above can be seen as almost a programme for that criticism, though I have not seen anywhere in the writings of its main proponents, like Professor Wiles and Professor Lampe, any direct reference to the works of Troeltsch in general or to the article that we have been considering in particular. That makes it all the more striking that from two different directions we are brought up against the problem that when we consider either the Bible or Christian doctrine, what we see is an essentially human process of argument, involving not only rational exploration and philosophical discussion, but also institutional pressure and machinations. *Errore hominum, providentia dei*, as the saying has it: by human error and divine providence. But there has been an awful lot of error; and precisely where, in the ongoing interrelated fabric of history, does God act, and just how does he do so?

In his most recent book, the 1986 Bampton Lectures entitled *God's Action in the World*,[35] that was the specific problem which Professor Wiles considered. And his answer was essentially a negative one, one which leads on from the writings of Troeltsch so directly that at times it is difficult to realize that such an interval separates them.

Professor Wiles argues for an understanding of creation which dispenses with specific divine interventions in history. Creation really is creation, to be understood as a continuing activity, and since God's concern is to create self-determining, independent creatures who are truly creative, he is logically bound not to interfere in their affairs in any way. He works out his plans for his creation in terms of a 'bias implanted in matter' (a phrase that he quotes from Hugh Montefiore)[36]; this bias is not a 'pre-packaged blueprint'[37] which everything must follow, but God's purposive activity proceeding flexibly in such a way as to take into account the response of his creatures, either positive or negative. Since creation is a continuous process, every part of it is in the broadest sense an expression of divine activities:

Differences within that process, leading us to regard some happenings as more properly to be spoken of in such terms than others, are dependent not on differing divine initiatives but on differing degrees of human responsiveness. The players in the improvised drama of the world's creation, through whom the agency of the author finds truest expression, are not ones to whom he has given some special information or advice, but those who have best grasped his intention and developed it.[38]

Thus the traditional Christian understanding is retrospective, looking back and interpreting what has happened. Miracles are striking events in the past in and through which the divine purpose can be seen to have been furthered.[39] Jesus is to be interpreted along similar lines. No changes in the structure of the natural world are to be associated with him because what his activity does is to make possible new ways of living in and responding to the world.[40]

Many of the reviews I have read of Professor Wiles' book criticized it for being in some way 'reductionist', for offering very much less than is claimed by traditional Christian faith (and by many modern biblical theologies of God's action in the world, including liberation theologies) for the workings of divine providence.[41] But in the present state of the theological discussion, those who criticize this kind of view which takes seriously the nature of history as described by Troeltsch have to do rather more than that. It is easy enough to cry 'This is dated theology reflecting the views of the Enlightenment'; harder to see where in the current world of theology any coherent and comprehensible alternatives are being offered. And comprehensibility (along, of course, with commitment to the truth) is a virtue sadly lacking in much modern theological writing. One is tempted to introduce into the discussion the comment from David Friedrich Strauss that I quoted at the end of the previous chapter.[42]

So at present it is not unreasonable to concede to Troeltsch that the only justification for the doctrinal basis of Christian tradition would seem to be miracle. Traditional Christian doctrine is committed to, and indissolubly bound up with, a belief in miracle, for only such a belief can save it from being a contingent part of the ongoing fabric of history.

'And what is wrong with that?', will come the retort; is that not precisely what Christianity is about: the miracle of God made man in Jesus of Nazareth, the Word made flesh and taking our human existence, to redeem it with a view to our eternal happiness? Given the miracle of the incarnation, why rule out other lesser miracles?[43]

Given that the earthly career of Jesus according to the Christian tradition begins and ends with a miracle, namely the virgin birth and the resurrection, and that Jesus himself is said in the Gospels to have performed a variety of miracles from healing the sick and raising the dead to turning water into wine, walking on water and stilling a storm, a book of this kind cannot pass over the question of miracle without at least some discussion. And here would seem to be an appropriate place, because Troeltsch's view of history and historical criticism, with its use of analogy and correlation, in principle rules out the possibility of miraculous intervention. The most natural criticism of Troeltsch's whole approach, and one that has often been made with some forthrightness, is that it would not know what to do with a miracle if it was directly confronted with one, because it has ruled out miracles from the start.

There is no denying that limitation to historical method, but instead of taking delight in having scored a major hit by pointing out the limitation, those who would appeal to miracle need to explore the material on which they rely rather more deeply than they usually do. For the miracles of Jesus and other miracles do not come down to us through accounts composed as they would have been had they been written by a neutral observer of our time, as statements of something that happened which can either be accepted or rejected. What we find in the Gospel tradition is not this kind of account but stories of 'wonders' bound up with a mixture of myth and symbolism, part of the interpretation of the life and death of a person which led those who believed in him ultimately to say that what had happened in him was the greatest of miracles. And before any use is made of miracles in arguments for Christian doctrine, the nature of that type of interpretation and the wonder stories it contains has to be carefully analysed. If we start on this process of analysis, taking into account what I have just said, we shall find a high proportion of pious legend, myth, symbolism and later development in these stories, and discover that the degree of historical reminiscence is usually very difficult to establish. The degree of the later elaborations is notably higher at those two points where Christian tradition most wants to see miracles: the virgin birth and the resurrection.

Although these two miracles are usually linked together, the virgin birth (or strictly speaking the virginal conception) of Jesus is altogether less significant in the New Testament than the resurrection. Whereas the resurrection can be found referred to in just about every type of material, the virgin birth is mentioned only in Matthew and Luke. The significance of the New Testament evidence about Jesus would be little different if these two passages were not contained in the New Testament, but that could hardly be said of the resurrection. Since we have no statement from the only person, Mary, who could have cast light on the matter, and it is by nature so private anyway, all arguments about the virginal conception must be indirect. Those hesitating, for the reasons advanced so far in this book, over accepting such a miracle at the beginning of the life of Jesus,could suggest various factors which helped to give rise to the belief: a mixture consisting of the credal affirmations about the Son of God made in early preaching, a theology of sinlessness, and the physical condition of Mary when she came to live with her husband.[44] But what complicates the whole discussion is the subsequent development, through the patristic period down to modern times, in which a whole series of theological, psychological and cultural developments played a part, producing a cult rivalling, and in some areas even overshadowing, the worship offered to Christ. Thus the whole issue is taken into areas in which it is impossible to discuss it rationally.[45]

We saw in Chapter 3 how difficult it was to reconcile the different presentations of the resurrection in the Gospels because at that point the portrait of Jesus seems to be almost purely theological. There are also various problems connected with the empty tomb, which like the virgin birth is confined in the New Testament to the Gospels: there is no mention of it at all, for example, in the letters of Paul. All this explains why many Christians feel that it is not intrinsically necessary for belief in the resurrection to be associated with the belief that a particular 'miraculous' event took place. And they would go on to say that when writers in the New Testament speak of the resurrection of Jesus, when they say that God raised him, these writers are talking not so much about particular events (say empty tomb or appearances) as about a whole complex of elements.These include the person of Jesus as he had been and was still believed to be, the work of God in him in life and death, the response to that person and that work in the subsequent life and thought of believers, and the significance of all these things in the ongoing history of the Jewish people and the world. To quote Professor Lampe again:

> We may leave aside the literal question concerning the where-abouts of Jesus' bones; for unless we believe... that they are located in a spatial heaven into which he ascended and where he now sits, or that in his case, uniquely, they were 'dematerialized' and transformed into a spiritual body, they cannot be supposed to be elsewhere than in Palestine. That question is of little importance. What we need to ask is whether the present experience of believers that they are 'in Christ' is directly related to, and dependent upon, a resurrection-event in the world of time and space, which took place at a particular moment in history – whether, in fact, what we understand as the active presence of God, the Spirit who was in Jesus, must, rather, be understood as a personal presence of the resurrected Jesus.[46]

As we shall see in the last chapter, Professor Lampe would go even further than that; but the position which he outlines is one that is quite widely held.

It remains to comment on the 'miracles' associated with Jesus during his lifetime. That he performed 'wonders', particularly in driving out demons and healing the sick, is attested in the tradition in so many ways that it had can hardly be doubted; but we may also note the way in which great religious figures tend to attract stories of miracle-working to them, and how these stories can vary widely, extending from symbolic attempts to express the significance of the figure to virtual conjuring tricks (this latter development can already be seen in the Synoptic Gospels[47] and runs riot in the many apocryphal Gospels, later writings about Jesus which were rightly excluded from the New Testament canon).[48] And because the early church interpreted Jesus in terms of the Old Testament and – as I pointed out in Chapter 8 – in the Gospels a good deal of symbolism is presented as event, we must see stories like the changing of water into wine with its message 'I came that they might have life, and have it abundantly' as essentially symbolic.[49] The insistence that every miracle in the Gospels must have happened just as the Gospels say that it did is a capitulation to rationalism.

We can see the complexity of the Gospel record from a very brief examination of the end of Mark 4 and the beginning of Mark 5. Here we have in immediate juxtaposition the stilling of a storm on the lake, ending with the question 'Who is this, that even wind and sea obey him?', and the stilling of the storm in a man which ends with a herd of pigs rushing down a cliff into the sea. As can be discovered from commentaries on the passage,[50] the former episode is full of mythological and Old Testament imagery, which must have been developed through constant use of the story; in the latter we not only have a possible continuation of this background, but in addition to that a hint that in going into Gentile territory for the first time in the Gospel, Jesus banishes uncleanness as symbolized in the pigs. But there may be yet a further, political, dimension.[51] The area in which the episode of the 'Gadarene swine' was set was under Roman occupation, and when the demon first introduced himself as 'Legion', any ancient hearer must immediately have thought of Roman troops. What historical events underlie all this is now quite impossible to discover; there is plenty of evidence to show that Jesus healed and performed exorcisms, but his actions have now been caught up into this complicated symbolic realm.

In a judicious dictionary article on miracles, Barnabas Lindars mentions two factors in contemporary thought which point the way for further discussion of miracles. They follow on well from what I have been saying in this chapter so it is appropriate to end my comments on miracle with them.

1. Quantum physics has questioned the concept of fixed laws of nature and substituted a more fluid view of the random effects of a fundamental indeterminacy. This gives broader (but still limited) scope for naturalistic interpretations of unusual events, but does nothing to prove divine origin. The crucial problem of the intervention of God remains open.

2. The observation that religion belongs to the human sciences points to the social function of belief in miracles. *Miracle stories attributed to a holy person* are testimonies to the impact of that person on society. *Claims to perform miracles* belong to the sphere of manipulation of power and come close to shamanism. *Personal experiences of miracles*, like special providences, have spiritual value only if they are received as free gifts from God, evoking

praise and dedication. For the person who receives them they are 'situations', whereby sensitivity to the hand of God in the *whole* of life is confirmed and enhanced.[52]

The debate over miracle will go on.[53] But I believe that what I have said about it is sufficient evidence that even less radical theological thinking about miracle today does not suggest that it is possible to base the whole edifice of Christian doctrine upon a miraculous intervention of God. It is a very far cry indeed from the nature of the miracle tradition in the Gospels (including virginal conception and resurrection) to the use of miracle as a theological justification for Christian doctrine. And that is quite apart from the question whether a God who introduced an intellectual edifice like Christian doctrine by a miracle and used similar miracles to buttress it would be a God worth the bother of believing in.

So the problems of doctrine remain as great as they were, and historical method seems unstoppable. But that does not lead to utter relativity. We shall be considering that problem when we look at criteria for theological truth in Chapter 12.

11 | The Finality of Christ?

One of the most serious problems raised by and for Christianity in a multi-cultural, pluralistic world is its inbuilt claim to superiority and finality as a religion, particularly when that claim is appropriated – as it often is – by sectarian groups with very narrow views of divine inspiration, conversion, authority and morality. We have already seen what devastating consequences Christianity from the New Testament onwards has had for the Jews, with its encouragement of antisemitism.[1] But that is not the only instance of Christianity having had a detrimental effect on other religions and cultures. The whole history of the missionary enterprise is full of examples, and it is perhaps as a growing realization of this that Christian missionary work within the more liberal traditions of the churches finds itself in crisis.

This makes the claim that in Jesus Christ God has acted once and for all, that Jesus has made a 'full, perfect, and sufficient sacrifice, oblation, and satisfaction, for the sins of the whole world',[2] that he is God's final revelation, such an important one to consider. The focus of that belief is not difficult to illustrate: right at the beginning of this book I quoted the saying of the Jesus of St John's Gospel which ends 'no one comes to the Father, but by me',[3] and in the Acts of the Apostles a sermon attributed to Peter testifies that there is salvation in no one else, 'for there is no other name under heaven given among men by which we must be saved',[4] words echoed by the famous saying, in Latin *extra ecclesiam nulla salus*: outside the church there is no salvation. One could add illustration after illustration, from all Christian traditions, down to the present day. And as I have said, for many Christians the consequence of this is still the claim that their faith is intrinsically superior to any other.

In the world of dialogue, particularly dialogue with Judaism and Islam, the other two great monotheistic religions, of course nothing is put so starkly as this. There is much that Judaism and Christianity have in common, not least because in the Western world they have gone through the same scientific and cultural revolutions together. The experience of the Holocaust, the Shoah, and Christian failure to react more firmly right from the beginning to Hitler's persecution of the Jews still casts its dark shadow,[5] and the existence and policies of the state of Israel are a source of tension, but nevertheless official Christian declarations increasingly emphasize the common ground.[6] Indeed there is even a tendency to see Judaism as part of a wider ecumenical movement.

However, the basic problem still remains even where dialogue is at its most friendly. If traditional Christian doctrine is that God is Trinity, Father, Son and Holy Spirit, and that God the Son was incarnate in Jesus of Nazareth, it inevitably follows that Christianity is not only different even from Judaism, but intrinsically, by virtue of its official doctrinal position, must claim to be superior.

Many Christians find no difficulty in that position. Thus Roman Catholics will even now reaffirm the view of the fifteenth-century Council of Florence that 'no one remaining outside the Catholic Church, not just pagans, but also Jews or heretics or schismatics, can become partakers of eternal life',[7] and fundamentalist evangelicals will have no difficulty with the message of the 1960 Chicago Congress of World Mission, that 'in the days since the war, more than one billion souls have passed into eternity and more than half of these went to the torment of hell fire without even hearing of Jesus Christ, who he was, or why he died on the cross of Calvary'.[8]

Karl Barth, whose approach we encountered in Chapter 10, advocated a particularly extreme version of this position. As we saw, he argued that Christian faith, properly understood, is not a religion at all, but the abolition of religion. He did so because he was particularly concerned in all his theology to make faith in God something which originates in God and God's revelation in Jesus. And faith, not religion, was for him the decisive element. The sections in Barth's *Church Dogmatics* which discuss 'The Revelation of God as the Abolition of Religion' are therefore headed 'The Problem of Religion in Theology', 'Religion as Unbelief' and 'True Religion'.[9]

The problem of religion in theology, Barth argues,

is not the question how the reality, religion, which has already been defined (and usually untheologically), can now be brought into an orderly and plausible relationship with the theological concepts, revelation, faith, etc. On the contrary, the question is uninterruptedly theological. What is this thing which from the standpoint of revelation and faith is revealed in the actuality of human life as religion?[10]

His answer is that religion is unbelief, the one great concern of godless man. True religion, or rather authentic Christian faith, is brought about by God, is entirely in God's giving, is to be found where God speaks in the name of Jesus Christ. Moreover this means that not all Christianity is authentic Christian faith; more often than not Christianity, too, is mere religion because it lacks that element of God-given faith which constitutes the church and establishes the relationship between God and the Christian through the person of Jesus Christ. Where this does not happen, Christianity stands under the same condemnation as non-Christian religions. By adopting this position at a time when, as a result of his admirable involvement in the Church Struggle in Germany, he had enormous influence which was continued by his subsequent great stature as a theologian, Barth contributed to keeping in being the view that, compared with faith in Jesus Christ, the other religions were inferior, if not godless. However, by including Christianity in its condemnation his view did not have the arrogance of less sophisticated theological positions.

A much cruder position of the latter kind, though less dialectical and with more first-hand knowledge of other faiths, is represented by the Dutch theologian Hendrik Kraemer, whose *The Christian Message in a Non-Christian World* has been one of the most influential of modern missionary textbooks,[11] apparently winning the unqualified support of such unlikely figures as Archbishop William Temple and the famous General Secretary of the World Council of Churches, Willem Visser 't Hooft.[12] The one advantage Kraemer had over Barth was that at least he had some first-hand knowledge of contemporary world religions: one feels that in post-First World War Germany and from the early 1930s in Basel, Barth's personal experience of Hindus, Buddhists and Sikhs must have been very limited indeed.

Kraemer's views were quite uncompromising, and unlike Barth

he became less, rather than more, mellow in his old age. In his view the *only* way of knowing true religion was through God's revelation in Jesus Christ and through nothing else, so that it could be said of other religions that 'in this light and in regard to their deepest, most essential purport they are all in error'.[13] 'If we are ever to know what true and divinely willed religion is, we can do this only through God's revelation in Jesus Christ and through nothing else.'[14]

Christians with wider horizons, who have more sympathy with men and women of other faiths and perhaps a greater capacity for listening as well as pronouncing, have found such a position most unsatisfactory. But if they want to maintain the traditional Christian attitude, their only alternative is to argue that in one way or another adherents of other religions are in fact worshipping Christ without knowing it and will discover the fact one day.

For this view, too, it is possible to refer to the New Testament, and particularly to the Acts of the Apostles, where Peter is made to say, 'Truly I perceive that God shows no partiality, but in every nation any one who fears him and does what is right is acceptable to him',[15] and Paul identifies the inscription which he finds on an altar in Athens 'to an unknown god' as referring to Jesus.[16] Those who hold such a view go on to argue that one of the problems which worried the early Christian Fathers was why God had waited so long to send Christ; they point to the way in which the Christian church came to identify Jesus with the Logos, the eternal principle of reason in which the whole human race shares (a development which we looked at in Chapter 5).

Perhaps the best known version of this alternative view is that put forward by the Roman Catholic theologian Karl Rahner, who developed the idea of the 'anonymous Christian'.[17] He argued that non-Christian religions could be said to be vehicles of salvation because they contain not only elements of a natural knowledge of God, compounded with human depravity as a result of the Fall, but also supernatural elements arising out of the grace given on account of Christ. Consequently, 'Christianity does not simply confront the member of an extra-Christian religion as a mere non-Christian but as someone who can and must already be regarded in this or that respect as an anonymous Christian.' So the church is not the exclusive source of salvation; it is the 'historically and socially constituted expression of what the Christian hopes is present as a hidden reality even outside the visible church'.[18]

Of all the world religions, Hinduism with its pluralism seems to Christians to be the most susceptible to the approach represented by Rahner, and therefore a good deal has been written on the relationship between Christianity and Hinduism.[19] One of the most widely read authors in this area is Raimundo Panikkar, though he starts from a different perspective.[20] While Panikkar personally associates the Lordship of Christ with the person of Jesus of Nazareth, he believes that the Lord can appear in innumerable forms. Christ is the link between the finite and the infinite, but in using that name Panikkar is not presupposing that Christ is identical with Jesus of Nazareth. 'Though a Christian believes that "Jesus is the Christ"... this sentence is not identical to "the Christ is Jesus".'[21] Jesus is the specific historical name 'for that name which is above every name, so that Christians should acknowledge that all religions recognize this Christ in one way or another', and the 'name above all names' can go by many historical names: Rama, Krishna, Isvara, Purusha, Tahagata.[22] This concern for what has come to be known as an 'inclusivist' view of Christianity has also been put forward by writers like Hans Küng[23] and John A.T. Robinson.[24]

This approach would certainly seem to be truer and more realistic than that of Barth and Kraemer, and to indicate more of an attempt to understand non-Christian religions from within. However, it is at least legitimate to ask how far it represents above all a discussion within Christianity focussed largely on a Christian audience and beginning from questions of concern to Christians. Moreover it is extremely doubtful whether it is appropriate even to seem to be suggesting to those of other faiths what they 'really' believe or will come to believe. In the past a similar approach has been bitterly contested by atheists who resent being told that they 'really' believe in God,[25] and the parallel is very close. It is hard to avoid the feeling that this is yet one more illegitimate piece of potential empire-building on the part of Christianity. And in the end, some prominent advocates of the approach still seem to end up by affirming the superiority of Christianity to all other religions, albeit in a more roundabout way. For the Hindu, Buddhist, Muslim or Sikh, could not the words with which Rahner concludes the discussion that we looked at earlier just as well be those of Karl Barth or Hendrik Kraemer?

> Non-Christians may think it presumptuous of the Christian to judge everything which is sound or restored (by being sanctified) to be the fruit in every man of the grace of his Christ, and to interpret it as anonymous Christianity; they may think it presumption for the Christian to regard the non-Christian as a Christian who has not yet come to himself reflectively. But the Christian cannot renounce this 'presumption' which is really the source of the greatest humility both for himself and the Church. For it is a profound admission of the fact that God is greater than man and the Church. The Church will go out to meet the non-Christian of tomorrow with the attitude expressed by St Paul when he said: What therefore you do not know and yet worship (and yet *worship*) that I proclaim to you (Acts 17.23). On such a basis one can be tolerant, humble and yet firm towards all non-Christian religions.[26]

And condescending? For when it comes to considering the relationship between Christianity and other religions, more than relatively abstract, theological factors have to be taken into account. Ideas are not developed in a vacuum but are the thoughts of men and women belonging to social groups which can look back on a long history which includes conflict, oppression and persecution. A good deal of rethinking and reinterpretation of the Christian Christ will have to be done before he can be mentioned in many of the contexts in which Rahner's theory or modifications of it would want to introduce him, as for example that of Jewish holocaust theology. And as we shall see shortly, it is highly doubtful whether such rethinking and reinterpretation is the right course to take.

Neither of the two positions which I have described is satisfactory. Moreover, they both fail completely to do justice to the problems that we have been looking at in previous chapters. They are based on a whole series of basic presuppositions which we have seen to be in need of re-examination. Therefore the next question must be: is there still any justification for insisting on the finality of Christ? That is not a question we have yet confronted directly. To do so we shall begin, not in the context of the dialogue between Christianity and other religions, but in that of the early church.

We have already seen how the early church was dominated by the expectation of an imminent end to the present age and the coming of God's kingdom.[27] That was the context against which the first Christians experienced the resurrection of Jesus. And in that context of apocalyptic hope the resurrection came to be understood as an anticipation of the final resurrection at the end of days and thus an anticipation of the end of history. Within the thought categories available to those who saw the resurrection in these terms this was tantamount to attributing a kind of absoluteness to Jesus, because absoluteness comes only at the end of history.[28]

But (again as we have seen)[29] in the course of time in the mainstream church the apocalyptic expectation faded and the church adapted its life-style and code of ethics to living in the world for a much longer period than had originally been expected. But this delay in the coming of the kingdom also raised an even more pressing theological question for Christians. If Jesus was the one chosen by God to usher in that kingdom, God's anointed one, God's messiah, God's Christ, and that kingdom had failed to come and Jesus had not returned, in what way could his life, death and resurrection be said to be significant for the world? The earlier conception of the way in which he was Christ was no longer viable, so people were faced with the stark alternative of either changing the focus of their understanding of him and putting it elsewhere, or giving up believing in him on the grounds that he had been mistaken.

They did the former, and did so by placing Jesus firmly at the centre of all things.[30] This may have been an ambitious claim, but within three centuries it had become so established that it was impossible to doubt (not least because state sanctions made certain that no one would try, openly). Circumstances favoured the claim of the centrality of Christ. For while Rome had unified the world politically, by military force, it had not succeeded in doing so ideologically, and therefore a crisis in values had developed. So by saying that Jesus was the centre of everything, Christians could fill a spiritual vacuum, and when Constantine became emperor and Christianity in due course became the state religion, the image of Christ at the centre was reinforced by that of his servant upon earth.[31]

This may have been a good strategical victory for Christianity, but the move shifted its perspective in a way from which it has never recovered. For once Christ was put at the centre, Christianity adopted the habit of constantly looking back over its shoulder, and became increasingly weighed down by the burden of its past, leaving expectations of the future (which never completely died) to become the property of marginal sects.[32] There is no doubt, as Professor Moltmann brought out in his own distinctive way in his much-read book *Theology of Hope*,[33] that the perspective of the Bible is forward-looking, the New Testament following the Old Testament in looking forward to what God was to do in the future: we shall be returning to the theme in the final chapters of this book. But once Christ was put at the centre the gaze of Christians was predominantly directed backwards, to what he *had* been and what *had* happened in him. It very soon came to be said that Jesus was himself the kingdom, that the kingdom had already come. And if you asked where that kingdom now was, it was to be seen in the church, the kingdom of God on earth, even 'the extension of the incarnation' (a particularly pernicious phrase). Moreover, although many Christians at the time of the Reformation found this claim intolerable, they did not change the emphasis back so that it again became forward-looking; with the exception of the sects referred to above they simply put the Bible, with Christ seen as its centre, in place of the Pope.

This view that Christ was at the centre of all things was not much questioned even in the hey-day of liberal Christianity, before Barth came to stress the centrality of Christ even more strongly than ever before. As Tom Driver, commenting on the developments outlined in the previous two paragraphs, has put it:

Liberal Christianity in the nineteenth and twentieth centuries does not seem to have addressed itself to a basic question which may be phrased like this: can the idea of an enduring *centre* of all things, including history, be compatible with the sense of 'history' that is presupposed in modern historical scholarship? I think that the answer to this question must be negative, but I do not hear this plainly from biblical, ecclesiastical, or theological historians. Specifically, I do not hear them say that since Christ is a historical concept referring to a historical person, then Christ must be a *movable* and *relative* figure, like all other historical phenomena. Instead of this, I hear that 'Jesus of Nazareth' is a historical figure, known only in the relativistic way that all history is known, but that 'Christ' is somehow above history – transcendent in such a way as to be not truly a subject of historical inquiry or judgment. This, I have long thought, is to have it both ways. It is no wonder that many conservative Christians have thought we liberals exhibit bad faith.[34]

Here we meet up with some of the issues that we have already considered in Chapter 10. And we meet up with the problems of emphasis on Christ as a central figure which we discussed in Chapter 6 and indeed with the discussion of the incarnation in Chapter 5. Tom Driver further comments that while we have learned that God has no need of a geographical centre like a temple or a holy city at Rome, Jerusalem or Mecca, we have not been taught that God also has no need of a temporal or historical centre.[35] So is this not the kind of pressure which is proving so strong that we are on the verge of that kind of paradigm-shift to which I referred earlier?[36]

Professor Hick has long argued that we have now reached a stage in human history where a change needs to take place in religious outlook precisely parallel to that which took place in astronomy with the Copernican revolution (which we looked at in Chapter 2). It is now necessary that Christ should be replaced by God at the centre of the religious universe. A whole series of arguments have been used to maintain the idea of Christ the centre, but the expedients which have to be devised in order to sustain them have become so complex that they resemble the epicycles which were introduced to make the old Ptolemaic system compatible with actual observations of the heavens. Like the theory of epicycles, these devices may go on propping up the traditional system for a while, but as our observations become more and more accurate they must inevitably collapse. And so Professor Hick concludes: 'We have to realize that the universe of faiths centres upon God, and not upon Christianity or upon any other religion. He is the sun, the originative source of light and life, whom all the religions reflect in their own different ways.'[37]

Anyone adopting this approach can point to the fact that the major world religions may be seen to have grown out of a particular period of religious experience – often denoted by a phrase coined by the German philosopher Karl Jaspers, 'the axial period', lasting roughly between 800 and 200 BC – but in different areas of the globe.[38] These different religions can be seen as different responses, conditioned by different cultures and geographical settings, to the same divine Spirit within the world, with individual types of response going on to develop in different ways (for example, Christianity and Islam developing out of the Jewish tradition).

If we look at these religions together as a group we can see that they have many parallel characteristics. Christianity is not the only religion to hold that it is the final one, that it can claim to have a superior insight into the nature of God and thus represent the centre of religious faith. John Hick describes one such claim as follows:

> The most striking example of this today in the religious realm is provided by contemporary philosophical Hinduism. This holds that the ultimate reality, Brahman, is beyond all qualities, including personality, and that personal deities, such as the God of the Bible or the Krishna of the Bhagavad Gita, are partial images of the Absolute created for the benefit of that majority of mankind who cannot rise above anthropomorphic thinking to the pure Absolute... The adherent of each system of belief can assume that his own system is alone fully true and that all the others are more or less true according as they approximate to or diverge from it.[39]

The great strength of the approach of which John Hick is a representative, an approach which is buttressed by the historical, biblical and doctrinal criticism that has compelled such a major rethinking of Christianity, is the soundness of its basically empirical method and the evidence which it can adduce in its support. It is firmly rooted in the world we know, and makes observations which cannot be denied. Thus John Hick has movingly described how his approach to people of other faiths was moulded by his time in the multi-cultural city of Birmingham, where he was not only an academic theologian at the university but also Chairman of a voluntary organization, All Faiths For One Race, formed to combat the activities and propaganda of the National Front, and Chairman of the Religious and Cultural Panel of the Birmingham Community Relations Committee, an official body set up by the government.

He also worked on producing a new multi-faith syllabus to be used in religious education.[40]

If personal encounter and shared activities and projects have been the primary motive force behind this new, pluralist approach, so too has been the impact of plain common-sense considerations on some of the more nonsensical views of traditionalist theologians.

There should have been no need to point out the degree to which the faith one has depends on the area in which one is born and the culture of which one is a member or the arrogance of supposing that all non-Christians are practising an inferior, superstitious, misguided form of religion from which they need to be converted. But in almost all areas the cause of religious pluralism has a long way to go before it even begins to gain a reasonable foothold in the churches. The main reason for that is there are still many otherwise responsible, learned, distinguished and highly-esteemed theologians and church leaders whose attitudes, when it comes to considering those of other faiths, tend to be at best condescending, reluctant to contemplate change and blind to the consequences of their position (far less to be ready to demonstrate repentance over past evils perpetrated in the name of Christianity), and at worst bigoted and intolerant; and there are 'ordinary' Christians who just do not want to think about the issues now facing them. The unfortunate result is that we can see theologians tying themselves in knots trying to rescue the supremacy and finality of Christianity, and lay people who have not even begun to see the problems posed by Christian theology in a multi-faith society, quite apart from its doubtful truth-claims. That is so particularly if they live in areas, like the depths of rural Britain or America, where they can pretend that the multi-cultural world of the cities does not exist or, if it does, has no relation to their beliefs.

I have already compared the attitude of what I suspect is the majority of Christians to that of their forebears in the last century when confronted with the discoveries of modern science. But worse is to come. In the case of other religions, where other human beings are involved, this already biassed attitude is accompanied by a kind of *Schadenfreude*, delight in other people's misfortunes. Christians actually give the impression of not wanting other religions to be right, to have a valid insight into the nature of God and his ways with human beings. As Professor Wilfred Cantwell Smith, one of the great contributors towards understanding between religions, has pointed out:

> If one's chances of getting to Heaven – or to use a nowadays more acceptable metaphor – of coming into God's presence – are dependent upon other people's not getting there, then one becomes walled up within the quite intolerable position that the Christian has a vested interest in other men's damnation. It is shocking to admit it, but this actually takes place. When an observer comes back from Asia, or from a study of Asian religious traditions, and reports that, contrary to accepted theory, some Hindus and Buddhists and some Muslims lead a pious and moral life and seem very near to God by any possible standards, so that, so far as one can see, in these particular cases at least faith is as 'adequate' as Christian faith, then presumably a Christian should be overjoyed, enthusiastically hopeful that this be true, even though he might be permitted a fear lest it not be so. Instead, I have sometimes witnessed just the opposite: an emotional resistance to the news, men hoping firmly that it is not so, though perhaps with a covert fear that it might be. Whatever the rights and wrongs of the situation theoretically, I submit that practically this is just not Christian, and indeed is not tolerable. It will not do, to have a faith that can be undermined by God's saving one's neighbour; or to be afraid lest other men turn out to be closer to God than one had been led to suppose.[41]

Similarly, one might have thought that mutual understanding, reciprocal dialogue, exploration of one another's standpoints might have been a high priority among Christians. If what they claim is really true, that God was in Christ reconciling the world to himself, and that this work of reconciliation represents the ultimate truth of the universe, one would have expected their prime concern to be to achieve reconciliation among men and women of all races and cultures, breaking down barriers and bridging divisions, not least because it is clear to any sensitive person in our age that our world needs to be one world and that lack of reconciliation among peoples of different faiths, and indeed within Christianity itself, is a major factor in tearing it apart. Moreover in all the inner cities of Britain and America Christians are living in communities where those who are adherents of other religions are neighbours, fellow-workers, owners of restaurants and shops, and so on.

Like Mount Everest, religious diversity is there. And because it is there, any system of Christian doctrine of creation must give an account of religious diversity; it must have something to say on the question why there are Buddhists, Sikhs, Hindus and Moslems with their different traditions, their different holy books. Indeed any presentation of the Christian faith generally is incomplete if it does not contain some worked-out view of the presence of those of other religions.

Any such presentation which points to the inadequacies of other religions or asserts that they are in error has a fundamental problem of method to deal with. How can one show that someone else's religion is false? We might say that we know our religion to be true because we have lived it ourselves and that our view is shared by millions upon millions of people down the centuries. But in the sphere of religious belief one cannot go on to say that if one's own beliefs are true it must follow that others' beliefs must be false. Beyond question there will be and are errors of belief and conduct in a religious faith, but that applies to all religions, including Christianity. As John Hick again points out, Christian practice has ranged from the saintly – in the persons of, say, St Francis of Assisi and Mother Teresa of Calcutta – to the demonic, as instanced in the history of Christian persecution of the Jews. And one can go on from this to argue that for each evil that the Christian can point to in other religious traditions, there is just as obvious an evil within the Christian tradition, and that one cannot realistically compare one religious tradition with another.

How are we to weigh the lethargy of many Eastern countries in relation to social and economic problems, so that they suffer from endemic poverty, against the West's ruthlessly competitive greed in the exploitation of the earth's resources – the Western capitalist rape of the planet at the expense of half the world and all future generations? How are we to weigh the effect of Hindu and Buddhist 'otherwordliness' in retarding social, economic and technological progress against the use of the Christian Gospel to validate unjust social systems in Europe and South America, and to justify and perpetuate massive racial exploitation in South

Africa? How are we to weigh the unjust caste-system of India against the unjust class-system and pervasive racism of much of the Christian West? How do we weigh the use of the sword in building great Muslim, Hindu and Buddhist empires against the use of the gun in building the great Christian empires? How do we weigh the aggressive Muslim incursion into Europe in the fourteenth century against the previous Christian incursion into the Middle East known as the Crusades? How do we weigh the hideous custom of the 'voluntary' burning of widows (*suttee*) in India against the equally hideous burning of 'witches' in Christian Europe and North America?[42]

A good deal more could be said in this connection, but this is not primarily a book about pluralism but about the significance of Jesus, and so we must leave the discussion at this point. It is likely to continue for some time to come, and now provides another interesting parallel to that over the doctrine of the Incarnation. A recent conference on the question of religious pluralism has led to the production of a volume, edited by John Hick and the American Paul Knitter, entitled *The Myth of Christian Uniqueness*.[43] The contributors are those who now feel it necessary to state publicly their adherence to a pluralistic view, with all the risks (given the predominant climate within Christianity) which that involves.

The Myth of Christian Uniqueness, like *The Myth of God Incarnate* before it, is notable not so much for the completely new insights it brings as for the way in which it can be seen as a summary and emphasizing of a debate already in progress for some time (though the contributions in it from Paul Knitter and Marjorie Suchocki are valuable for the way in which they show how a revision of the status of Christianity would bring changes to the insights of liberation theology).[44] Certainly the contributors are well aware of the difficulties that still face them, as is clear from two memorable images which emerged at the public forum held during the conference itself. A contributor, from the platform, described her image of pilgrims ascending the mountain of religion.

> They could not see its summit because they were making their way up through the clouds, but after a long time they climbed to heights above the clouds and stood on the upper reaches of their mountain under a clear sky. Then they could see, to their surprise,

that there were other mountains. And on their peaks, beyond the valleys that lay concealed beneath the clouds, were other pilgrims. So the pilgrims cry out over the distance, 'Halloo!' 'Halloo!' And that is all that they communicate.[45]

A member of the audience responded. She referred to the Hindu belief in the existence of a mountain that is upside down. Like an inverted pyramid, it is narrow at the bottom, wide and broad at the top. A persistent religious seeker, climbing this mountain with great difficulty, finds at the end of the climb a broad summit where dwell every variety of creature and all manner of Gods.[46]

There is, though, one factor on which little stress is placed in *The Myth of Christian Uniqueness* and in the debate over the relationship between religious faiths and religious pluralism generally. The usual assumption made by those involved in that dialogue is that the discussion is taking place between the representatives of relatively solid, relatively coherent religious traditions, and that, for example, on the Christian side there is an agreed Christianity for which a Christian representative can speak. But, as we saw in Chapter 4, for Christians the very identity of Christianity is a problem. Perhaps in some respects discussion with those of other faiths does serve to highlight overall features of the Christian perspective which differ markedly from those of other religions, but this is true only to a limited degree, and less so in dialogues with Judaism and Islam than in dialogues with, say, Eastern faiths.

In fact the Christian tradition is disintegrating, and disintegrating in a particularly complicated way, which would be worth much further attention than it can be given here: I can touch on it only in passing. For Christianity has become bound up with a post-religious, secular, technological attitude to the world which, as a result of Western success in the commercial, military and paramilitary spheres and the global activity of the media, multinational corporations and international finance houses, is steadily spreading all over the world. And so this secularized version of Christianity can be seen as a threat to any form of traditional religion, including Christianity itself. And that again complicates the whole question of the finality of Christianity and its Christ.

The disintegration of the Christian tradition and the problems with which it is confronted might seem to make the step that the contributors to *The Myth of Christian Uniqueness* feel that they are taking perhaps less drastic than they make out. The editors describe how their project came to be referred to as the crossing of a theological Rubicon. That it may well prove to be. But I remember from my classical training that the Rubicon was a pretty insignificant river, and that no one is quite sure where it was.

12 | Criteria for Christianity

We are now virtually at the end of a long series of questions. At this stage we can look back and see not only the wide range of issues that they have covered but also the variety of reasons for which they have emerged. Some have been questions about Jesus raised by the clash between modern critical methods and the Christian tradition; some have been questions raised by the collapse of the world of Christendom and the very new context in which the church and individual believers find themselves. Others have arisen through the problem of sustaining claims about Jesus against the background of much widened horizons which can often show up those claims as they have been previously made as being problematical, even arrogant (as in case of the discussion of the finality of Christ in the previous chapter). Yet others have been raised because it would seem – and this is a point to which we shall be returning – that because of heightened moral susceptibilities and deeper insights, some images of Christ and arguments derived from them do not match our higher standards. In another area, some forms of belief in Christ exercise illegitimate psychological pressure or do not live up to our best understanding of what it is to be human: one need only think of the reaction that the threat of hell-fire more than once attributed to the Jesus of the Synoptic Gospels has provoked among humanist critics of Jesus.

Not only have we seen a series of reasons why the questions which we have been considering have arisen; we have also seen how questions do not just have a negative role. Certainly many of the questions that I have been asking do make deep inroads into Christian tradition, and if they are accepted and followed through cannot leave traditional Christianity as it has been: as I said at the beginning they are deeply disturbing. But although they are there and will not go away, by their existence they also provide a positive safeguard against Christian imperialism, institutionalism, the tradition in its worst, quasi-totalitarian form, and the ideological dangers that go with it.

In Chapter 8 we saw the darker side of the tradition – and while it has not been the purpose of this book to dwell on that darker side, we must never forget that it is there. In particular those who nostalgically hanker after 'traditional' Christianity, like those who hanker after Victorian values, need to remember everything that went with a more confident, more authoritarian age, and not just pick out – one suspects above all for their reassurance – those parts which they find most congenial (we need to remind ourselves of the links between the virgin birth and antisemitism, between the resurrection and an excessive use of power in the name of religion). Historical questions and the understanding of the historical nature of our consciousness can have a positive and liberating effect if they lead to a relativizing of dogmas and ideals so that in a transitory and changing world these cannot be claimed to have a permanence and absoluteness which they do not possess. Questions are also important in coming to terms with the need to achieve at the very least satisfactory dialogue between the many religious traditions in our pluralistic world, with their very different values. So all has not been loss.

If one single result emerges from all this it is surely that the symbols of Jesus and the Christ – as I said at the beginning, these are to some degree separate figures in the tradition and have almost irrevocably come to be associated with two very different sets of values – occupy too prominent a place in Christianity. They have accumulated too much power; so much power indeed that in many contexts the figure of Jesus has come to eclipse that of God. Of course belief in God has not been without its problems as a result of yet another set of questions, not considered here, which have arisen over the last two centuries. But that would be the topic for another book. The important thing to be noted in this context is that Jesus has become a distorting factor, an irrational element which, rather than exercising influence that comes from the person Jesus of Nazareth himself (we have seen how difficult it is to know anything for certain about him), is in fact a symbol that is used to dominate and manipulate. This may be manipulation through the aspects of the symbol which support power ('Christ the Lord')[1] or manipulation through those aspects of it which represent weakness (the crucified Christ: one might think, for example of the use in two world wars of the Johannine text about 'laying down one's life for one's friends';[2] Malachi Martin in a telling passage calls this the 'bleeding lord' image[3]).

But, it may be argued, it is all very well pointing out the value of questioning as an antidote to a dominant and authoritarian tradition or as a means of increasing openness in discussion between those of different faiths, but one cannot live on questions alone. What is to be said to those who are dimly aware of most of these questions and are prepared to accept them, but in addition are looking for something more positive (which perhaps they had hoped, somehow, still to be able to find in Jesus), the beginnings of a faith to live by? Surely, such people might rightly say, far too much contemporary theology resembles nothing so much as a community living in an old, rambling and dilapidated house, with suspect foundations, structural problems demanding constant attention, leaks from the plumbing and draughts, all of which sorely tries the patience of the inhabitants. And among its inhabitants, the more radical solutions for improving the situation are always rejected by those who have lived in the house for a very long time, often with parents and grandparents before them who always appeal to the restrictions imposed by some divine planning order. No wonder that occupants are steadily moving out, often finding it more tolerable to camp in the open air than to put up with the atmosphere inside.

That justified hope and desire for some answers is accompanied by an equally justified fear. If one moves too far in the direction of the historical relativism discussed in Chapter 10, even more if one accepts the kind of non-realist view of the world and consequently of belief put forward by Don Cupitt in his two most recent books,[4] does one not arrive at a position of utter relativity? Christian theologians of different ages have had their own different mental terrors (each age has a terror that has not occurred to previous ages and does not frighten later ones), and the terror of many theologians of our age is cultural relativism.[5] If you abandon the finality of Christ, do you not end up in a world in which everything is relative to everything else: 'it's all a matter of opinion', and 'anything goes'?

Such a panic reaction does not help clear thinking, and at this point it is all too easy to lose one's head and lapse into some kind of doctrinal or biblical fundamentalism simply because the apparent alternative, complete relativism, is so intolerable. But little can be said for such a reaction other than that it satisfies a craving for security and certainty. However, the fact of the matter is that security, certainty and finality are not to be had in this world – from any source, no matter how time-hallowed, no matter what divine authority it claims. This was recognized in the nineteenth century by F.D.Maurice, who suffered for his insistence on the point;[6] and it was also recognized, in what now seem to be the distant 1960s, by Ian Ramsey, when he wrote that 'the desire to be sure in religion, however natural, however dangerous, seems in our age doomed to disappointment by an intellectual, practical and evangelistic context of appalling complexity',[7] and concluded that in our circumstances a tentative theology is in no way a euphemism for scepticism, does not suppose that all theologies are equally good and is not an excuse for sloth and ignorance, but is an apt counterpart to our vision of God.[8]

It may perhaps help if we begin by identifying this issue with which we are now concerned in a more precise way. In the light of what I have said so far, I think that it can reasonably be formulated in one last question, which goes like this. We have seen that the Christian claim that Jesus Christ is the sole source of truth, the final revelation, the way, the truth and the life is open to serious objections and cannot of itself serve as a criterion. So what criteria do we use for judging Christ, Christianity and religious faith generally, and where we get them from?

To have got as far as formulating that question is already to have come a long way, simply because of what the question presupposes. As I have just said, it is a question that many Christians will not entertain and will not ask, because its implications are terrifying. Once the questions about the Christ of Christianity get too pressing, the one sure place on which it seems possible to stand in an uncertain and shifting world gives way and believers feel abandoned defenceless to the quicksands. But it is the question that we must ask.

As Ian Ramsey reminds us, when we consider these criteria, we are not looking for criteria which will enable us to appeal to finality, centrality, certainty. We are looking for criteria by which to live our lives authentically, by which we can be true to ourselves, true to those among whom we live, and responsive to the needs of the world, always with our gaze fixed on a purpose, aim and goal transcending all this which is worth striving for. Here we are in fact in harmony with a theme which runs through the Bible from beginning to end: that of the pilgrimage, the journey, without complete clarity as to the ultimate destination except by virtue of the use of metaphorical terms like the promised land, the heavenly city, the kingdom of God, the presence of God, when all will become clear and all will be well.[9]

To have that kind of hope is already to have come down on one side of the stark alternative with which we are all confronted, that life either has meaning, or is meaningless. In a famous modern parable John Hick illustrated the contrast between these perspectives by describing two travellers on the same road, the only road there is. One believes that it leads to the Celestial City, interpreting the pleasant parts as encouragements and the obstacles as trials of his purpose and lessons in endurance, bringing about a process of growth; the other finds only the road itself and the luck of the road in good weather and bad.[10] We all have to identify with one or other of these travellers if we are to follow the questioning where it leads or decide that it is not worth bothering with; to decide whether we see the world as having meaning or being meaningless. To take the latter position makes the whole of this book, like the rest of life, pointless, and indeed it may be. No one who has not at some time or other truly struggled with the prospect, the threat, of meaninglessness, can be aware of the risk of the venture of faith. Our quest is quite likely to be interrupted and may need to be taken up time and again, for often we may find the threat of meaninglessness very real. Here again is a weakness of much of the currently most fashionable conservative theology, for it seems to underestimate the degree to which one can have a faith which is full of questions yet is nevertheless faith.

The criteria that we are looking for in this chapter, then, are those we need to help in exploration, journeying, so that we remain true to ourselves and all that we know. But we are not trying to find explanations for everything, for that is to go beyond our nature as human beings. What kind of criteria will these be?

Above all, the indications are that they must be ethical. We have already seen this point made by Michael Langford,[11] the sub-title of the book by Tom Driver from which I have already quoted several times is 'Towards an Ethical Christology',[12] and the point was reiterated by Stewart Sutherland when he attempted to set out a series of standards for viable religious convictions in the contemporary world. Among these he includes the criterion that any religious belief which runs counter to our moral beliefs is unacceptable.[13] Theological judgments, then, may be said to be subject to ethical testing. However, it might be objected that this hardly improves the situation. Is there not constant revision in ideas of what is good? Does not the notion of good change from society to society and from age to age? Here the spectre of relativity again begins to creep in. Since it can be demonstrated that ethics, too, has a history, are we not still confronted with the same basic problem?

Ethics certainly has a history, like everything else, but the effect of a historical critique of ethics is not as devastating as that of a historical critique of Christian theology. For example, in his influential *After Virtue*, the philosopher Alasdair MacIntyre has used an account of historical changes in ethical theory and outlook as a basis for criticizing the relativity and shallowness of many contemporary ethical arguments. He begins the book by comparing such arguments with the way scientific arguments might look if a catastrophe had so reduced resources that all that were left were fragments detached from the theoretical context which gave them any significance.[14] Established terms might be used, but the beliefs which they presuppose would have been lost and the resultant situation would inevitably seem one of arbitrariness. Reconstruct the situation, and the predicament and the inadequacy of many modern ethical approaches becomes clear. If we see what happened to classical 'virtue', it is easier for us to consider what comes 'after virtue'. Among other things this survey demonstrates that relativism by no means has the last word.[15]

That this is the case is made even clearer by another study of ethics by the English philosopher Renford Bambrough, *Moral Scepticism and Moral Knowledge*. The author makes clear from the start his opposition to the idea that there can be no objectivity in moral philosophy:

My proof that we have moral knowledge consists essentially in saying, 'We know that this child, who is about to undergo what would otherwise be painful surgery, should be given an anaesthetic before the operation. Therefore we know at least one moral proposition to be true.' I argue that no proposition that could plausibly be alleged as a reason in favour of doubting the truth of the proposition that the child should be given an anaesthetic can possibly be more certainly true than that proposition itself. If a philosopher produces an argument against my claim to *know* that the child should be given an anaesthetic, I can therefore be sure in advance that *either* at least one of the premises of his argument is false, *or* that there is a mistake in the reasoning by which he purports to derive from his premises the conclusion that I do not know that the child should be given an anaesthetic.[16]

From here Renford Bambrough goes on, for example, to establish a case for moral objectivity by arguing that it is no more necessary to believe in moral absolutes in order to believe in moral objectivity than it is to believe in the existence of absolute space or absolute time in order to believe in the objectivity of temporal or spatial relations and of judgments about them.[17] Or he can contest the famous assertion that there is no legitimate argument from what *is* the case to what *ought* to be the case by pointing out that the transition from is to ought is made in any argument which seeks to constrain another party to accept its premises.[18] There is no need to repeat all of his arguments here, but to my mind the evidence of his book, taken alongside that of Alasdair MacIntyre, is enough to show that there are good grounds for arguing for a degree of objectivity in moral criteria (something which is generally accepted in common-sense judgments) as opposed to utter relativity. Historical relativism does not entail complete relativism. At any rate, there is good reason for more exploration along these lines. And we can progress further by means of it.

Assuming, on the basis of the discussion in the previous paragraphs, that there is more to be said than is commonly accepted for supposing morality to be a given, to be part of the structure of our world, it makes sense to talk of historical developments leading to heightened moral awareness, to the discovery by human beings of new insights which make them feel that what might have been tolerated in the past is no longer tolerable in the present. Those who have such insights may be in no position to implement them: they may themselves be weak and unprivileged; they may be poets and mystics and visionaries and artists. But it is beyond question that insights into moral demands have been developed in our century which were not there before, sometimes in response to new increased threats from perceived evil and sometimes because of a deeper realization of circumstances which have prevailed for a long time, and that these insights have changed many people's understanding of what is acceptable in religious belief.

We can see that in a number of areas. One obvious one is the movement for women's liberation, which has impressed on us that from the way in which we use our language to the way in which we order our churches and societies, half the human race has been marginalized and oppressed. That is not an insight that can be traced back very far but it is nevertheless an authentic one. Another similar insight is the realization of the injustice in the distribution of the world's natural resources, and the degree to which the exploitation of the poor has provided and still provides the comfort of the rich. From our perspective we have a completely different view of the Old Testament prophets from our ancestors because we prize them primarily because of their stress on social justice, while at the same time feeling that their transformation into foretellers of Jesus, a role accepted down Christian history, was a distortion of their concern.[19] In the same way, we may single out for commendation from other passages in Paul's letters his affirmation 'there is neither Jew nor Greek, there is neither slave nor free, there is neither male nor female, for you are all one in Christ Jesus',[20] even if this often seems as far from realization as ever.

We may not forget, then, that among our best insights, if not in the realization of them, there is real progress. As some obvious examples, it is worth remembering that, for instance, the John Newton who wrote the famous hymn 'How sweet the name of Jesus sounds in a believer's ear', with its song of love to his Lord, was involved in slave trading even as a converted Christian.[21] The use of child labour and the treatment of the poor which was taken for granted by Christian industrialists and Christian society generally in the Victorian age is recognized for the inhumanity it was.[22] And examples could be multiplied here. The process is still going on.

The motive power behind the heightening of moral insight and the recognition of oppression and injustice stems from the tension between what is, in an immoral world, and what could be. That vision spreads, and gains power – the sort of power, for example, generated by Martin Luther King's famous 'I have a dream' speech[23] – when those who have hitherto been forced for one reason or another to remain speechless are given a voice. It is when one is open enough to hear the perspective of the other – the black voices, the women's voices, the cry of the poor, the marginalized, the imprisoned, those facing death – that the necessary content of the vision, if it is an authentic one, becomes that much wider.

But at this point we are again thrown back on the question of meaning or meaninglessness. We have to ask whether all those visions which in one way or another express some kind of 'happy ending'(this ending may be expressed in terms of the kingdom of God or in some other less direct way) are visions of a real possibility or are just delusions – the use of a kind of religious language which is not, however, backed up by the reality to which it was once thought to refer.[24] In other words, we are brought up against that reality to whom the Christian and Jewish traditions, among others, refer as God. For only if there is that reality behind the language of exploration, vision, faith and hope that we use do these terms have any worthwhile meaning by that standard which we must apply to any analysis of human life in our world – the life of the dispossessed, the despairing, the starving, the oppressed, those with no earthly future.

At this stage we are already pointed beyond the ethical sphere to what might be called the sphere of transcendence. So that such a term does not become too abstract, we might note here the role of what the Roman Catholic theologian Edward Schillebeeckx talks of as 'experiences of contrast'.[25] There are certain experiences which inevitably come to all men and women – those of finitude and contingency in which they cry out for something different. Men and women should not suffer; they should not be hurt and oppressed; they should not be made to weep. And even in their best moments, when men and women seem almost to begin to transcend their finite natures, as when they reach out to each other in mutual love, there is nevertheless a consciousness of just how fragile this love is, accompanied by a conviction that it should be something more than a transient moment in our humanity.

Despite all our negative experience, Schillebeeckx continues, there still seems to be in most people something like a fundamental trust, the trust that in the end all will be well. And this trust leads him to the conclusion that there is something in humankind which is not of ourselves and which as it were constantly seizes us despite ourselves, the power of the creative action of a God who is concerned for salvation.[26] To put it in a more basic way: the tension between what is and what ought to be cries out for something more, something beyond what seem to be our everyday realities. So Schillebeeckx and others, as indeed I myself, would want to say in our own particular ways that we believe there to be 'a power at the heart of things who makes for good and who confronts, judges and absorbs what makes for bad; who is available as Spirit, to support struggles for good, confront the work of evil and to renew people in the struggle and innovate hopefully'. Or that 'the world is somehow or other transfused with a power and a possibility who intends purpose, direction and promise for those whom he calls to know him'.[27]

But since this book is above all one of questions and the examination of arguments, this is not yet the point to move to confessions of faith. The theme of this chapter needs to be taken further.

Developing the criterion that religious belief must be ethical has brought us to a second sphere. If we are ruthless in our examination of our own experience and the world around us, and reject half truths, despite the arguments against this sort of approach, especially as advocated by Karl Barth,[28] we may nevertheless find ourselves directed towards a transcendent dimension. At this point individual explorations become more personal, and those looking for a guide have many to choose from. Here I mention just two books which I have found helpful and are never likely to figure among the theological books which I part with because I am never likely to look at them again.

The first is the German theologian Gerd Theissen's *On Having a Critical Faith*. As he explains in his Preface, during his student days he kept asking himself 'How can theologians go on working, day after day, when they cannot even give a convincing answer to the suspicion that God is an illusion?'[29] And he resolved either to find an answer of his own or to give up theology altogether. His answer resulted in his book. Another of his comments is worth bearing in mind:

Many theologians often know nothing about the real convictions of those with whom they are talking: what they accept or what they reject. One disillusioned comment which I heard recently was that theologians are no longer concerned with the truth. That I refuse to believe. It would be utter disaster. But I do hope at least that this book will show all my colleagues and students more clearly than is possible in brief seminars and discussions why I still continue to identify myself with our religious traditions, and how far I do, despite the fact that I have become involved in such 'godless' matters as sociology and psychology. Given the present situation in the church and in theology, it may sound portentous to say so, but I do think that the greatest problem for theology is the question of the truth, and that the hallmark of the theological teacher must be his openness and honesty. This book means more to me than all my other writings.[30]

And he goes on to tackle head-on, and work his way through to a positive conclusion, the criticism of religion as an ideology; sociological, psychological and empiricist criticism of religion; and the problems of historical relativity. Not the least important feature of his approach is that an exploration is really being carried forward, in real issues, in the real world, with full personal commitment, in questioning involvement, for if God is, it is in reality that God is to be found.[31]

The second is a remarkable short book by the English writer and journalist Philip Toynbee. In a succinct 'Tract for the Times' which he produced in 1973, a rigorously argued essay entitled *Towards the Holy Spirit*, consisting of 237 numbered paragraphs, Philip Toynbee began by pointing out the way in which old confidence had been eroded among both orthodox theologians and scientific materialists by the inkling that a good deal of reality may be inconceivable to the human mind. Traditional Christian theology cannot withstand the moral arguments to which it is vulnerable (particularly the problem of evil) and logical positivism is unable to cope with the kind of language that physicists feel compelled to use to describe their findings. Far from old problems being solved, new ones are constantly being added, confronting thinkers with the unthinkable.[32]

The crucial argument, he went on, was how best, most convincingly and most usefully in present circumstances, to interpret the whole of human existence. Any attempt to do this comes up against a whole series of 'intractable' words which refuse to be reduced to something else: identity, love, beauty, freedom, art, death, truth, vision, eternity and so on. These do not denote unsolved problems, but mysteries (and here he uses the term in a legitimate way). These mysteries denote areas of experience to which too little attention is paid by both scientists and philosophers. Among all the evidence to be taken into consideration in interpreting the whole of human existence is that of those who claim to have had mystical experience. Here is evidence from the widest imaginable range of sources, from men and women of the utmost integrity, who claim that the order of reality with which they find themselves in contact is infinitely superior by any criterion of value to anything else that they have ever encountered: more joyful, more beautiful, more real. It must therefore be accounted for.[33]

Of course there is a tendency to dismiss this experience; it is explained away, it is vetoed as illegitimate speculation, or it is appropriated by some attempt to revive the old Christian dogmas. But none of these expedients really does justice to the experiences attested:

> It is as if Captain Cook had returned to England and reported the existence of a great southern continent, only to be told by those who had stayed at home that he was certainly suffering from an illusion, due to the Captain's inordinate love of his mother; or to his social origins; or to his drunkenness; or to sea-sickness; or simply to his passionate *desire* to make a great discovery (wish-fulfilment).[34]

Philip Toynbee rejected the attempt to reintroduce traditional theological statements at this point because they did not seem to get to the heart of the matter: their certainties are inappropriate to our gropings for truth and they over-simplify our problems as much in one direction as scientific reductionism does in another. So what was he – what are we – left with?

First of all, he argued, when it comes to talking about mysteries all our language must be metaphorical. At the limits of exploration the language that has to be used needs to be 'a ghostly language: a language of hint and suggestion, of echo and paradox: something much closer to the untranslateable communications of music than to the demonstrations of logic'[35] – and he went on to point out, four years before the position was argued for in *The Myth of God Incarnate*, that the major error of all systematic theologies was their attempt to use a non-metaphorical language when only metaphor would do (adding that to attempt to turn into metaphor what were originally meant as literal statements would not do either).

Unable at this stage (though his thinking developed later, as is evidenced in subsequent writings) to accept either a Christian creator God as traditionally presented or a Jesus worshipped as Son of God, Philip Toynbee seized on the Holy Spirit as an interpretation of what stood out for him as a result of his exploration of the phenomena with which he found himself confronted, arriving at a conclusion which, by its stress on the need to resist certainty and yet rule out certain positions which were demonstrably unsatisfactory, both avoided relativism and yet remained open to revision and development, development which he himself continued to work out up to his death in 1981.[36]

So he could write:

The greatest gift is the gift of religious understanding, for this can enable us to receive as much of heaven's light as we are ever able to receive. Other gifts are inner freedom (for the natural world knows nothing but necessity); the knowledge of good and evil (for the natural world knows nothing but advantage and disadvantage), art, love; joyful perception of beauty in the uncreated world around us; ardour for truth; redeeming pain... When we see, or feel, these gifts in action, surely they seem like mysterious colonists from some more splendid realm of being than our own?

So the supreme function of men and women is to receive God's gifts, the light of heaven, as fully as they can. Some people are congenitally better attuned to the will of God, more permeable to heaven's light; but all of us can work continually to make ourselves more receptive – by encouraging whatever we can find in ourselves of faith and hope; by prayer and meditation; by reading; by self-attrition; by alert attention to even the most familiar and everyday experiences. But above all, by practising the art of love. 'I am come that ye might have life and that ye might have it more abundantly.'[37]

We have seen two instances of explorations of reality which press beyond moral criteria, opening up an area which one can find touched on in a wide variety of artists and visionaries.[38] But there is yet one further step that must be taken in our discussion of criteria, which leads us beyond the criteria themselves, and that can be indicated by more words from the Gospel of John: 'If you know these things, blessed are you if you do them.'[39] Theory is not enough. As I remarked at the beginning, the whole of the discussion in which we have been engaged really strikes home only in those whose religious attitudes also involve a degree of commitment.

Where talk of criteria, the images of exploration and the journey are not enough is in their inadequate indication of the imperative need for action as well. To go back to Schillebeeckx's 'experiences of contrast': confronted with such experiences which point to transcendence the proper response is not to say, 'Ah yes, there is a pointer beyond the situation, towards God'; it is to do something about the experience. No one can deny the moving character of Philip Toynbee's exploration, and what he says about the world in which we live is very important, but as well as the sceptics and the traditional believers he also has to argue against those who see the need for action against the injustices of the world as so pressing that it must take priority over everything else.

The right response to some problems is not intellectual, but practical; not a reasoned response, but action. The most difficult problem in all theology, indeed in all of human existence, is the problem of evil. Countless attempts have been made to explain it, and to justify the possibility of belief in a good God against the background of such an evil world. But the existence of evil cannot be explained; it is ultimately a mystery, and the proper response to its existence is to combat it, with authentic, creative symbol and with action.[40] Similarly, at the opposite extreme the proper response to the question whether God exists is ultimately not a verbal demonstration of that possibility (such a demonstration can never do more than indicate possibility), but hope, trust and worship. For example, the proper response to seeing the tension between the condition of the poor and the vision of what would be justice for them as a cry to God is to take their side and remove that injustice. In other words, the answer to many theological questions has to be worked out in practice – but in a much wider company. And that need not involve any theology at all (though obviously beliefs which shape individuals and groups will have at least an indirect influence on their actions).

So in this chapter we have seen the basis for an alternative approach, rooted in reality, taking account of the theoretical question and aware of the need for theory to be expressed in action. Inevitably, in the context, only the skeleton of this approach has emerged, and at this stage it is only a beginning. But it does offer grounds for hope. And there will be more to be said in that connection in the final chapter.

13 | Living with Questions

It began to emerge during the previous chapter that there would be much to be said for giving less prominence to the symbols of Jesus and the Christ, and focussing more on the two poles of humankind and God. (To anticipate a common objection: we shall see in this last chapter that the result need not necessary be an individualistic form of belief which has abandoned all the rich dimensions of the Christian tradition.[1]) We can now see how natural it was during the development of Christianity for the symbol of Christ to attract so much to it by its snowball effect; during a period of the intellectual and social decline of Christianity[2] some reversal of that process, however difficult it may prove, seems to be a necessary step. Of course the symbol of Jesus, or the Christ, is with us to stay in one form or another, but it can no longer be used authentically in the innocent and almost naive way that it has been used in the past, because that was possible only on the assumption that a whole interrelated structure of belief still held together. And that is demonstrably no longer the case, as it has been one of the purposes of this book to show.

The observation that too much prominence is given to the person of Jesus is again not new. It has been echoed by theologians from very different traditions in the last half-century or so. In America in the 1950s, Professor H. Richard Niebuhr was saying:

> The significance of Jesus Christ for the Christian church is so great that high expressions about his centrality to faith are the rule rather than the exception in the language of preaching and of worship. Yet it is one thing for Christians to look forward to the day when 'every tongue [will] confess that Jesus Christ is Lord, to the glory of God the Father' – to use the words of an ancient liturgical hymn – and another thing for theology as well as popular

piety to substitute the Lordship of Christ for the Lordship of God. At various times in history and in many areas of piety and theology Christianity has been transformed not only into a Christ-cult or a Jesus-cult but into a Christ- or Jesus-faith. The person through whom Christians have received access to God, the one who so reconciled them to the source of being that they are bold to say 'Our father who art in heaven', the one who in unique obedience, trust and loyalty lived, died, and rose again as Son of God, is now invested with such absolute significance that his relation to the One beyond himself is so slurred over that he becomes the centre of value and the object of loyalty. The confidence that is expected of Christians is confidence in him; the formulation of the confidence in creed and theology becomes a set of assertions about Jesus Christ; theology is turned into christology. And with this turn there is also a frequent turn to ecclesiasticism in so far as the community that centres in Jesus Christ is set forth both as the object of his loyalty and of the Christian's loyalty. To be a Christian now means not so much that through the mediation and the pioneering faith of Jesus Christ a man has become wholly human, has been called into membership in the society of universal being, and has accepted the fact that amidst the totality of existence he is not exempt from the human lot; it means rather that he has become a member of a special group, with a special god, a special deity and a separate existence.[3]

Twenty years later a conservative Roman Catholic figure, Abbé Jean Milet of Paris, was making just the same point for his tradition:

Since the beginning of this century Roman Catholicism has tended increasingly to favour belief in Christ over belief in God. For many people now, to be a Christian is first and foremost to 'believe in Christ', to 'live in conformity to Christ', and to spread Christianity is to 'proclaim Jesus Christ'. Belief in God is virtually hidden; there are those who go so far as to think and say that it is belief in Jesus Christ which will lead to belief in God, the latter coming as a kind of bonus. Others, finally, push things so far – within Catholicism, which they still claim to profess, presenting themselves as its interpreters – that they have come to talk of a 'Christianity without God'. There is no longer need to put one's trust in a God; belief in the historical Christ should be enough and should suffice for all needs: to satisfy the spirit, to gratify man's desires and to ensure his spiritual and moral salvation.[4]

And one might add the ironical comment which at one time went the rounds, that the World Council of Churches had become unitarian – of the Son.[5]

I shall be leaving on one side here specific theological developments like Barth's implacable insistence on the centrality of Christ and the influence of the theological stance of the World Council of Churches, which we looked at in Chapter 11.[6] What needs to be noted at this point is that the language and imagery of public worship and what might be called confessional language in connection with prayer and spirituality are key factors in this over-stressing of the person of Jesus. Intellectually, the arguments I have put forward might seem compelling, but those who go to church regularly or become involved in current spirituality are likely to be subjected to constant conditioning in the opposite direction by the language and imagery used there, which can only be changed by deliberate action, and as we saw right at the beginning of the book, one feature of our age is the virtually complete divorce between liturgy and spirituality on the one hand and critical thinking on the other.

In a whole series of areas within Christian worship, discussion and statement it would be a helpful step to subject the occurrence of the names Jesus or Christ to close and careful scrutiny and to see what is being said by them. It would almost certainly prove healthier in many cases if they were replaced by 'God'. After all, one of the strengths of the Christian tradition as of the Jewish tradition before it has been its vision that takes in the whole universe and sees God and his spirit as being active outside the community of believers.[7]

The problem which would seem to necessitate this sort of exploration has been put by Professor Lampe in the context of those experiences of 'Jesus' which play such a prominent role in the evangelical tradition:

We do not see him, recognize him, speak to him, listen to his voice. It is true that many people do in fact claim to meet him. Indeed, they say that they are encountered by him, addressed by him, and listened to by him. But they use this language in a very special and peculiar sense. They do not actually meet a first-century person, except in so far as that historical figure can be said to come alive for the reader in the pages of the Gospels. It is, in fact, hard to imagine how a person known only from first-century records could actually be communicated with by us today, even if he were somehow present to our senses; either such a person would have somehow remained unchanged, in which case he could be recognized, but would belong to a world so remote from our own that he would turn out to be a stranger, or he would have changed with time and no longer be recognizable. Those who talk of meeting and speaking to Jesus would find it hard to explain the difference between that experience and encountering, or being encountered by, God.[8]

In view of the issues we looked at in the previous chapter, is there not an alternative approach which would better take into account the variety of approaches there are to the exploration of that realm which points towards the transcendent and the degree to which these approaches are relative to one another and interconnected, rather than being through sectarian and allegedly privileged communities?

To take one specific example, is not the whole matter of 'conversion' a much more complex, far wider-ranging experience than, say, evangelical accounts make it out to be?[9] In the light of all the questions that we have considered in this book, can we really put experience of 'Jesus', 'the Christ' in a totally separate compartment from all those 'unattended moments' the descriptions of which by a wide variety of figures down the ages seem to contain 'echoes of that twilight *terra incognita* beyond the limits of which words fail though meanings still exist'?[10]

Dag Hammarskjöld, the Secretary General of the United Nations, whose *Markings* has become a classic of twentieth-century spirituality, had an experience on Whit Sunday 1961 which he described like this:

I don't know Who – or what – put the question, I don't know when it was put. I don't even remember answering. But at some moment I did answer *Yes* to someone – or Something – and from that hour I was certain that existence is meaningful and that, therefore, my life, in self-surrender, had a goal.[11]

He, too, read deep in the Gospels, but his whole approach, that

of twentieth-century cultured man *par excellence*, was very different
from that of an 'evangelical'. Therefore the effect of his experience
was different, too, but cannot be said to be any less authentic. In
his account of 'unattended moments' Michael Paffard commented:
'Whether a writer describes the unattended moment as religious or
aesthetic he would often say also that it made him feel good, living,
benevolent, altruistic. There really does seem to be a mysterious
affinity binding together the trinity of religious truth, aesthetic
beauty and moral goodness.'[12] And that also happens to people who
do not have the literary skill to describe such moments. But if one
insists that these experiences must be demonstrably experiences of
Jesus and can be worked out in only one way, the insoluble questions
come flooding back. How do you tell whether it is *Jesus* whom
you are experiencing? Why not God? How can you convey your
experience to anyone else – and how can you pass judgment on
anyone else's experience? What criteria do you use? Can you
really say that the particular experience is completely different and
superior?[13]

I am in no way doubting that those who talk like this have had
some overwhelming experience which has changed their lives. That
should be made quite plain. But the interpretation of that experience
is certainly open to examination and discussion. After a century of
the insights of the psychoanalysts, those who use such an experience
and make it a yardstick for everything and the great absolute in their
lives ought to be rather more sophisticated in the way in which
they interpret it, and be aware of the real dangers that some
interpretations can carry in their wake, not to mention the inadequate ethical and pastoral attitudes to which narrow-minded stress
on such an experience may lead.[14]

As things stand, the natural tendency for a very high proportion
of Christians who have an experience of 'Jesus' of the kind which
we have just been considering to gravitate towards a community of
those who value and share their experience is consolidated by the
social consequences and conditioning to which it leads. By becoming
members of that community (which is always a basically closed one)
they are led to share the terminology and experience of their group.
Indeed the existence and background of evangelical groups will
obviously colour such experience. And once individuals join the

group their life as Christians will be controlled by the norms of that group (we noted all this in Chapter 2).

Is it not equally possible, however, to argue that the characteristics of a 'personal experience of Jesus' may also be had in other contexts, leading to similar but different consequences, and that such an experience and consequences may not be equally authentic as an experience of God?

This re-examination of Jesus-imagery is even more needed in the area of public worship, because it is there that symbols are allowed to exercise their power with far too little critical control of their use. There is a current tendency to highlight the worshipping community as being the heart of Christianity; for example the climax of Professor Stephen Sykes' book *The Identity of Christianity*, which I quoted earlier, is the statement that: 'The identity of Christianity consists in the interaction between its external forms and an inward element, constantly maintained by participation in communal worship.'[15] But first, this fails to take account of the sheer frustration and barrenness experienced by congregations at so much of Christian worship, including eucharistic worship, which is confirmed by a steady exodus from the pews of traditional churches and the growth of charismatic groups and 'house churches'. Liturgical revision has done little to halt this,[16] so that there is in fact something like a 'myth of Christian worship'. Moreover, secondly, Professor Sykes' approach fails to allow sufficiently for the distortions that Christian worship produces. We have already considered that issue earlier in connection with doctrine, in Chapter 5.

There we saw the way in which over-enthusiastic communal worship could prove so dominant as to distort doctrinal insights, and in the twentieth century the same factors are still at work, this time lulling the critical faculty or preventing it from being developed by the constant presentation of material from distant periods in the past, in different conceptuality and unable now to command the authority that it once had, as though it could speak – against all the rules – directly to the present day. The complaints of members of the churches about the mental gymnastics they have to go through in order to be able to join in, say, the creeds, or some of the hymns and psalms, are legion and represent a deep cause for concern – but they seem constantly to be ignored.

While public worship is a battleground fought over and largely controlled by outdated factions – as it tends to be in the Church of England, at any rate – hopes for an actual change in the situation cannot be considered great. Popular custom from an earlier age is still very powerful. For example the service of Nine Lessons and Carols and the Seven Last Words from the Cross still exercise a substantial attraction, though the former is based on the argument from prophecy which we have seen to be both outmoded and dangerous, and the latter on a totally uncritical view of the Gospels. And the more popular hymns used regularly outside the liturgy exercise the same conditioning effect.

It would have been healthy if a body of criticism like that surrounding, say, music, opera, theatre and art (or even a habit of regular criticism to identify its strengths and weaknesses) had grown up around public worship to exercise some control and guidance over it. After all, the relationship between liturgy and various art forms is very close indeed, from the sublime examples of liturgy to the ridiculous ('I don't get nothing from church. Have you ever been to a badly acted play' is a comment from a survey of recent attitudes of religion in the inner city).[17] Whether in cathedrals or in inner-city churches, there is room for the asking, in a new perspective, of a series of different questions about worship which goes far deeper and allow the changes in belief and attitudes which exist outside church services to make more of an impact. This could usefully be accompanied by more concern that liturgy should, at whatever level, meet up with the expectations over its presentation which are raised by the standards of the present-day media.

Such a radical revision of worship – indeed of Christianity generally – would not need to lead to wholesale iconoclasm, though this is what those who are opposed to it imagine. Here again parallels from the way in which past works of art – painting, music or theatre, for example – can speak to the present, or to a wider audience, have much to teach us; perhaps the crisis which the revision of liturgy has posed to many Christians would not have arisen had greater attention been paid to them. There are ways of living with the expressions of Christianity, particularly with the best historical forms of its worship and traditions, even when these seem to come from a different world from ours, with a very different conceptuality and approach to God, without engaging in quite so many mental gymnastics.

One example which I have found particularly helpful as a model that can be applied in a variety of contexts is given by Professor Stewart Sutherland. He relates how, in 1617, during the building of St Peter's, Rome, some relics were found which were believed to be fragments of the True Cross. In honour of the discovery Monteverdi wrote and arranged the performance of a particularly beautiful five-part motet. It is doubtful in the extreme whether the relics were genuine, so the occasion for the composition of the motet was an illusion. But the motet itself has been preserved and is still performed regularly; it is beautiful and speaks to us in its own right as music, regardless of the reason for which it was composed.[18] Is not much in the Christian tradition now like that to many people? We may not be able to accept the motive behind its origin; we may have all kinds of reservations; it would be impossible for us to put things as they were once put in the past; nevertheless the tradition provides many vehicles – from cathedrals to the writings of the Fathers – through which *something* comes to us. But in an age of so much doubt and uncertainty, coupled with so many manipulative pressures, that something is inevitably Philip Toynbee's 'ghostly language: a language of hint and suggestion, of echo and paradox'.[19] And there are parts of the tradition which need to be ruthlessly discarded or repudiated. Discarding elements in the tradition has often happened almost imperceptibly in the past, along with the tacit adoption by a generation of insights for which a minority in a previous generation had to engage in virtually a life or death struggle, but the almost underhand way in which this has sometimes been done is not good enough for us now. For it goes to suggest the permanence and the immutability of a tradition which, as we saw in Chapter 4, has always been varied and regularly in a process of major change.

Against this background it is very hard to see a role for authoritarianism in matters of belief. Communities may need to have rules for membership and sanctions against those who infringe them in order to keep the nature of the community, and practical rules for living may need to be laid down in some of them. Discussion of that whole area would take us far beyond the scope of this book. But the religious quest which is currently going on outside as well as inside the organized churches is not something for which rules can be prescribed in advance if it is to continue to be what it always has been, an exploration in faith. Churches must be 'open' churches.

And above all they – and Christians – must be open to the future. We saw in Chapter 11 how Christianity moved at an early stage from a forward-looking perspective to one which looked back to Christ at the centre. Jesus and his first followers may have been mistaken about the coming of the kingdom, but the way in which they directed their gaze firmly towards the future was surely the indication of a fundamentally correct insight into the nature of the relationship between humankind and God. Faith must always be an ongoing quest into new territory, supported by the expectation that there is always more to learn and discover.

In this book we have already had one analogy from scientific understanding of the universe, the Copernican revolution. Perhaps it would not be inappropriate at this stage to introduce another. Professor Cantwell Smith has pointed out that thinkers in the West, especially Protestants, have tended to interpret the history of religion in terms of a 'big-bang' theory of origins.[20] In other words, a religion begins with one great seismic event, as it were: a cosmic happening within history, in the reverberations and resonance of whose explosive power the faithful subsequently live. But because there is a fear that the explosion might not be powerful enough to leap across the increasing gap of time that separates us from it theologians must make sure that the battery is fully charged and that the spark-plugs are clean. Hence the constant concern to get back to origins.

But what religions are about is the quest for God, relationship with that ultimate reality for whom neither 'He', 'She', nor 'It' are sufficient words, for whom indeed there are no words. So what we have is not so much a 'big bang' as a 'steady state', with the focal points primarily in the present and the future – though always related to the past, since we never start with a clean slate but have in our understanding all the confused and inadequate presuppositions with which we have been brought up, presuppositions which have constantly to be refined.

Even if we were not persuaded of the need for a future-orientated approach and a recognition of the way in which faith is an ongoing response and commitment to God, or whatever other name we might use for reality, the problems of the world's future that confront us should force it home on us. The themes of the energy crisis, the tension between North and South, and between rich and poor in individual countries, the spread of Islamic fundamentalism and Christian Evangelical and Catholic conservatism, the nuclear threat, world famine and all those other issues the existence of which we are seldom allowed to forget, are also part of a theological agenda, simply because they are part of that world in which the churches exist. They are especially related to the communal religious quest, and in present circumstances any personal religious quest that does not take them into account becomes a personal luxury.[21]

It is impossible to expand on this further here, and fortunately that is not necessary, because the issues which arise have been explored attractively and in detail in one of the best books of modern theology, Dietrich Ritschl's *The Logic of Theology*. From it I quote just his description of the theologian of the future (and he does not just mean professional theologian):

> The model for the theologian of the future is the wise man (and for man, of course, also read woman throughout). The wise man... does not force himself on others and does not want to overwhelm them with what he thinks he knows. He is concerned with clarification and understanding. He wants to acts as a catalyst rather than convince, because he has more confidence in the Spirit of God than in the human capacity for knowledge. But he differs from the hermit by the passion of his involvement in the social life of his time. Here he also incurs guilt and appears to many people to be unwise.[22]

A future-orientated approach will also be inspired by a vision of how things could be, and if it is not to be wishful thinking or day-dreaming, it will call for changes in those cumbersome and restrictive structures which often seem necessary only for shoring up an increasingly dilapidated past. Here the insights of liberation theology and its stress on the priority of what it calls *praxis*, seeing theology as secondary reflection on what is already being put into practice by the community in everyday life, are particularly important. But as I have argued, liberation theology is in danger of being an ideology, a group of ideologies, and still has many questions that it will have to ask one day about the ultimate truth of its claims and its tendency to dogmatism and attempted manipulation.

One cannot easily fight battles with 'it depends what you mean' and 'it seems open to question whether', so there may well be times and places, as during the German Church Struggle, when assertion leading to action, or stemming from action, even at the risk of seeming ideological in the bad sense, may be the only possible course. But they are probably rarer than is commonly thought. If one further message emerges from the survey which we have been undertaking, it is that to be authentic, every approach in faith and theology must by nature be approximate and tentative, always subject to revision. One cannot say too often that this uncertainty and tentativeness is all that we have been given by way of knowledge, though that need not prevent us from having a boundless trust that somehow in the end all will be well, however much it sometimes seems to be against all the odds.

And what remains of Jesus in all this? That a whole book can be devoted to questions about him, ranging over such a variety of areas of human history, culture and experience shows that in that which begins with him there is something quite special that still has a strange if elusive power. But the question 'what remains of Jesus?' is not one that I can answer here: it is one that I am still working out, as everyone must work out who has been brought under his uncanny spell. I have shared my particular quest as far as it has gone. The future remains to be seen.

For the moment, my last task is to finish this book, and writing the last pages has proved the most difficult part of the whole undertaking. They have gone through many drafts, and been read by a variety of readers, and reactions have been very varied. Some have regretted that I have attempted any kind of positive counterpart to the questions and would have preferred the book to end with them, leaving the reader, as John Kent's brilliant analyses of modern theology leave him or her, under a dark and leaden sky.[23] Others have asked for more answers and a more outspoken confession of faith. Neither alternative quite seems to work, yet I take the point of both of them. For like others, I suspect, when confronted with the dark and leaden sky I feel compelled to say, and believe, that this *cannot* be all there is to it; and when it comes to confessions of faith there is always 'but what about…?'

I can only try to be myself, and since I tend to think better in the company of others, that means my continuing with more of the comments I received in what can almost be called the concluding discussion of the book. So the next thing of which I have to take account is the piece of paper in front of me with the words 'Why bother?' written on them in very large letters. Why bother with all this questioning? Why bother with Jesus and the Christian tradition? Surely it is only worth bothering about if there is something in it – but what is that something? Does it not get analysed away in all the questions?

I do not think that it does. In *The Quest of the Historical Jesus*, Albert Schweitzer wrote: 'There is no historical task which so reveals a man's true self as the writing of a Life of Jesus. No vital force comes into the figure unless a man breathes into it all the hate or all the love of which he is capable.'[24] I believe that also to be true of the asking of questions about Jesus. In the things about Jesus we do seem to have a clue to how the world is, to how we are, to how God is, even if at times the clue seems cryptic beyond our understanding.

Why bother? Because although it may be the case that in the Western world most of the people most of the time do not seem concerned to ask ultimate questions, that does not mean that none of them ever do. I have found that the ultimate questions ('Who am I? What am I here for? What will happen to me?') are asked at one time or another (and not just in moments of crisis) by a surprising number of people, and it seems to be at those moments when we do find ourselves asking ultimate questions that we are most authentically ourselves. Or, to put it in a better way, it is when we find ourselves asking ultimate questions about *other* people ('What will happen to them?', and so on – a lot of theology is hopelessly selfish and egotistic) that we are most authentically ourselves. These questions may begin by being what could be called merely existential questions, but if their implications are taken further they do point, as Philip Toynbee indicated, to questions of transcendence, of religion, of God. And I would argue that the questions which are raised in connection with Jesus are among the most searching questions we can ask.

But is there nothing but questions? At each of the two large gatherings at which I gave the paper from which this book grew a member of the audience commented: 'That's all very well, but what about those of us who have to preach?' My answer was and is that asking questions is one activity and preaching is another, and that the relationship between them needs to be worked out in the doing. I preach, too, and have never been told that my sermons are negative and questioning, though they may have questions in them. Asking questions may at times, as here, also include something of a confession of faith. But to suppose that we may not ask penetrating questions because a gospel has to be preached is to set out on a course which can only lead to an intellectually barren and ideological church.

Then there is the matter of action. I have made some rather hard comments in passages in this book about liberation theology, and that is in fact something which has surprised me, since when I began writing I had a much more positive attitude to it. But again the comments of some of those who read earlier drafts of the book showed how many of the questions it raises are ones for which liberation theology does not have an answer either. There is no disputing the need for liberation of the oppressed, the poor, the marginalized; but whether the theological motivation offered by liberation theologians is adequate is another matter.

But there is more than questions and action. Those who identify themselves with the movement that began with Jesus, and indeed those of other faiths would also want to say, as I do, that what we do, our questions and our actions, are sometimes met with that which, the One who, comes to us from beyond ourselves, that to which, or the One to whom, traditional talk of the grace and love of God refers. That it is difficult to talk about this in our language, in our world, does not mean that it does not happen. We can experience it, and hear the accounts of experiences of it from those who are not confessedly Christians as well as those who are. That is something which changes the whole picture for those who are aware of this dimension. Even though for our worship we may have to look beyond the Christian liturgy with all the current malaise surrounding liturgical worship, it is in the liturgy that we find the most open talk of this nevertheless loving Other, not extinguished even by hatred and evil. A few years ago I collected what seems to me to be the greatest riches of the centuries-old Jewish-Christian liturgical tradition, words that have become a part of me, in a short anthology entitled *By Heart*.[25] What I have written here is, for me, the counterpart of that book. To ask questions about Jesus and what he led to in an attempt to see where we have come so far makes sense only if the questions put in a positive vision of the future, and a vision of the future is a luxury or a sedative unless it is accompanied by questioning leading to action. So I end with an old collect, which for me embodies that vision more than any other:

O God, who hast prepared for them that love thee such good things as pass man's understanding: Pour into our hearts such love toward thee, that we, loving thee above all things, may obtain thy promises, which exceed all that we can desire.[26]

Notes

Preface

1. See T.G.A.Baker, *Questioning Worship*, SCM Press 1977, 20-34. He criticizes familiar passages in services which ultimately came to be included in the Church of England's *Alternative Service Book 1980* like the Peace and the Offertory Prayer 'Yours, Lord' as being torn out of context in such a way as to distort their content, and deplores the addition of 'This is the word of the Lord' to the Epistle as suggesting a disastrous identification of the time-conditioned words of a particular author with the word of God. Since there is a close link between Anglican and Roman Catholic versions of the eucharist, the point is of wider application. See also below, 198, 201-3.

2. See Chapter 5 below, 74ff.

3. See especially Chapter 11 below, 179f.

4. See e.g. 94–101 below.

5. See further the beginning of Chapter 1 below, 2ff.

6. Judith Herrin, *The Formation of Christendom*, Blackwell and Princeton University Press 1987, 8.

7. Cf. Primo Levi, *If Not Now, When?*, Michael Joseph 1986.

1. By Way of Introduction

1. Dietrich Bonhoeffer, *Letters and Papers from Prison. The Enlarged Edition*, SCM Press and Macmillan, New York 1971, 279, letter of 30 April 1944.

2. See especially below, 37, 79f.

3. The two most commonly used English synopses are H.F.D.Sparks, *A Synopsis of the Gospels*, Vol.1, *The Synoptic Gospels with Johannine Parallels*, A.&.C.Black ²1970 (there is a second volume of St John with Synoptic parallels), and Burton H.Throckmorton, *Gospel Parallels*, Thomas Nelson, Nashville ⁴1979.

4. Quoted in H.J.Kraus, *Geschichte der historisch-kritischen Erforschung des Alten Testaments*, Neukirchen 1956, 236f.

5. Ernst Troeltsch, 'Über historische und dogmatische Methode in der Theologie', *Gesammelte Schriften* II, Tübingen 1913, 734.

6. For the origins of doctrinal criticism see Maurice Wiles, 'Looking into the Sun', in *Working Papers in Doctrine*, SCM Press 1976, 148-163,

especially 152ff., who refers in particular to Professor George Woods.

7. See Acts 11.26, 'In Antioch the disciples were for the first time called Christians'; for comments on this passage in Acts see Ernst Haenchen, *The Acts of the Apostles*, Blackwell 1971, 368f.; Gerd Lüdemann, *Das frühe Christentum nach den Traditionen der Apostelgeschichte*, Göttingen 1987, 144. The statement is an isolated one, not integrated into the context. See also E.Bickerman, 'The Name of Christians', *Harvard Theological Review* 42, 1949, 109-24. Judith Herrin, *The Formation of Christendom*, 55 n.1, points out that the first evidence of the use of *Christianos* in Egypt is not until AD 256.

8. For a survey of approaches to the interpretation of Jesus' teaching about the kingdom of God see Norman Perrin, *The Kingdom of God in the Teaching of Jesus*, SCM Press 1963. Bruce Chilton (ed.), *The Kingdom of God*, SPCK and Fortress Press 1984, provides a collection of representative articles by New Testament scholars on the theme; here, as on other issues of this kind, Christopher Rowland, *Christian Origins*, SPCK 1985, gives a lucid summary and further literature (133-6).

9. See Albert Schweitzer, *The Mysticism of Paul the Apostle*, A.& C.Black 1931; Ernest Best, *One Body in Christ*, SPCK 1955; John Ziesler, *Pauline Christianity*, Oxford University Press 1983, 47ff.

10. An important book entitled *The So-Called Historical Jesus and the Historic, Biblical Christ* was written by Martin Kähler in 1892; an English translation was published by Fortress Press in 1964. Kähler argued that the 'real' Christ was the one who was 'historic' by virtue of the impact he made, not 'historical' in the sense of having been discovered by historians.

11. See especially Jack T.Sanders, *The Jews in Luke-Acts*, SCM Press and Fortress Press 1987; E.P.Sanders, *Paul and Palestinian Judaism*, SCM Press and Fortress Press 1977; Lucas Grollenberg, *Unexpected Messiah*, SCM Press 1988.

12. See especially Richard L.Rubenstein and John K.Roth, *Approaches to Auschwitz*, SCM Press and John Knox Press 1987.

13. John Bowden, *Voices in the Wilderness*, SCM Press 1977, 80f.

14. Dietrich Ritschl, *The Logic of Theology*, SCM Press and Fortress Press 1986, 67.

15. Aaron Esterson, 'Judaism and Wholeness', in *Soul Searching. Studies in Judaism and Psychotherapy* ed. Howard Cooper, SCM Press 1988, 170.

16. Jonathan Magonet, 'The Question of Identity', in ibid., 190.

2. Christianity and Truth

1. John 18.38.

2. I Cor.13.12.

3. Adrian Hastings, *Christianity in Britain 1920-1985*, Collins 1986, 61.

4. For ideology see especially Karl Mannheim, *Ideology and Utopia. An Introduction to the Sociology of Knowledge*, Routledge and Kegan Paul

1936, especially 49-96; there is also a useful short article by Nicholas Lash in *A New Dictionary of Christian Theology* ed. John Bowden and Alan Richardson, SCM Press and Westminster Press 1983, 279f.

5. Mannheim, *Ideology and Utopia*, 54.

6. Lash, art. cit. 280.

7. For an extended account of the nature of historical consciousness see John Lukacs, *Historical Consciousness or The Remembered Past*, revised and enlarged edition, Schocken Books 1985.

8. Beryl Smalley, *The Study of the Bible in the Middle Ages*, Blackwell ³1984, xxx-xxxii.

9. Ibid., 26.

10. For the following discussion I am particularly indebted to Klaus Scholder, *Ursprünge und Probleme der Bibelkritik im 17.Jahrhundert*, Christian Kaiser Verlag 1966. I should warn those assiduously following the notes for information about further reading that many of the notes in this chapter document my sources, which in this area are more than usually sparse and inaccessible.

11. For the introduction of epicycles see John Hick, *The Second Christianity*, SCM Press 1983, 81f.

12. For the idea of 'paradigm shift' see the now classic book by Thomas S.Kuhn, *The Structure of Scientific Revolutions*, Chicago University Press ²1970, in which he argues that the development of scientific knowledge does not take place by the constant accumulation of information but by the adoption of a perspective (a 'paradigm') in the light of which phenomena are investigated and interpreted. Every now and then pressure has developed at a particular point in a perspective, indicating that it is becoming inadequate, and when that pressure becomes too great the old perspective is abandoned and another one adopted ('paradigm shift').

13. For Galileo see Stillman Drake, *Galileo*, Oxford University Press 1986, and the literature listed there on pp.94-6. See by comparison Bertolt Brecht, *Life of Galileo*, Methuen 1974.

14. Scholder, *Ursprünge*, 66.

15. The letter itself is published in *Opere di Gaileo Galilei*, Edizione Nazionale V, 1895, 307-48; there is an English translation in S.Drake, *Discoveries and Opinions of Galileo*, Doubleday, New York 1957. For its contents see Scholder, 72ff.

16. See Scholder, 98ff.

17. Martin Luther, *Supputatio annorum mundi* (1541), Weimar Edition 53, 22ff.

18. This was the view of Johann Heinrich Alsted in his *Thesaurus chronologiae*; cf. Scholder, 93.

19. See Scholder, 94ff.

20. Ibid., 99. Richard H.Popkin, *Isaac La Peyrere (1596-1676)*, Brill 1987, appeared too late for me to make use of it.

21. Scholder, 100.

22. Ibid.

23. Ibid., 103.

24. For a more detailed discussion of the rise of theology in the Middle Ages and the influences on it see G.R.Evans, *Old Arts and New Theology*, Oxford University Press 1980.

25. For a detailed account of this stage see Henning Graf Reventlow, *The Authority of the Bible and the Rise of the Modern World*, SCM Press and Fortress Press 1984.

26. James Barr, Preface to Reventlow, *Authority*, xiii.

27. Here again Judith Herrin, *The Formation of Christendom*, is very illuminating.

28. The classic account is Albert Schweitzer, *The Quest of the Historical Jesus*, A.& C.Black ³1954, reissued SCM Press 1981. Unfortunately the English translation does not represent the final text of Schweitzer's work, which is available only in German as *Die Geschichte der Leben Jesu Forschung*, Siebenstern Taschenbuch Verlag 1966 (two volumes); for details of the differences see D.E.Nineham, 'Schweitzer Revisited', in *Explorations in Theology* 1, SCM Press 1977, 112-33. The quest is usually supposed to begin with Reimarus, see below, 34f.

29. For Spinoza see S.Hampshire, *Spinoza*, Penguin Books 1951; Roger Scruton, *Spinoza*, Oxford University Press 1986: Spinoza's *Theologico-Political Treatise* has been reissued by Dover Books 1951.

30. For a rather conservative account of D.F.Strauss see Horton Harris, *David Friedrich Strauss and his Theology*, Cambridge University Press 1974, especially 58-65. Strauss's *The Life of Jesus Critically Examined* (1840), translated by George Eliot (reissued SCM Press and Fortress Press 1973), and still well worth reading, is one of the great nineteenth-century books about Jesus; it proved controversial for the way in which it applied the 'mythical' point of view to the Gospels.

31. F.D.Maurice was removed from his chair at King's College, London in 1853 for teaching a 'dangerous' doctrine on the punishment of the wicked. See e.g. Owen Chadwick, *The Victorian Church*, Part One. 1829-1859, A.& C.Black ³1971, reissued SCM Press 1987, 546-9.

32. For W.Robertson Smith see J.S.Black and G.Chrystal, *The Life of William Robertson Smith*, London 1912.

33. Alfred Loisy (1857-1940) was a French New Testament scholar dismissed from his professorship in 1893 and excommunicated in 1908, after which he became Professor of the History of Religions at the College de France. See e.g. A.R.Vidler, *A Variety of Catholic Modernists*, Cambridge University Press 1970, 20-56.

34. George Tyrrell (1861-1909) was a prominent Catholic 'Modernist' who was first retired from active work and was ultimately excommunicated for his departures from the orthodoxy of the time. It is to be hoped that Nicolas Sagovsky's moving account of his life will be published in due course. Meanwhile see the classic *Autobiography and Life* (two volumes, 1912) by Maud D.Petre.

35. For Hans Küng see Peter Hebblethwaite, *The New Inquisition?*, Fount Books 1980, 76-102.

36. For Schillebeeckx see Hebblethwaite, *The New Inquisition?*, 9-59; Ted Schoof (ed.), *The Schillebeeckx Case*, Paulist Press 1984.

37. Leonardo Boff was summoned to Rome by the Prefect of the Sacred Congregation for the Doctrine of the Faith in 1984 for statements made in his *Church: Charism and Power*, originally published in Portuguese in 1981 (English translation SCM Press and Crossroad Publishing Company 1985). He was subsequently banned from writing for a period of one year.

38. The case of Jacques Pohier is movingly described in his autobiographical *God in Fragments*, SCM Press and Crossroad Publishing Company 1986.

39. See John Hick, *Problems of Religious Pluralism*, Macmillan 1985, 1-4; recently John Hick has also been suspended by the Presbyterian church in California as a result of his involvement in *The Myth of Christian Uniqueness* (for which see 178–80 below).

3. What can we really know about Jesus?

1. I have described the background to this conclusion in the history of New Testament scholarship in my article 'Jesus', in *A New Dictionary of Christian Theology* ed. Alan Richardson and John Bowden, 306-12. There are so many books on the topics covered in this chapter that it has not been possible for me even to begin to refer to the range of literature. However, the books mentioned in the notes all point the way forward to further reading.

2. Cf. A.E.Harvey, *Jesus and the Constraints of History*, Duckworth 1982, 6.

3. John Baker, *The Foolishness of God*, Darton, Longman and Todd 1970, 138.

4. Ibid., 152.

5. This information consists essentially of short passages in Josephus, Tacitus, Pliny, Suetonius and the Talmud. These are conveniently collected and discussed in Howard Clark Kee, *Jesus in History. An Approach to the Study of the Gospels*, Harcourt, Brace Jovanovich ²1977, 42-53.

6. There is an English translation of Reimarus' 'Concerning the Intention of Jesus and his Teaching' together with an extended introduction in *Reimarus: Fragments* ed. Charles H.Talbert, Fortress Press and SCM Press 1971.

7. Albert Schweitzer, *The Quest of the Historical Jesus*, A.& C.Black ³1954, reissued SCM Press 1981, 397.

8. For the messianic secret see William Wrede, *The Messianic Secret*, James Clarke 1971, and the critical comments by Martin Hengel, *Studies in the Gospel of Mark*, SCM Press and Fortress Press 1985, 41ff.; cf. also Christopher Tuckett (ed.), *The Messianic Secret*, SCM Press and Fortress Press 1983. There is, of course, more to Wrede than this and the questions

that he was already raising at the end of the last century are still very important. Cf. Robert Morgan, *The Nature of New Testament Theology*, SCM Press 1973, 68-116.

9. Schweitzer, *Quest*, 4.

10. Surveys of such books can be found in John H.Hayes, *Son of God to Superstar: Twentieth-Century Interpretations of Jesus*, Abingdon Press 1976; Barnes Tatum, *In Quest of Jesus*, SCM Press and John Knox Press 1982; Malachi Martin, *Jesus Now*, Fount Paperbacks 1975.

11. For a history of research see W.G.Kümmel, *The New Testament: The History of the Interpretation of its Problems*, SCM Press and Abingdon Press 1973, especially 74-88, 325-341.

12. The classic account of the synoptic problem is that of B.H.Streeter, *The Four Gospels*, Macmillan 1924. For a shorter and more recent account cf. Keith Nickle, *The Synoptic Gospels. An Introduction*, SCM Press and John Knox Press 1981. These results have not gone undisputed; it has been argued, for instance, that the sayings source never existed and that the passages usually assigned to it have come into being as a result of Matthew copying Luke or vice versa (the classic study is Austin Farrer, 'On Dispensing with Q', in *Studies in the Gospels. Essays in Memory of R.H.Lightfoot* ed. D.E.Nineham, Blackwell 1955, 55-88). The priority of Mark has also been denied in favour of that of Matthew. For the priority of Matthew see e.g. B.C.Butler, *The Originality of St Matthew*, Cambridge University Press 1951; W.R.Farmer, *The Synoptic Problem. A Critical Analysis*, Macmillan, New York 1964. Michael Goulder, *Luke: A New Paradigm*, JSOT Press 1988, thinks that Luke worked from Matthew. As far as the point in question is concerned, all this simply goes to highlight the difficulties involved and to indicate that the agreed solution is far from solving them all.

13. The main exception to this is John A.T.Robinson, *The Priority of John*, SCM Press 1985 and Meyer-Stone 1987, but his view has not carried conviction. However, in this book, as in his *Redating the New Testament*, SCM Press 1976, he did succeed in demonstrating the fragility of many arguments used by New Testament scholars.

14. Almost all recent studies of the Fourth Gospel see it as emanating from a community in which the author was an honoured and loved leader: see e.g. Oscar Cullmann, *The Johannine Circle*, SCM Press 1976; R.E.Brown, *The Community of the Beloved Disciple. The Life, Loves and Hates of an Individual Church in New Testament Times*, Paulist Press and Geoffrey Chapman 1979. Another perspective on the 'school' has been offered by Martin Hengel in his Stone Lectures, delivered at Princeton in 1987, to be published by SCM Press and Fortress Press in 1989.

15. This was especially as a result of Schleiermacher's 'one-sided preference' for the Fourth Gospel; see Schweitzer, *Quest*, 62-7, especially 66.

16. Perhaps the easiest way to see how Matthew and Luke work from Mark and at the same time alter his text is to look closely at the scene of Jesus' baptism: Mark 1.9-11/Matt.3.13-17/Luke 3.21-22.

17. See, for example, the numerous differences in the words of Jesus often

referred to as 'the conditions for discipleship': Mark 8.34-91/Matt.16.24-28/ Luke 9.23-27.

18. Studying the way in which these portraits are built up is known as redaction criticism: see especially Raymond F.Collins, *Introduction to the New Testament*, SCM Press and Doubleday 1983, 196-230; also Joachim Rohde, *Rediscovering the Teaching of the Evangelists*, SCM Press 1969; Norman Perrin, *What is Redaction Criticism?*, Fortress Press and SPCK 1969.

19. Mark 16.9-20 are now recognized to be a later addition and are printed in different type or relegated to a footnote in many Bibles. At one time it was argued that the Gospel originally had a different ending which is now lost, but this view no longer commands much consent. See C.F.Evans, *Resurrection and the New Testament*, SCM Press 1970, 67ff.

20. Evans, *Resurrection*, 67-127; Norman Perrin, *The Resurrection Narratives. A New Approach*, SCM Press 1977.

21. C.F.Evans, *Resurrection and the New Testament*, 128.

22. Raymond E.Brown, *The Birth of the Messiah*, Geoffrey Chapman and Doubleday 1977, 497.

23. This source is usually referred to as Q, the initial of the German for source, *Quelle*. The first passage in the Gospels usually attributed to Q is the preaching of John the Baptist in Matt.3.7-10; Luke 3.7-9; others can easily be seen from a synopsis.

24. Matt. 5-7; Luke 6.17-49. The setting and content is different in each Gospel and Luke's version, much shorter, is usually known as the Sermon on the Plain; for discussions of the material see W.D.Davies, *The Sermon on the Mount*, Cambridge University Press 1966. Professor Davies begins by pointing out that 'the view propounded by scholars in our day about the contents and structure of Matt.v-vii seems to compel the conclusion that the whole section is merely a collection of unrelated sayings of diverse origins, a patchwork, which cannot possible retain the pre-eminence once accorded to it as the authoritative source for the teaching of Jesus' (p.1). His book certainly indicates some of the problems in coping with this view.

25. See also Norman Perrin, *Rediscovering the Teaching of Jesus*, SCM Press 1967.

26. The best general introduction to all these issues for those unfamiliar with them is Linda Foster, *Four for the Gospel Makers*, SCM Press 1986. For some important reflections on the theological factors involved in shaping the Gospel tradition and its relation to the apocryphal Gospels see Helmut Koester, 'One Jesus and Four Primitive Gospels', in James M.Robinson and Helmut Koester, *Trajectories through Early Christianity*, Fortress Press 1971, 158-204, especially 204: 'The Gospels of the church cannot claim and should not be understood to reflect the preaching and the works of the earthly Jesus in a straight line of tradition. They are primarily Gospels *about* Jesus.'

27. Though this is disputed. For Mark see especially D.E.Nineham, *Saint Mark*, Pelican Gospel Commentaries, Penguin Books 1969; Norman Perrin,

The New Testament. An Introduction, Harcourt, Brace, Jovanovich ²1982 (with Denis B.Duling), 233-61; Martin Hengel, *Studies in the Gospel of Mark*, SCM Press 1985. In view of the current interest in the literary character of the biblical books (e.g. *A Literary Companion to the Bible* ed. Robert Alter and Frank Kermode, Harvard University Press and Collins 1987), I should perhaps point out that that approach is concerned with rather different issues from those discussed in the present chapter and elsewhere in this book.

28. One important question asked by scholars in connection with Mark is whether or not he had an outline of the ministry of Jesus into which he could fit the individual units of which his Gospel is made up. In the 1930s C.H.Dodd did argue that Mark had such an outline, but his approach was devastatingly criticized by D.E.Nineham in 'The Order of Events in St Mark's Gospel – An Examination of Dr Dodd's Hypothesis' (originally in *Studies in the Gospels. Essays in Memory of R.H.Lightfoot* ed. D.E.Nineham, Blackwell 1955, 223-40); in connection with the Gospel tradition Professor Nineham's studies on 'Eye-witness Testimony and the Gospel Tradition' are particularly important. For both see *Explorations in Theology* 1, SCM Press 1977, 7-23 and 24-60 respectively.

29. Joachim Jeremias, *New Testament Theology*, Vol. 1, *The Proclamation of Jesus*, SCM Press and Scribner 1971, 38, comments: 'It can be shown, as I believe, that the whole of the Gospel of Mark consists of complexes of tradition... In these circumstances the search for a systematic structure of the gospel is a lost labour of love.' Scholars have produced elaborate explanations of the construction of the Gospel, but here as elsewhere the variety of their solutions gives one much food for thought.

30. For example, John puts the cleansing of the temple at the beginning of Jesus' ministry, whereas the Synoptics put it at the end; they could not in fact put it earlier because according to them Jesus only goes up to Jerusalem shortly before the crucifixion; according to John he goes up several times.

31. Study of the way in which these stories were formed is called form criticism. The pioneering scholar here was K.L.Schmidt, *Der Rahmen der Geschichte Jesu*, Berlin 1919, reissued Wissenschaftliche Buchgesellschaft, Darmstadt 1964, e.g. 317: 'There is no life of Jesus in the sense of an evolving biography, no chronological sketch of the story of Jesus, but only single stories, *pericopae*, which are put into a framework.' The two classic books on this are Martin Dibelius, *From Tradition to Gospel*, reissued James Clarke 1971, and Rudolf Bultmann, *History of the Synoptic Tradition*, Blackwell and Harper and Row 1963.

32. See more recently Edgar V.McKnight, *What is Form Criticism*, Fortress Press 1969; Raymond F.Collins, *Introduction to the New Testament*, Doubleday and SCM Press 1983, 156-95. There is now much more doubt about the nature of the process of tradition but the phenomena which led to this approach still call for explanation and no better explanation has been produced.

33. For an introduction to the question why Matthew and Luke wrote their Gospels see Nickle, *The Synoptic Gospels*, 94-151. For Matthew, cf. e.g. Perrin, *Introduction*, 263-9; Günther Bornkamm, Gerhard Barth, Heinz Joachim Held, *Tradition and Interpretation in Matthew*, SCM Press ²1971; for Luke the classic study is Hans Conzelmann, *The Theology of St Luke*, Faber 1960, reissued SCM Press 1982. For further literature see the bibliographies on Acts in the books mentioned in n.37 below.

34. See e.g. John Reumann, *Jesus in the Church's Gospels*, Fortress Press 1978 and SPCK 1980.

35. There is a good example of how this might have happened in Gerd Theissen, *The Shadow of the Galilean*, SCM Press and Fortress Press 1987, 99. 'I asked myself whether Hannah had heard all the stories about Jesus which she had told to Miriam. Had she perhaps invented some of them to comfort little Miriam? I believe that if she had run out of stories, I myself would have added some and invented some.' For those wanting a readable picture of the Synoptic Jesus in narrative form which takes account of all the limitations of our knowledge, this book could hardly be bettered.

36. For I Corinthians 15 see, for example, C.F.Evans, *Resurrection and the New Testament*, 41-55.

37. The best commentary on the Acts of the Apostles is still Ernst Haenchen, *The Acts of the Apostles*, Blackwell and Westminster Press 1971; cf. also Hans Conzelmann, *Acts*, Hermeneia, Fortress Press 1987; Gerd Lüdemann, *Das frühe Christentum nach den Traditionen der Apostelgeschichte*, Vandenhoeck and Ruprecht 1987.

38. For details of these clashes see John Knox, *Chapters in a Life of Paul*, A.& C.Black and Abingdon Press 1950; Paul Jewett, *Dating Paul's Life*, SCM Press and Fortress Press 1979; G.Lüdemann, *Paul, Apostle to the Gentiles*, SCM Press and Fortress Press 1984.

39. For Paul see e.g. Günther Bornkamm, *Paul*, Hodder and Stoughton 1971; Lucas Grollenberg, *Paul*, SCM Press and Westminster Press 1978; John Ziesler, *Pauline Christianity*, Oxford University Press 1983; Calvin J.Roetzel, *The Letters of Paul*, John Knox Press ²1982, SCM Press 1983; Wayne Meeks, *The First Urban Christians*, Yale University Press 1983. E.P.Sanders, *Paul and Palestinian Judaism*, SCM Press and Fortress Press 1977, is essential reading for understanding Paul's background, so often misrepresented by Christian scholars in the past. We shall be looking at some of the issues raised by Paul's attitudes in Chapter 8, 123, 126f. below.

40. The problem was fully explored by F.Gerald Downing in *The Church and Jesus*, SCM Press 1967.

41. Norman Perrin, *Rediscovering the Teaching of Jesus*, SCM Press 1967.

42. Perrin, op.cit., 39-43.

43. E.P.Sanders, *Jesus and Judaism*, SCM Press and Fortress Press 1985, 13.

44. Sanders, op.cit., 11.

45. F.Gerald Downing, *Jesus and the Threat of Freedom*, SCM Press 1987, 151f.

46. Downing, op.cit., 152.

47. John Knox, *The Death of Jesus*, Abingdon Press and Collins 1958.

48. Ibid., 37-9.

49. C.H.Dodd, *The Founder of Christianity*, Fontana Books 1973, was hailed as one such book.

50. E.g. Günther Bornkamm, *Jesus of Nazareth*, Hodder and Stoughton and Harper and Row 1960, which George Newlands describes as 'the most scholarly and reliable life of Jesus in our time' (*The Church of God*, Marshall, Morgan and Scott 1984, 19).

51. See my comments below, 116f.

52. It is always necessary to take into account the bias of the evangelists and the geographical and chronological distance separating them from the events they describe, along with the symbolism of the Gospel tradition. Cf. below 138ff., 162ff. and for the subtlety of the symbolism see already R.H.Lightfoot, *History and Interpretation in the Gospels*, Hodder and Stoughton 1935; id., *Locality and Doctrine in the Gospels*, Hodder and Stoughton 1938.

53. Joachim Jeremias, *The Parables of Jesus*, SCM Press 1963, is one of many New Testament scholars who stress how much the parables of Jesus tell us about life in first-century Palestine, even though in so many cases they were adapted at a later stage by the church so that their original intention is not always clear.

54. For a more detailed discussion of the development of early Christianity cf. e.g. W.H.C.Frend, *The Rise of Christianity*, Darton, Longman and Todd 1984, 86-160; Walter Bauer, *Orthodoxy and Heresy in Earliest Christianity*, Fortress Press 1971 and SCM Press 1972; Helmut Koester, *Introduction to the New Testament*, De Gruyter and Fortress Press 1982, Vol.2; James D.G.Dunn, *Unity and Diversity in the New Testament*, SCM Press 1977.

55. See F.Gerald Downing, *Jesus and the Threat of Freedom*, especially 126-60.

56. See e.g.Romans 15.19ff.

57. For the first stage see Gerd Theissen, *The First Followers of Jesus*, SCM Press 1978 (US title: *Sociology of Early Palestinian Christianity*, Fortress Press 1978); for the second see Wayne E.Meeks, *The First Urban Christians*; John Stambaugh and David Balch, *The Social World of the First Christians*, SPCK and Fortress Press 1986, 138-67.

58. The text of the Didache can be found in *Early Christian Writings*, Penguin Books 1968, 225-37.

59. This attitude is documented, e.g. in W.G.Kümmel, *The New Testament. The History of the Interpretation of its Problems*, Abingdon Press 1972 and SCM Press 1973.

60. The title of the book by Wayne Meeks (see n.39 above).

61. Meeks, *The First Urban Christians*, 190-2.

62. See Gerd Theissen, *Social Reality and New Testament Research*, SCM Press and Fortress Press 1988.

63. For events leading up to the fall of Jerusalem see Josephus, *The Jewish War*; there is a translation conveniently available in Penguin Classics, Penguin Books ³1981. Reading Josephus, who also wrote a history of the Jews entitled *Jewish Antiquities*, is the best way of sensing the atmosphere of Jesus' time.

64. See below, pp. 75ff. For Judaism in the first century AD see E.Schürer, *The Jewish People in the Time of Jesus Christ*, revised edition by G.Vermes and F.Millar, four volumes, T.& T.Clark 1973ff.; S.Safrai and M.Stern, *The Jewish People in the First Christian Century*, Assen 1974-76; Geza Vermes, *Jesus and the World of Judaism*, SCM Press and Fortress Press 1983, and E.P.Sanders, *Paul and Palestinian Judaism* (n.39 above).

65. Some of the letters of Paul seem to have been put together from fragments; e.g. II Corinthians 7-8 is often regarded as a separate letter, and Romans 16 seems out of place in its present position. From this it is argued that they were collected together at a later stage and that letters were added to the collection which bore the name of Paul but were not by him. There is some doubt as to whether Colossians and Ephesians (which have close similarities) were actually written by Paul; the arguments against I and II Timothy and Titus (usually called the Pastoral Epistles), on grounds of both style and content are very much stronger. See especially Calvin J.Roetzel, *The Letters of Paul* (above n.39). John C.Hurd Jr, *The Origins of I Corinthians*, SPCK 1965, gives a good idea of how this fragmentation can be traced; for the authorship of the Pastoral Epistles see W.G.Kümmel, *Introduction to the New Testament*, SCM Press and Abingdon Press ²1975, 366-86.

66. See e.g. I Tim.3; II Tim.2.22-26; Titus 2.1-10.

67. For a discussion of the varieties of Christianity in the earliest period see Chapter 4 below.

68. For what follows see Elizabeth Schüssler Fiorenza, *In Memory of Her*, Crossroad Publishing Company and SCM Press 1983, and above all Susanne Heine, *Women and Early Christianity*, SCM Press 1987 and Augsburg Publishing House 1988, 83-105.

69. These include Martha and Mary of Bethany, Mary Magdalene, Salome, Joanna wife of Chuza and Suzanna, as well as many whose names are not recorded, chief among them the unknown woman of Mark 14.3-9. See Elisabeth Moltmann-Wendel, *The Women around Jesus*, SCM Press and Crossroad Publishing House 1982.

70. Mark 16.1-8.

71. See Matt.21.31f.

72. John 7.53-8.11. This passage is usually relegated to a footnote, since on stylistic grounds alone it is quite different from the rest of the Gospel; moreover in some manuscripts of the New Testament it also appears at the end of the Gospel or after Luke 21.38.

73. See Rom. 16.1-16; Col.4.15; Phil.4.2f.; Acts 16.4.

74. I Tim.2.11-15; cf.also I Cor.14.33b-36. If one reads the text from I Cor.14.33a to v.37 passing over this passage, there is no feeling of any gap, and vv.33b-36 are in complete contradiction to what Paul says elsewhere, being more reminiscent of the Pastoral Epistles; consequently it has been argued that this is a later interpolation (see Susanne Heine, *Women and Early Christianity*, 135f.). This view has, however, been challenged.

4. The Kaleidoscopic Christ

1. Hebrews 13.8.
2. Ninian Smart, *The Phenomenon of Christianity*, Collins 1979, 13-31.
3. See Judith Herrin, *The Formation of Christendom*, Blackwell and Princeton University Press 1987.
4. See Marina Warner, *Alone of of All Her Sex. The Myth and Cult of the Virgin Mary*, Weidenfeld and Nicolson 1976; Michael Carroll, *The Cult of the Virgin Mary. Psychological Origins*, Princeton University Press 1986.
5. Smart, *Phenomenon*, 31-49.
6. Ibid., 49-64.
7. Ibid., 65-85.
8. Ibid., 86-105.
9. For African Christianity see Adrian Hastings, *A History of African Christianity 1950-1975*, Cambridge University Press 1979.
10. For Christianity in South-East Asia see John C. England, *Living Theology in Asia*, SCM Press and Orbis Books 1981.
11. For Christianity in Latin America see e.g. Trevor Beeson and Jenny Pearce, *A Vision of Hope*, Fount Paperbacks 1984; Philip Berryman, *The Religious Roots of Rebellion*, Orbis Books and SCM Press 1984; Rubem Alves, *Protestantism and Repression*, Orbis Books and SCM Press 1985.
12. See especially Theo Witvliet, *The Way of the Black Messiah*, SCM Press 1986 and Meyer-Stone 1987.
13. *World Christian Encyclopaedia* ed.David B.Barrett, Oxford University Press 1982, v.
14. As anyone not in a position to encounter it at first hand could discover from the pages of Adrian Hastings, *A History of Christianity 1920-1985*, Collins 1986 or any issue of the *Church Times* or *Church of England Newspaper*.
15. Ninian Smart, op.cit., 11.
16. Jaroslav Pelikan, *Jesus Through the Centuries*, Yale University Press 1986.
17. For a detailed introduction to Christian iconography see Gertrud Schiller, *Iconography of Christian Art*, Volume 1: *Christ's Incarnation – Childhood – Baptism – Temptation – Transfiguration – Works and Miracles*, Lund Humphries 1971; Volume 2: *The Passion of Jesus Christ*, Lund Humphries 1972. Cf. also Denis Thomas, *The Faces of Christ*, Paul Hamlyn 1979.

18. See Pelikan, *Jesus*, 21-33; Herrin, *Formation of Christendom*, 3-6. The introduction of the dating system backwards from Christ into the indefinite past, BC, was introduced much later, in Europe in the eighteenth century: see O.Cullmann, *Christ and Time*, SCM Press and Westminster Press ²1965, 17-18, 32f.

19. Pelikan, *Jesus*, 34-8; for these developments see Herrin, *Formation*, 55ff.; Robin Lane Fox, *Pagans and Christians*, Viking 1986, 609ff.

20. Pelikan, *Jesus*, 46-56.

21. See above, 220 n. 65.

22. See below, 82f.

23. Pelikan, *Jesus*, 57-70.

24. The literature on the Son of Man is unending. There is a very brief introductory survey of the problems in Christopher Rowland, *Christian Origins*, SPCK 1985, 182-6. Arguments from the imagery current in the New Testament period and the possible background to the use of the term 'Son of Man' must now take into account the arguments of Margaret Barker, *The Older Testament*, SPCK 1987.

25. Pelikan, *Jesus*, 78-82.

26. Ibid., 83-94.

27. For icons and the iconoclastic controversy see Herrin, *Formation*, 306-43.

28. Michael Carroll, *The Cult of the Virgin Mary*, 86ff.

29. For Constantine and his special version of the cross, the labarum, see Robin Lane Fox, *Pagans and Christians*, 609-18; Alistair Kee, *Constantine versus Christ*, SCM Press 1982, esp. 141-52.

30. Pelikan, op.cit., 95-108

31. Ibid., 109-32.

32. Ibid., 133ff. Umberto Eco, *The Name of the Rose*, Secker and Warburg 1983 (Pan Books 1984), has a discussion on the theme of Christ's lack of possessions, on which the fourteenth-century Pope John XXII pronounced, declaring that the belief that Jesus had no possessions was a heresy! See the execution of Brother Michael, 236f.

33. 'Lord of the Dance' seems to be inspired by the Apocryphal Acts of John; see E.Hennecke, W.Schneemelcher and R.McL.Wilson, *New Testament Apocrypha* 2, Lutterworth Press 1965, 229, 232f. Cf. e.g. 'To the Universe belongs the dancer... He who does not dance does not know what happens' (229); 'I leaped, but you do not understand the whole...After the Lord had so danced with us, my beloved, he went out' (232). I am grateful to J.L.Houlden for pointing this out.

34. See John H.Hayes, *Son of God to Superstar*, Abingdon Press 1976; Malachi Martin, *Jesus Now*, Fount Paperbacks 1975; Barnes Tatum, *In Quest of Jesus*, SCM Press and John Knox Press 1982.

35. Lord Beaverbrook, *The Divine Propagandist*, Heinemann 1962.

36. Joseph Klausner, *Jesus of Nazareth*, Macmillan, New York 1929; Geza Vermes, *Jesus the Jew*, Collins 1973 reissued SCM Press 1983.

37. Rudolf Bultmann, *Jesus and the Word*, Scribner 1934, reissued Fontana Books 1958; Günther Bornkamm, *Jesus of Nazareth*, Hodder and Stoughton and Harper and Row 1960.

38. Edward Schillebeeckx, *Jesus. An Experiment in Christology*, Collins 1979.

39. Dietrich Bonhoeffer, *Letters and Papers from Prison. The Enlarged Edition*, SCM Press and Macmillan 1971, 381.

40. Hugh Schonfield, *The Passover Plot*, Hutchinson 1965.

41. Joel Carmichael, *The Death of Jesus*, Macmillan 1962; S.G.F.Brandon, *Jesus and the Zealots*, Manchester University Press 1967.

42. Edmund Wilson, *The Scrolls from the Dead Sea*, Oxford University Press 1955; C.F.Potter, *The Last Years of Jesus*, Fawcett Publications 1958.

43. Dan Otto Via, *Kerygma and Comedy in the New Testament*, Fortress Press 1975.

44. Morton Smith, *Jesus the Magician*, Gollancz and Harper and Row 1978; John Hull, *Hellenistic Magic and the Synoptic Tradition*, SCM Press 1974.

45. Tim Rice and Andrew Lloyd Webber, *Jesus Christ Superstar*, MCA Music 1969.

46. Alfred A.Lovejoy, *The Great Chain of Being*, Harvard University Press 1936, 6.

47. Don Cupitt, 'One Jesus, Many Christs?', in *Christ, Faith and History. Cambridge Studies in Christology* ed. S.W.Sykes and J.P.Clayton, Cambridge University Press 1972, 142, 144.

48. Bamber Gascoigne, *The Christians*, Jonathan Cape 1971, 294.

49. James D.G.Dunn, *Unity and Diversity in the New Testament*, SCM Press and Westminster Press 1977, 373f. He argues that all this is held together by Christ, but that raises the problem that we shall have to go on to consider.

50. Don Cupitt, 'One Jesus, Many Christs?', 140f.

51. For Gnosticism see below, 77f.

52. For the following portraits I am indebted to Robert L.Wilken, *The Myth of Christian Beginnings*, Doubleday and SCM Press 1979, 165ff.

53. See e.g. Walter Bauer, *Orthodoxy and Heresy in Earliest Christianity*, SCM Press and Fortress Press 1973; Helmut Koester, *Introduction to the New Testament*, De Gruyter and Fortress Press 1982.

54. Luke is, of course, aware that his Gospel is only the first part of a two-volume work, which is continued in the Acts of the Apostles; see below.

55. In addition to the books on Acts already mentioned, for what follows see Wilken, op.cit., 31-7.

56. For Matthias see Acts 1.15-26: Haenchen, *Acts of the Apostles*, 157-65; Conzelmann, *Acts*, 10f.; Lüdemann, *Das frühe Christentum*, 37-42 (for full bibliographical details see Chapter 3, n.37).

57. For James see Rowland, *Christian Origins*, 263f.; W.Schmithals, *Paul and James*, SCM Press 1963.

58. For 'the Seven' see M.Simon, *St Stephen and the Hellenists in the Primitive Church*, Longmans 1958; Haenchen, *Acts*, 259-70; Conzelmann, *Acts*, 44-6; Lüdemann, *Das frühe Christentum*, 79-85.

59. Controversy particularly centres on the number of visits Paul made to Jerusalem; in addition to the books already quoted in Chapter 3, nn.37,38 above see Paul Nickle, *The Collection*, SCM Press 1966.

60. The three 'journeys' are described in Acts 13.1-14.28; 15.16-18.22; 18.23-23.35.

61. See further Nickle, *Collection* (n.59 above).

62. There were Christians in Rome to whom Paul wrote: cf. e.g. Wayne Meeks, *The First Urban Christians*, Yale University Press 1983.

63. This name is in fact erroneous. The creed recited at the eucharist is the Niceno-Constantinopolitan creed, which dates from the Council of Constantinople in 381. See J.N.D.Kelly, *Early Christian Creeds*, Longmans 1950, 205-62, 296-331.

64. A modern translation of Eusebius is available as Eusebius, *The History of the Church*, ed. G.A.Williamson, Penguin Books 1965; the older standard edition with commentary is Eusebius, *The Ecclesiastical History* ed. by H.J. Lawlor and J.E.L.Oulton, SPCK 1927. For what follows see Wilken, op.cit., 53-76. For Eusebius see also Robin Lane Fox, *Pagans and Christians*, 607-30; Alistair Kee, *Constantine versus Christ*, 51-8.

65. Wilken, op.cit., 185.

66. What follows is based on Elizabeth Maclaren, *The Nature of Belief*, Sheldon Press 1976, 89-91.

67. For a representative of this last approach see Rudolf Bultmann, e.g. *Jesus Christ and Mythology*, Scribner and SCM Press 1960.

68. Maclaren, op.cit., 91f.

69. David Perman, *Change and the Churches. An Anatomy of Religion in Britain*, Bodley Head 1977, 229.

70. See the series *Jesus depuis Jesus*, published by Editions du Cerf, Paris 1987ff.; volumes are to cover: From Jesus of Nazareth to the churches; the Jewish-Christian, apocryphal and Gnostic Jesus; the Manichaean Jesus; the Christ of doctrinal controversy, East and West; the Christs of the islands; the Christ of the barbarians; the imperial Christs; Jesus the hostage of Jews; Christians and Moslems in early mediaeval Spain; the incarnation of Jesus in the West; the Jesus of the Greek empire; Christ at the Reformation; the Christ of the conquistadors; the pietist and Enlightenment Jesus; the Slavonic Christ; the Christ of the barricades; the scientific Christ; the colonial Jesus and the contemporary Jesus.

71. Michael Carroll, *The Cult of the Virgin Mary*, 90-112.

72. Ibid., 86f.

73. Ibid., 89.

74. Ibid., 61ff., 86ff.

75. The development of images of Mary can be traced much further into the mediaeval period and beyond. Marina Warner, *Alone of All her Sex*, is a popular and somewhat rambling study; however, most of the systematic

treatments are available only in German, cf. the bibliography in F.L.Cross and E.A.Livingstone, *The Oxford Dictionary of the Christian Church*, Oxford University Press ²1974, 883f.

76. Dietrich Bonhoeffer, *Letters and Papers from Prison*, The Enlarged Edition, 381.

77. John A.T.Robinson, *Honest to God*, SCM Press and Westminster Press 1963, chapter 4, 64-83.

78. Leonardo Boff, *Jesus Christ Liberator*, SPCK and Orbis Books 1978, though see 131 below.

79. Mark 7.24-30; Matt. 15.21-28 (for whom she is a Canaanite).

80. Matt. 10.5,6.

81. Mark 14.7; Matt.26.11.

5. Problems with the Incarnation

1. The Chalcedonian Definition, quoted from T.H.Bindley, *The Oecumenical Documents of the Faith*, Methuen ⁴1950, 234f. Since this statement is generally recognized as the touchstone for the doctrine of the Incarnation, I do not see how we are helped by those who take pains to say that Christianity has had doctrines of the Incarnation in the plural rather than just one. Of course it has, but the mainstream has rejected that plurality which does not match up to Chalcedon.

2. For events leading up to the Council of Chalcedon see R.V.Sellars, *The Council of Chalcedon. A Historical and Doctrinal Survey*, SPCK 1953; W.H.C.Frend, *The Rise of Christianity*, Darton, Longman and Todd and Fortress Press 1984, 741-85.

3. For Arius, see below, 80.

4. The most persistent opposition to the Chalcedonian position came from the Monotheletes, those who argued that Christ had only a divine will, not a human will (a particularly striking instance of the constant reluctance throughout Christianity to see Christ as fully human). For this Monotheletic opposition see Judith Herrin, *The Formation of Christendom*, Blackwell and Princeton University Press 1987, 207-10, 213-15, 217-19, 250-9, etc.

5. The most monumental study is that by Aloys Grillmeier, *Christ in Christian Tradition*, Volume 1, revised edition Mowbrays 1975; also Frances Young, *From Nicaea to Chalcedon*, SCM Press and Fortress Press 1983.

6. The Athanasian Creed is printed under its two opening words in Latin, Quicunque vult, in the *Book of Common Prayer*, after Morning and Evening Prayer. For the nineteenth-century controversy see Owen Chadwick, *The Victorian Church*, Part 2, 1860-1901, A.& C.Black ²1972 reissued SCM Press 1987, 150.

7. These included certain letters of Cyril of Alexandria and the 'Tome' of Leo: see e.g. Bindley, *Oecumenical Documents*, 207-31.

8. The fatal accident in which the emperor Theodosius fell off his horse:

for a discussion see David E.Jenkins, *God, Miracle and the Church of England*, SCM Press 1987, 59-70.

9. See most recently Lucas Grollenberg, *Unexpected Messiah*, SCM Press 1988.

10. For the Christian use of the Old Testament, see especially Barnabas Lindars, *New Testament Apologetic*, SCM Press 1961.

11. For the question of what claims Jesus may have made for himself see e.g. James D.G.Dunn, *Christology in the Making*, SCM Press and Westminster Press 1980; Christopher Rowland, *Christian Origins*, SPCK 1985, 174-86, and the vast range of literature cited in these two books. It is doubtful whether he ever referred to himself as Son of God or Messiah. For the trial of Jesus see Rowland, *Christian Origins*, 164-73; E.Bammel (ed.), *The Trial of Jesus. Cambridge Studies in Honour of C.F.D.Moule*, SCM Press 1970; Paul Winter, *The Trial of Jesus*, De Gruyter, Berlin [2]1974; Ellis Rivkin, *What Crucified Jesus?*, Abingdon Press 1984 and SCM Press 1986.

12. See especially the three volumes edited by E.P.Sanders and published by SCM Press and Fortress Press, *Jewish and Christian Self-Definition*: 1. *The Shaping of Christianity in the Second and Third Centuries*, 1980; 2. *Aspects of Judaism in the Graeco-Roman Period*, 1981 (edited with A.I.Baumgarten and Alan Mendelson); 3. *Self-Definition in the Graeco-Roman World*, 1982.

13. Lawrence F.Schiffman, 'At the Crossroads: Tannaitic Perspectives on the Jewish-Christian Schism', *Jewish and Christian Self-Definition* 2, 115-56; the quotation comes from 147f.

14. In addition to *Jewish and Christian Self-Definition* 2 and the books mentioned in Chapter 3 n.54 see Samuel Sandmel, *The First Christian Century in Judaism and Christianity*, Oxford University Press, New York 1969.

15. See especially Paul's discussion of food offered to idols in I Corinthians 8 and the controversy with Peter in Galatians 2.

16. Paul's farewell speech to the elders in Miletus (Acts 20.18-35) is thought by many scholars to contain a 'forecast' of this attributed by the author to Paul after this development had begun. Because 'Gnosticism' can cover so many trends, there is considerable argument as to when Gnosticism (with a capital as opposed to a small g) can be said to begin. See Rowland, *Christian Origins*, 294-7; R.McL.Wilson, *Gnosis and the New Testament*, Blackwell 1968, and for subsequent developments Frend, *The Rise of Christianity*, 195-221 and the bibliography there.

17. For a brief summary see R.McL.Wilson, 'Gnosticism', in *A New Dictionary of Christian Theology*, 226-30, and the bibliography listed there.

18. Translations of Gnostic texts are available in James M.Robinson, *The Nag Hammadi Library*, E.J.Brill, Leiden [2]1984 and Bentley Layton, *The Gnostic Scriptures*, Doubleday and SCM Press 1987.

19. R.McL.Wilson, 'Gnosticism', 227.

20. A very positive view of Gnosticism has been taken by Elaine Pagels,

The Gnostic Gospels, Penguin Books 1982, but see Susanne Heine, *Women and Early Christianity*, SCM Press 1987 and Augsburg 1988, 106-23.

21. For the history of the formation of the Jewish canon see e.g. P.R.Ackroyd, 'The Old Testament in the Making', in *The Cambridge History of the Bible*, Cambridge University Press 1970, 67-112; O.Eissfeldt, *The Old Testament. An Introduction*, Blackwell 1965, 560-70. The Dead Sea Scrolls have provided evidence of the complexity of the situation before AD 70.

22. Giovanni Garbini, *History and Ideology in Ancient Israel*, SCM Press and Crossroad Publishing Company 1988, 151-69, gives reasons for supposing that canonical Ezra did not reach its final form until the first century AD.

23. These can be found in the Old Testament Pseudepigrapha; there is an older collection in R.H.Charles, *The Apocrypha and Pseudepigrapha of the Old Testament*, Oxford University Press 1913 reissued 1963; a more recent and more extensive collection is J.H.Charlesworth, *The Old Testament Pseudepigrapha* (two volumes), Darton, Longman and Todd and Doubleday 1983, 1985; both have introductions and notes to the works they contain. See also H.F.D.Sparks, *The Apocryphal Old Testament*, Oxford University Press 1984. For the term 'pseudepigrapha' and pseudepigraphy see Chapter 7, n.18 below.

24. For example, parts of the book of Enoch were preserved in Ethiopic and Slavonic.

25. For inspiration and exegesis see James Barr, *Old and New in Interpretation*, SCM Press 1966; R.P.C.Hanson, 'Biblical Exegesis in the Early Church', *Cambridge History of the Bible* 1, 412-53.

26. For the formation of the New Testament canon see Hans von Campenhausen, *The Formation of the Christian Bible*, A.& C.Black and Fortress Press 1972; C.F.Evans, 'The New Testament in the Making', in *Cambridge History of the Bible*, 232-83; W.G.Kümmel, *Introduction to the New Testament*, Abingdon Press and SCM Press ²1975, 475-93.

27. For what follows see C.F.Evans, *Is 'Holy Scripture' Christian?*, SCM Press 1971, especially 21-36.

28. C.F.Evans, 'Tradition and Scripture', in op.cit., 17f. This same point is brought up again by John Barton, *Reading the Old Testament*, Darton Longman and Todd 1984, 101, but disappointingly he mentions 'the curse of the canon' only in passing and does not enlarge on the phrase.

29. For Arius see Maurice Wiles, 'In Defence of Arius', *Working Papers in Doctrine*, SCM Press 1976, 28-37; Robert C.Gregg and Dennis E.Groh, *Early Arianism*, Fortress Press and SCM Press 1981; Rowan Williams, *Arius*, Darton, Longman and Todd 1987.

30. H.M.Gwatkin, *Studies in Arianism*, ²1882, 274, quoted by Maurice Wiles, op.cit., 28.

31. An extensive bibliography is given in James D.G.Dunn, *Christology in the Making* (see n.11 above), which is probably the best introductory book on the question.

32. Dunn, *Christology*, 253f.

33. For this see J.L.Houlden, 'The Doctrine of the Trinity and the Person of Christ', *Explorations in Theology* 3, SCM Press 1978, 25-40.

34. Ibid., 35.

35. Ibid.

36. Maurice Wiles, *The Making of Christian Doctrine*, Cambridge University Press 1967, 123-5. There is an edition of Tertullian's *Against Praxeas* ed. E.Evans, SPCK and Macmillan, New York 1949.

37. Wiles, *Making*, 125f.

38. The problem of the development of doctrine was, of course, one with which Newman struggled in his famous *Essay on the Development of Christian Doctrine*, Penguin Books 1974 (1845 edition). His solution, much discussed, can hardly be said to be satisfactory.

39. See also below, 198–202.

40. Wiles, *Making.*, 89f.; cf. Michael Carroll, *The Cult of the Virgin Mary*, Princeton University Press 1986.

41. Wiles, *Making.*, 101-7; cf. his 'The Unassumed is the Unhealed', *Working Papers in Doctrine*, 108-121.

42. For what follows see his 'Does Christology Rest on a Mistake?', in *Working Papers in Doctrine*, 122-31.

43. Ibid., 127.

44. G.W.H.Lampe, *God as Spirit*, Oxford University Press 1977, reissued SCM Press 1983.

45. Ibid., 13.

46. Ibid., 17.

47. Ibid., 14ff.

48. For 'process' theology see David Pailin, 'Process Theology', in *A New Dictionary of Christian Theology* ed. Alan Richardson and John Bowden, SCM Press and Westminster Press 1983, 467-70 and the bibliography there.

49. Lampe, *God as Spirit*, 23f.

50. G.W.H.Lampe, *A Patristic Greek Lexicon*, Oxford University Press 1969.

51. For the controversy over *Essays and Reviews* see Owen Chadwick, *The Victorian Church*, Part 2, 75-97.

52. John Hick (ed.), *The Myth of God Incarnate*, SCM Press and Westminster Press 1977, ix.

53. John Hick, *The Second Christianity*, SCM Press 1983, 31f.

54. It is significant that there were substantial sales of *The Myth of God Incarnate* to Moslem groups and at least one Moslem wrote and had published a learned discussion on it.

55. John A.T.Robinson, *Honest to God*, SCM Press and Westminster Press 1963, 74 (his italics).

56. Nineham, in *The Myth of God Incarnate*, 188.

6. Can Jesus be Everyman?

1. Tom Driver, *Christ in a Changing World*, Crossroad Publishing Company and SCM Press 1981, 32.

2. See F.W.Dillistone, *The Christian Understanding of Atonement*, SCM Press ²1984.

3. See above, 46–8.

4. See above, 83.

5. The whole of the passage is much more difficult than most popular commentators (or the translations) let on. For some of the difficulties cf. J.L.Houlden, *Paul's Letters from Prison*, SCM and Westminster Pelican Commentaries 1977, 82-4. He mentions the problem of giving 'meaning to *hyper*, the prefix to the verb translated "exalted" in v.9, which would most naturally imply that after his death Christ received a status higher than that which he before possessed'.

6. Cf. e.g. Vincent Taylor, *The Atonement in New Testament Teaching*, Macmillan 1940; Leon Morris, *The Atonement. Its Meaning and Significance*, Inter-Varsity Press 1983; Frances Young, *Sacrifice and the Death of Christ*, SPCK 1975, reissued SCM Press 1983.

7. For a summary and bibliography see the article by F.W.Dillistone, 'Atonement', *A New Dictionary of Christian Theology* ed. Alan Richardson and John Bowden, SCM Press and Westminster Press 1983, 50-3.

8. The theory of *anakephalaiosis* put forward by Irenaeus of Lyons.

9. This was the view of Origen in the third century; the ransom was paid to Satan who had acquired rights over humankind as a result of the fall.

10. For this see especially Gustav Aulen, *Christus Victor*, SPCK 1931.

11. For the theory of satisfaction, cf. Anselm's *Cur Deus Homo*.

12. For the theory of substitution see especially Calvin, who taught that Jesus 'bore in his soul the tortures of a condemned and ruined man'.

13. F.R.Barry, *The Atonement*, Hodder and Stoughton 1968.

14. Dillistone, *The Christian Understanding of Atonement*, 410.

15. Ibid., 415.

16. See below, 159.

17. See above, 85–7.

18. Rosemary Ruether, *To Change the World. Christology and Cultural Criticism*, SCM Press and Crossroad Publishing Company 1981, 45f.

19. Ibid., 46.

20. See e.g. Willem Zuidema, *God's Partner*, SCM Press 1987, 71.

21. Hugh Montefiore, *For God's Sake*, Collins and Fortress Press 1969, 182.

22. *Newsweek*, 7 August 1967, 83.

23. William E. Phipps, *Was Jesus Married? The Distortion of Sexuality in the Christian Tradition*, Harper and Row 1970.

24. Id., *The Sexuality of Jesus. Theological and Literary Perspectives*, Harper and Row 1973.

25. Phipps, *Was Jesus Married?*, 187.

26. Nikos Kazantzakis, *The Last Temptation*, Faber 1961, 458ff.

27. Elisabeth Moltmann-Wendel, *The Women around Jesus*, SCM Press and Crossroad Publishing Company 1982, 85.

28. Matt.19.12. For Origen's castration of himself see Joseph Wilson Trigg, *Origen*, John Knox Press 1983 and SCM Press 1985, 53-4.

29. Elisabeth Moltmann-Wendel, *The Women around Jesus*, 82.

30. In addition to Michael Carroll, *The Cult of the Virgin Mary*, see also e.g. Thomas Boslooper, *The Virgin Birth*, SCM Press and Westminster Press 1962; Marina Warner, *Alone of All Her Sex*, Weidenfeld and Nicolson 1976.

31. Mary Daly, *Beyond God the Father* (1973), The Women's Press 1986, 81. However, I should qualify my approval here by saying that is impossible for me to follow Mary Daly in her later books, *Gyn/ecology* The Women's Press 1979, and *Pure Lust*, The Women's Press 1984.

32. Rosemary Ruether, in *Womanguides. Readings toward a Feminist Theology*, Beacon Press 1985, 105f.

33. Ibid., 112.

34. See Susanne Heine, *Christianity and the Goddesses*, SCM Press 1988, Chapter 5.

35. Anselm, 'Prayer to St Paul', in Benedicta Ward (ed.), *The Prayers and Meditations of St Anselm*, Penguin Books 1973, 153-6.

36. Quoted in Grace Jantzen, *Julian of Norwich*, SPCK 1987, 123f.

37. Julian of Norwich, *Revelations of Divine Love*, Chapter 60. For comments on this whole question see Grace Jantzen, *Julian of Norwich*, 116-24.

38. See Don Cupitt, 'One Jesus, Many Christs', *Christ, Faith and History. Cambridge Studies in Christology* ed. S.W.Sykes and J.P.Clayton, Cambridge University Press 1973, 138.

39. Mary Daly, *Beyond God the Father*, 129.

40. Ibid., 96.

41. See my comments above and the books cited in n.30.

42. Manas Buthelezi is a Lutheran bishop; these comments from lectures given in Heidelberg in 1972 are quoted in Theo Witvliet, *A Place in the Sun*, SCM Press and Orbis Books 1985, 77.

43. James H.Cone, *God of the Oppressed*, Seabury Press 1975, quoted in Theo Witvliet, *A Place in the Sun*.

44. Ibid. For the whole matter of black theology see Theo Witvliet, *The Way of the Black Messiah*, SCM Press and Meyer-Stone 1987.

45. Tom Driver, *Christ in a Changing World*, 45.

46. See Franz Fanon, *The Wretched of the Earth*, Penguin Books 1967. This was one of the first and most powerful expressions of the sufferings of those on the 'underside of history', to use another moving expression, this time from Gustavo Gutierrez.

47. Stevie Smith, 'Was He Married?', *The Collected Poems*, Allen Lane, The Penguin Press and New Directions, New York 1975, 389f.

48. Stevie Smith, 'Oh Christianity, Christianity?', ibid., 416.

7. Jesus and Ethics

1. John Austin Baker, *The Foolishness of God*, Darton, Longman and Todd 1970, 138.

2. He does not give a reference, and I have not been able to find the exact phrase, but cf. C.G.Montefiore, *The Synoptic Gospels*, 1, Macmillan 1927, 170.

3. Baker, *The Foolishness of God*, 137.

4. Bertrand Russell, *Why I am Not a Christian*, George Allen and Unwin 1957, 22.

5. Richard Robinson, *An Atheist's Values*, Clarendon Press 1964, 146.

6. Ibid., 148-50.

7. Matt.8.22; Luke 9.60.

8. John Knox, *The Ethic of Jesus in the Teaching of the Church*, Abingdon Press 1961 and Epworth Press 1962, 29f.

9. C.G.Montefiore, op.cit., II, 86.

10. H.J.Cadbury, *The Peril of Modernizing Jesus*, Macmillan, New York 1937, 102.

11. See below, 112 cf. n.15.

12. Cadbury, *Peril*, 88.

13. Michael J.Langford, *The Good and the True. An Introduction to Christian Ethics*, SCM Press 1985, 29.

14. Ibid., 2-31. Michael Langford goes on to give four reasons why it does not follow, in his view, that the life and teaching of Jesus are of little importance for ethics. 1. Where the Christian church lays obligations on its members derived from particular words of Jesus, the members have a duty to fulfil those obligations, as they have a duty to respond to Jesus' command at the last supper, 'Do this in remembrance of me.' But what about the question of ideology raised in Chapter 2? 2. While what is right may in principle be open to rational testing and systematization, in practice we tend to learn from example. The role of specially inspired teachers and example is very important. For the Christian, Jesus is the supreme example of such a teacher. But in the previous chapter and so far in this one we have been looking at the problems attached to this view. 3. relates to what Langford calls inspiration of the heart rather than the mind. But if Jesus has the effect that he had on a sensitive person like Stevie Smith, does not the problem connected with the previous point remain? 4. The inspiration of Jesus leads to a new spiritual grace. Now there is no doubt about the importance of this whole area. But it is a different area from that of ethics.

15. Wayne E.Meeks, *The Moral World of the First Christians*, SPCK 1986, 16.

16. Mark 10.1-12; Matt. 19.1-9.

17. For the degree to which other hands have probably contributed to e.g. the Sermon on the Mount cf. above Chapter 3 n.24, and especially W.D.Davies, *The Sermon on the Mount*, Cambridge University Press 1966.

18. The practice is known as pseudepigraphy. Since concepts of authorship

were very different in post-exilic Judaism and early Christianity, for a variety of reasons, books were often written under the name of an authoritative figure. From the Old Testament one might single out the Book of Daniel – and both Proverbs and Ecclesiastes purport to have been written by Solomon; at least the Gospel of Matthew and II Peter from the New Testament would fall into the same category. There is a whole genre of literature usually referred to as Pseudepigrapha amounting to well over fifty works, the alleged authors of which go as far back as Adam! See James H.Charlesworth, *The Old Testament Pseudepigrapha* (two volumes), Doubleday and Darton, Longman and Todd 1983, 1985 and the other literature mentioned in Chapter 5 n.23 above.

19. See below, 113f.

20. Albert Schweitzer, *My Life and Thought*, George Allen and Unwin 1954, 53, quoted in D.E.Nineham, *Explorations in Theology 1*, SCM Press 1977, 130.

21. E.P.Sanders, *Jesus and Judaism*, SCM Press and Fortress Press 1983.

22. Cf. Mark 9.1 (note the way in which this is changed in Matt.16.28/ Luke 9.27: it evidently caused them problems); Matt.19.28/Luke 22.30; Matt.10.23.

23. I Thess.4.15-18.

24. I Cor. 15.51-52.

25. For this point cf. also p.46 above.

26. Cf. Rom.15.24-28.

27. John A.T.Robinson, *Jesus and His Coming*, SCM Press 1957.

28. For discussion see the books referred to in Chapter 3 above.

29. For a discussion of the evidence see Eduard Schweizer, *Church Order in the New Testament*, SCM Press 1961, 20ff.; Hans Freiherr von Campenhausen, *Ecclesiastical Authority and Spiritual Power in the Church*, A.& C.Black and Fortress Press 1969, 1ff.

30. The history of the use of Matt.16.18 in defence of the papacy is a complex one and is bound up with the history of the increase in the influence of the Roman church and the Pope in the eighth century, cf. Judith Herrin, *The Formation of Christendom*, Blackwell and Princeton University Press 1987, 386ff., 420.

31. John 21.20-23.

32. For this verdict see W.G.Kümmel, *Introduction to the New Testament*, Abingdon Press and SCM Press ²1975, 429-34; the main reasons are the work's literary dependence on Jude and the church situation presupposed.

33. II Peter 3.4f.

34. II Peter 3.8f.

35. Martin Werner, *Die Entstehung des christlichen Dogmas*, Bern 1941, abbreviated translation *The Formation of Christian Doctrine*, A.&.C.Black 1957, is an often wrong-headed but important book here.

36. This is generally thought to be the background to I Corinthians, cf. e.g. Kümmel, *Introduction*, 274: 'The whole letter manifests a front against a Gnostic perversion of the Christian message which attributes to the

pneumatics... a perfect redemptive state and an unconditional moral freedom.' Cf. the commentaries on I Corinthians listed there and for Gnosticism above, 77f.

37. In addition to the passage quoted below, such material can also be found in Ephesians, I Peter and the Pastoral Epistles.

38. Col.3.18-23. Cf. Kümmel, *Introduction*, 345: 'The household admonitions in Col.3.13-4.1 show a remarkably small christianizing' (sic!).

39. F.W.Beare, 'The Epistle to the Colossians', *The Interpreter's Bible* 11, Abingdon Press 1955, 226.

40. For later developments see W.H.C.Frend, *The Rise of Christianity*, Fortress Press and Darton, Longman and Todd 1984, 131ff., esp.133: 'The code of conduct expected of Christians recalls the requirements of righteousness set out in intertestamental writings, more than the stark demands of Jesus.' But here too we should not forget the variety of Christianity.

41. J.T.Sanders, *Ethics in the New Testament*, SCM Press and Fortress Press 1975, reissued SCM Press 1986, 29.

42. Ibid., 1986, xii.

8. Jesus, Power and Politics

1. See especially Alastair G.Hunter, *Christianity and Other Faiths in Britain*, SCM Press 1985, which explores this issue in some detail.

2. See 56, 75, 84, 121, 225 n. 4 above.

3. See Judith Herrin, *The Formation of Christendom*, Blackwell and Princeton University Press 1987, 207-18, 221-38, 250-59, etc., for the Arians and Monotheletes; for the iconoclastic controversy see above, Chapter 4, n.27.

4. For this cf. e.g. Martin Kähler, *The So-called Historical Jesus and the Historic, Biblical Christ* (1896), Fortress Press 1964.

5. See S.W.Sykes, *The Identity of Christianity*, SPCK 1984, 77.

6. This is evident from the way in which, say, in the 1950s and for some time afterwards German theologians could be categorized as belonging to the schools of e.g. Barth, Bultmann, Cullmann, von Rad and so on. This had a decisive effect on the staffing of universities.

7. For 'the rapture' and the attitude associated with it see the countless pamphlets written by Gordon Lindsay and published by Christ for the Nations in Dallas; e.g *Rapture: Rapture and the Second Coming of Christ*; also John F.Walvoord, *The Rapture Question*, Zondervan 1970. For the evangelical Right see Alistair Kee, *Domination or Liberation*, SCM Press 1986, 87-121; Gore Vidal, *Armageddon?*, André Deutsch 1987.

8. For these developments see e.g. Klaus Scholder, *The Churches and the Third Reich*, Vol.1, SCM Press and Fortress Press 1987; J.S. Conway, *The Nazi Persecution of the Churches*, Weidenfeld and Nicolson 1968; Eberhard Bethge, *Dietrich Bonhoeffer*, Fount Paperbacks 1977.

9. See Galatians 2.11ff.

10. Sykes, *The Identity of Christianity*, 23.

11. See above, 107.

12. This adoption of the exodus symbolism by Christianity was a step which has had particular repercussions in contemporary liberation theology, in which 'exodus' is often the main symbol. Because, as we shall see, liberation theology has problems in its christology, it finds a Christianized exodus theme an important alternative.

13. For the misinterpretation of first-century Judaism and a more balanced present-day understanding see above, Chapter 3 nn.39, 64.

14. For one pattern see Robin Lane Fox, *Pagans and Christians*, Viking 1986, 681.

15. See Michael Carroll, *The Cult of the Virgin Mary. Psychological Origins*, Princeton University Press 1986, 90-112.

16. For Christendom see, of course, Judith Herrin, *The Formation of Christendom*.

17. For an introduction see e.g. Theo Witvliet, *A Place in the Sun*, SCM Press and Orbis Books 1985, 8-18; Kenneth Cracknell, *Towards a New Relationship. Christians and People of Other Faiths*, Epworth Press 1986, 17-24. Both books contain useful bibliographies.

18. For a terrifying picture of the power exercised by these communities see Jacques Pohier, *God in Fragments*, SCM Press and Crossroad Publishing Company 1986.

19. Sykes, *The Identity of Christianity*, 54f.

20. Graham Shaw, *The Cost of Authority*, SCM Press and Fortress Press 1983; with this should also be read the sequel *God in Our Hands*, SCM Press 1987, which extends this investigation of manipulation into the Psalms and Christian prayer.

21. Shaw, *The Cost of Authority*, 181f.

22. Ibid., 24.

23. See Robin Lane Fox, *Pagans and Christians*, 609; W.H.C.Frend, *The Rise of Christianity*, Fortress Press and Darton, Longman and Todd 1984, 473-505.

24. For a thorough discussion see Alistair Kee, *Constantine versus Christ*, SCM Press 1982, 17-22; Robin Lane Fox, *Pagans and Christians*, 615-20.

25. See above, 63.

26. Norman Baynes, 'Eusebius and the Christian Empire' (1933), *Byzantine Studies and Other Essays*, The Athlone Press 1955, 168-72, quoted by Kee, *Constantine versus Christ*, 129.

27. *Life of Constantine* I.84, in *Nicene and Post-Nicene Fathers* 1, *Eusebius*, Oxford 1840 reissued Grand Rapids nd.

28. For the far-reaching consequences of the identification of Jesus with the pre-existent Logos see above, 82f.

29. For instances, see Herrin, *Formation of Christendom*.

30. See e.g. Edward Schillebeeckx, *The Church with a Human Face*, SCM Press and Crossroad Publishing Company 1985, 163ff., 192ff.

31. For overall surveys of liberation theology see e.g. Rosino Gibellini, *The Liberation Theology Debate*, SCM Press 1987; Deane W. Ferm, *Third*

World Liberation Theologies, Orbis Books 1985; Theo Witvliet, *A Place in the Sun*, SCM Press and Orbis Books 1985. I should stress that I am not attempting a balanced assessment of liberation theology (or, more properly, theologies) here. I am just pointing to some aspects which seem to me to be misguided or sinister.

32. See above, 28f.

33. Alfredo Fierro, *The Militant Gospel*, SCM Press and Orbis Books 1977, 152f.

34. For a survey of the discussion see Rosemary Ruether, 'Jesus and the Revolutionaries', in *To Change the World. Christology and Cultural Criticism*, SCM Press and Crossroad Publishing Company 1984, 7-19.

35. Thus e.g. S.G.F.Brandon, *Jesus and the Zealots*, Manchester University Press 1967; Joel Carmichael, *The Death of Jesus*, Macmillan, New York 1962.

36. Thus e.g. Oscar Cullmann, *Jesus and the Revolutionaries of his Time*, Harper and Row 1971.

37. See e.g. Gustavo Gutierrez, *A Theology of Liberation*, Orbis Books 1973 and SCM Press 1974, 225-32.

38. E.g.Gutierrez, op.cit. 317. The situation is not substantially altered by the appearance of José Míguez Bonino, *Faces of Jesus. Latin American Theologies* (1977), Orbis Books 1984.

39. See J.Andrew Kirk, *Liberation Theology. An Evangelical View of the Third World*, Marshall, Morgan and Scott 1979, 123.

40. Leonardo Boff, *Jesus Christ Liberator*, Orbis Books and SPCK 1978.

41. Jon Sobrino, *Christology at the Crossroads*, Orbis Books and SCM Press 1978.

42. H.Assmann, *Theology for a Nomad Church*, Orbis Books 1976; it is vitally important to understand this perspective and method of liberation theology; see Rosino Gibellini, *The Liberation Theology Debate*, 1-6.

43. The problems of christology in Latin American theology are further shown by Rosemary Ruether (though that is not her intention) in 'Christology and Latin American Theology', *To Change the World*, 19-30. Here the stress is on 'Jesus' preferential option for the poor' (20), for which we have seen that there is not sufficient basis in the Gospels (above 70f.); having covered that, Rosemary Ruether is forced to shift her theme, for lack of material, to the kingdom of God.

44. See Fierro, *The Militant Gospel*, 157.

45. Sykes, *The Identity of Christianity*, 18-20.

9. Problems with History

1. See James Barr, 'Which Language did Jesus Speak? Some Remarks of a Semitist', *Bulletin of the John Rylands Library* 53, 1970, 11-27. For a general comment on languages used in Palestine in the first century see John Stambaugh and David Balch, *The Social World of the First Christians*, SPCK 1986, 87f.

2. For Hellenization after Alexander the Great see especially Martin Hengel, *Judaism and Hellenism*, SCM Press and Fortress Press 1974; id., *Jews, Greeks and Barbarians*, SCM Press and Fortress Press 1980.

3. A number of Church Fathers believed that Matthew the disciple of Jesus collected the sayings of Jesus – or wrote a Gospel – in Hebrew, but this was probably a misunderstanding of a brief saying in Papias, one of the earliest pieces of external evidence to the books of the New Testament.

4. Hebrew can in fact make comparisons by saying that x is *min/me* (from) y (e.g. life is better than death = *hayyim memawet*). I am grateful to Robert Carroll for this point.

5. Matt.6.24; Luke 16.13.

6. It is interesting that the Bible says very little generally about problems of communication between those of different languages; with rare exceptions it is taken for granted that everyone can understand everyone else. For a comment on this see Giovanni Garbini, *History and Ideology in Ancient Israel*, SCM Press and Crossroad Publishing Company 1988, 44-7. Language difficulties were a contributory factor to the increasing split between East and West during the first Christian millennium; cf. Judith Herrin, *The Formation of Christendom*, Blackwell and Princeton University Press 1987, 11-12, 79-81.

7. See C.F.Burney, *The Poetry of our Lord*, Oxford University Press 1925; Matthew Black, *An Aramaic Approach to the Gospels and Acts*, Oxford University Press [3]1967.

8. See Walter Bauer, W.F.Arndt and F.W.Gingrich, *A Greek-English Lexicon of the New Testament and Other Early Christian Literature*, Chicago University Press [2]1979, cols.296f.

9. See Origen, *De Oratione*, 27.7. For further discussion see C.F.Evans, *The Lord's Prayer*, SPCK 1963, 46-56: Ernst Lohmeyer, *The Lord's Prayer*, Collins 1965, 141-5.

10. Preface to *The New English Bible*, New Testament, Oxford University Press and Cambridge University Press [2]1970, viii.

11. Ibid., vii.

12. Ibid.

13. *The Good News Bible* (the English version of the American *Today's English Version*), Collins/Bible Societies 1976.

14. See Bruce Chilton, *Beginning New Testament Study*, SPCK 1986, 98f.: thus in John 2.4 Jesus' words rendered in the Revised Standard Version 'O woman, what have you to do with me?' become 'You must not tell me what to do' in the *Good News Bible*.

15. See C.H.Dodd, *The Parables of the Kingdom* (1935), revised edition Fontana Books 1961 ([4]1983).

16. See above, 113.

17. Dodd, *Parables*, 43. I have already noted that this saying was a problem to the later evangelists, Matthew and Mark. See above, Chapter 7, n.22.

18. Chilton, *Beginning New Testament Study*, 111.

19. Ibid., 106.

20. Rudolf Bultmann, *Jesus Christ and Mythology*, SCM Press and Scribner 1960; see also 'New Testament and Mythology' (1941), in H.W.Bartsch (ed.), *Kerygma and Myth*, SPCK 1953, 1-44, now in Schubert M.Ogden (ed.), *New Testament and Mythology and Other Basic Writings*, Fortress Press and SCM Press 1985.

21. See *New Testament and Mythology*, 11.

22. The proclamation of the New Testament 'cannot be saved by reducing the amount of mythology by picking and choosing', ibid., 8.

23. For detailed accounts of Bultmann's approach see Walter Schmithals, *An Introduction to the Theology of Rudolf Bultmann*, SCM Press 1968; John Macquarrie, *An Existentialist Theology*, SCM Press 1955; id., *The Scope of Demythologizing*, SCM Press 1960; Schubert M.Ogden, *Christ without Myth*, Collins 1962.

24. See e.g. the difference between Mark and Luke in the story of the healing of the paralysed man (Mark 2. 10-12; Luke 5.17-26). Mark says that to gain access to Jesus the four men carrying him dug up the roof; Luke changes this to removing the tiles. Joseph A.Fitzmyer, *The Gospel According to Luke I-IX*, Anchor Bible, Doubleday 1981, 582, comments: 'The roof of the common Palestinian house was made of wooden beams placed across stone or mudbrick walls; the beams were covered with reeds, matted layers of thorns, and several inches of clay. It was sloped and usually rolled before the rainy season. Such a roof could have been dug through (see Mark 2.4). Luke, however, has changed the description, introducing the tiled roof of Hellenistic houses in the eastern Mediterranean area – making the action more intelligible to Greek-speaking Christian readers outside of the Palestinian context.'

25. See for example the influence of the book of Zechariah, Psalm 22, and other Old Testament passages on the passion narrative; cf. the commentaries and Barnabas Lindars, *New Testament Apologetic*, SCM Press 1961; Lucas Grollenberg, *Unexpected Messiah*, SCM Press 1988.

26. For an extremely complicated and 'scientific' discussion of the star which led the wise men see David Hughes, *The Star of Bethlehem Mystery*, Dent 1979.

27. Mark 15.33; Matt. 27.45; Luke 23.44.

28. H.J.Cadbury, *The Peril of Modernizing Jesus*, Macmillan, New York 1937, 5.

29. Ibid., 8f.

30. Lionel Trilling, *The Liberal Imagination*, Mercury Books 1964, 186. I am indebted for this reference and its application to D.E.Nineham, *The Use and Abuse of the Bible*, Macmillan 1976 reissued SPCK 1978, 192f.

31. Cadbury, *Peril*, e.g.37f., 72f.

32. See above, 22-31.

33. Cadbury, *Peril*, 120-53.

34. Luke 12.50.

35. Cadbury, *Peril*, 129.

36. Ibid., 41. This is challenged by E.P.Sanders, *Jesus and Judaism*, SCM Press and Fortress Press 1985, 19ff. but not to my mind convincingly. Professor Sanders is comparing intention in an individual with intention in movements and organizations.

37. See especially Lucas Grollenberg, *Unexpected Messiah*, SCM Press 1988.

38. Luke 9.51.

39. See above, 36f.

40. See above, 36f.

41. For the atonement, see above, 92-4.

42. In Mark 8.31; 9.31; 10.34 Jesus three times predicts that the Son of Man will suffer and die and after three days rise. If these passages are the work of Mark they tell us nothing of Jesus' actual intentions. If they are authentic, they raise the problem of the significance of a death that Jesus, in intimate communion with the Father, has always known would be followed by a resurrection. There is a third possibility, that Jesus had a different picture of the future from anything we can now trace in the Gospels, which included some sort of vindication, and that references to this picture were subsequently altered in the light of what had actually happened.

43. Joseph Klausner, *Jesus of Nazareth*, Hodder and Stoughton 1925.

44. Geza Vermes, *Jesus the Jew*, Collins and Fortress Press 1973, reissued SCM Press 1973; id., *Jesus and the World of Judaism*, SCM Press and Fortress Press 1983.

45. E.P.Sanders, *Paul and Palestinian Judaism*, SCM Press and Fortress Press 1977.

46. See for example the parallels from Cynicism in Gerald Downing, *Jesus and the Threat of Freedom*, SCM Press 1987.

47. Albert Schweitzer, *The Quest of the Historical Jesus*, A.& C.Black ³1954 reissued SCM Press 1981, 397.

48. I noted this quotation in 1976 and now cannot find the source.

49. Not to mention the many different popularizations and harmonies.

50. Dennis Nineham, 'The Use of the Bible in Modern Theology', in *Explorations in Theology* 1, SCM Press 1977, 111.

51. Don Cupitt, *The Leap of Reason*, Sheldon Press 1976, 123.

10. History, Doctrine and Miracle

1. G.E.Lessing, *On the Proof of the Spirit and of Power*, in H.Chadwick (ed.), *Lessing's Theological Writings*, A.& C.Black 1956, 53.

2. Ibid., 55.

3. For historical consciousness see above, 20, 62, 74.

4. Ernst Troeltsch, 'Über historische und dogmatische Methode in der Theologie', *Gesammelte Schriften* 2, Tübingen 1913, 729-53.

5. The first scholars to try to approach this variety of materials consistently and systematically were the members of the so-called 'History of Religions School' in Germany ('Religionsgeschichtliche Schule'), who included Wilhelm Bousset (1865-1920), Hermann Gunkel (1862-1932) and Wilhelm Heitmüller (1869-1925). They have their chronicler in German in C.Colpe, *Die Religionsgeschichtliche Schule*, Göttingen 1961, but not in English. Their concerns are long overdue for a revival.

6. Over-hasty parallels drawn between biblical texts and Babylonian literature led to what was referred to as the 'Bibel-Babel' (Bible-Babylon) school, again in Germany. That the concerns of this school were not utterly wide of the mark has been shown recently by Giovanni Garbini, *History and Ideology in Ancient Israel*, SCM Press and Crossroad Publishing Company 1988.

7. Published in Tübingen between 1912 and 1925. The first volume contains his famous *The Social Teaching of the Christian Churches*, translated into English by Olive Wyon, Lutterworth Press (two volumes) 1931.

8. For more details see my *Karl Barth. Theologian*, SCM Press 1983, 24f.; Eberhard Busch, *Karl Barth*, SCM Press and Fortress Press 1976, 81-3.

9. The most vivid account of how this came into being and its main concerns is still the correspondence between Karl Barth and Eduard Thurneysen in the second and third decades of this century, a selection from which is published as *Revolutionary Theology in the Making* ed. James D.Smart, John Knox Press and Epworth Press 1964.

10. See above, 122.

11. For more details see the books mentioned in Chapter 8 n.8.

12. For more details see below, 152f.

13. See below, 166.

14. Karl Barth, *Evangelical Theology. An Introduction*, Fontana Books 1965, 34.

15. Karl Barth, *How I Changed My Mind*, John Knox Press and St Andrew Press 1969, 69.

16. See for example Rudolf Bultmann, *The Gospel of John*, Blackwell and Westminster Press 1971; *Primitive Christianity in its Contemporary Setting*, Thames and Hudson 1956, reissued 1983; Fontana Books 1960.

17. Rudolf Bultmann, *The Historical Jesus and the Kerygmatic Christ*, ed. C.E.Braaten and R.H.Harrisville, Abingdon Press 1964, 20: 'Paul and John, each in his own way, indicate that we do not *need* to go beyond the "that" [the fact that Jesus existed, italics his].'

18. See the books mentioned in Chapter 9, n.23 above.

19. See especially Schubert M.Ogden, *Christ without Myth*, Collins 1962.

20. For further details see James M.Robinson (ed.), *The Beginnings of Dialectical Theology*, John Knox Press 1968; Rudolf Bultmann, *Faith and Understanding*, SCM Press 1969: id., *Essays Philosophical and Theological*,

SCM Press 1956.

21. For the 'new quest of the historical Jesus' see above all James M.Robinson, *A New Quest of the Historical Jesus*, SCM Press 1959, reissued with additional essays on the theme by Fortress Press 1983. Robinson began by noting a shift in this direction in the later thought of Bultmann himself; other authors who were highlighted in this way were Günther Bornkamm, *Jesus*, Harper and Row and Hodder 1960; Ernst Käsemann, 'The Problem of the Historical Jesus', in *Essays on New Testament Themes*, SCM Press 1964; Ernst Fuchs, *Studies of the Historical Jesus*, SCM Press 1964.

22. Scottish theologians have always been more sensitive to this dialogue than those in England.

23. For biblical theology see James D.Smart, *The Interpretation of the Bible*, Westminster Press and SCM Press 1961, 232-304; id., *The Past, Present and Future of Biblical Theology*, Westminster Press 1979; W.J.Harrington, *The Path of Biblical Theology*, Gill and Macmillan 1973; James Barr, *The Semantics of Biblical Language*, Oxford University Press 1961 reissued SCM Press 1983; id., *Biblical Words for Time*, SCM Press ²1969; id., *The Bible in the Modern World*, SCM Press 1973.

24. The article is directed against Niebergall, 'Über die Absolutheit des Christentums'; Troeltsch himself wrote on the *Absoluteness of Christianity*, see below n. 28.

25. Ernst Troeltsch, 'Über historische und dogmatische Methode in der Theologie', 730.

26. For more details see my *What about the Old Testament?*, SCM Press 1969, 29, and J.W.Colenso, *The Pentateuch and the Book of Joshua Critically Examined*, London 1862.

27. Troeltsch, op. cit., 733f.

28. James Luther Adams, in his introduction to Ernst Troeltsch, *The Absoluteness of Christianity*, John Knox Press 1971 and SCM Press 1972, 9f.

29. Troeltsch, 'Überhistorische und dogmatische Methode', 734.

30. Ibid., 740.

31. Ibid.

32. Ibid., 741.

33. Ibid., 742.

34. Ibid., 744.

35. Maurice Wiles, *God's Action in the World*, SCM Press 1986.

36. Wiles, *God's Action*, 36; cf. Hugh Montefiore, *The Probability of God*, SCM Press 1985, 161.

37. Wiles, *God's Action*, 104.

38. Ibid., 108.

39. Ibid., 47f., 97.

40. Ibid., 93f.

41. E.g. Grace Jantzen, *The Times Literary Supplement*, 20 March 1987; Keith Ward, *The Tablet*, 31 January 1987.

42. See above, 146.

43. This was particularly the position of C.S.Lewis, *Miracles*, Fontana Books 1960.

44. See Raymond Brown, *The Birth of the Messiah*, Doubleday and Geoffrey Chapman 1977, 517-33.

45. See the books mentioned at Chapter 4, n.4 above.

46. G.W.H.Lampe, *God as Spirit*, 158f.

47. See the coin in the fish's mouth in Matt.17.27.

48. A favourite instance is the infant Jesus making good his father's mistakes in carpentry: 'Infancy Gospel of Thomas', in *The Apocryphal New Testament* ed. M.R.James, Oxford University Press 1924, 52f.

49. For this whole question see Howard Clark Kee, *Miracle in the Early Christian World. A Study in Sociohistorical Method*, Yale University Press 1983.

50. See e.g. D.E.Nineham, *Saint Mark*, Penguin Books 1963, 149ff.

51. For the political dimension see Gerd Theissen, *Miracle Stories of the Early Christian Tradition*, T.&.T.Clark 1983, 254f.

52. Barnabas Lindars, 'Miracles', in *A New Dictionary of Christian Theology* ed. Alan Richardson and John Bowden, SCM Press and Westminster Press 1983, 372.

53. For an enjoyable history of the interpretation of miracle see Ernst and Marie-Luise Keller, *Miracles in Dispute. A Continuing Debate*, SCM Press and Fortress Press 1969.

11. The Finality of Christ?

1. See above, 13.

2. From the prayer of consecration in the 1662 *Book of Common Prayer*.

3. John 14.6.

4. Acts 4.12.

5. For the lukewarm Christian response to the events of 1933 in Germany see Klaus Scholder, *The Churches and the Third Reich*, Volume 1, SCM Press and Fortress Press 1987, 254-79.

6. For a selection of these declarations see *Stepping Stones to Further Jewish-Christian Relations*, compiled by Helga Croner, Stimulus Books 1977; *More Stepping Stones to Jewish-Christian Relations*, compiled by Helga Croner, Stimulus Books and Paulist Press, New York 1985.

7. Denzinger, *Enchiridion Symbolorum Definitionum et Declarationum de Rebus Fidei et Morum*, [36]1976, no.714, quoted by John Hick, 'Religious Pluralism and Absolute Claims', in *Problems of Religious Pluralism*, Macmillan 1985, 51.

8. J.O.Percy, *Facing the Unfinished Task: Messages Delivered at the Congress on World Mission*, Eerdmans, Grand Rapids 1961, 9, quoted often by John Hick, e.g. ibid., 51, 68; id., *The Second Christianity*, SCM Press 1983, 72.

9. Karl Barth, *Church Dogmatics* I.2, T.&.T.Clark 1962, 280ff., 297ff., 325ff.

10. Ibid., 296f.

11. Hendrik Kraemer, *The Christian Message in a Non-Christian World*, Edinburgh House Press 1938.

12. See Alan Race, *Christians and Religious Pluralism*, SCM Press 1983, 21f.

13. Kraemer, *Christian Message*, 93.

14. Ibid., 79.

15. Acts 10.35.

16. Acts 17.22-31.

17. Cf. Karl Rahner, 'Christianity and the Non-Christian Religions', *Theological Investigations* 5, Darton, Longman and Todd and Seabury Press 1966, 115-34.

18. Rahner, *Theological Investigations* 5, 133.

19. See e.g. J.N.Farquhar, *The Crown of Hinduism*, 1913; Bede Griffiths, *Vedanta and Christian Faith*, Dawn Horse Press, Los Angeles 1973; id., *Return to the Centre*, Collins 1976; Klaus Klostermaier, *Hindu and Christian in Vrindaban*, SCM Press 1969; M.M.Thomas, *The Acknowledged Christ of the Indian Renaissance*, SCM Press 1971; Raimundo Panikkar, *The Unknown Christ of Hinduism*, Darton, Longman and Todd 1964.

20. For Raimundo Panikkar see Paul F.Knitter, *No Other Name? A Critical Survey of Christian Attitudes toward the World Religions*, Orbis Books, Maryknoll and SCM Press 1985, 152-7.

21. Raimundo Panikkar, *The Unknown Christ*, p.24.

22. Raimundo Panikkar, *The Trinity and the Religious Experience of Man*, Orbis Books, Maryknoll 1973, 53f.

23. For Hans Küng see *On Being a Christian*, Fount Paperbacks 1978, 123-6, and more recently *Christianity and the World Religions*, Fount Paperbacks 1985.

24. John A.T.Robinson, *Truth is Two-Eyed*, SCM Press and Westminster Press 1979.

25. Marghanita Laski was an atheist who particularly resented this approach and made it quite clear that she did.

26. Karl Rahner, *Theological Investigations* 5, 134.

27. See above, 113-16.

28. See Wolfhart Pannenberg, *Jesus God and Man*, SCM Press and Westminster Press 1968 and Maurice Wiles, 'Looking into the Sun', in *Working Papers in Doctrine*, SCM Press 1976, 159f.

29. See above, 48-50.

30. For this and the following see Tom F.Driver, *Christ in a Changing World*, SCM Press and Crossroad Publishing Company 1981, 32-57.

31. See in particular the comments on Constantine on 127f. above and the books by Robin Lane Fox and Judith Herrin cited there.

32. For example the Montanists in the early church, the thirteenth-century Joachimites, the Anabaptists, German pietists from the seventeenth century on and countless sects in Britain and the United States in the nineteenth and twentieth centuries including the Irvingites, the Plymouth

Brethren and the Adventists.

33. Jürgen Moltmann, *Theology of Hope*, SCM Press and Harper and Row 1967. Note the final conclusion that he draws on p.338: 'The world is not yet finished, but is understood as engaged in a history. It is therefore the world of possibilities, the world in which we can serve the future, promised truth and righteousness and peace. This is an age of diaspora, of sowing in hope, of self-surrender and sacrifice.'

34. Driver, *Christ in a Changing World*, 42f.

35. Ibid., 43.

36. Ibid., 44f.

37. John Hick, *God and the Universe of Faiths,* Macmillan 1973, 131.

38. First put forward in Karl Jaspers, *The Origin and Goal of History*, Routledge and Kegan Paul and Yale University Press 1953, Chapter 1.

39. John Hick, ibid.

40. John Hick *Problems of Religious Pluralism*, Macmillan 1985, 5-10.

41. W.Cantwell Smith, in John Hick and Brian Hebblethwaite (ed.), *Christianity and Other Religions*, Fount Paperbacks 1980, 99.

42. John Hick, *Problems of Religious Pluralism*, 84f.

43. John Hick and Paul Knitter (eds.), *The Myth of Christian Uniqueness*, Orbis Books and SCM Press 1988.

44. See Marjorie Suchocki, 'In Search of Justice', *Myth*, 149-62; Paul Knitter, 'Toward a Liberation Theology of Religions', *Myth*, 178-200.

45. Ibid., 213f.

46. Ibid., 214.

12. Criteria for Christianity

1. See Chapter 8 above.

2. John 15.13. See Alan Wilkinson, *The Church of England and the First World War*, SPCK 1978.

3. Malachi Martin, *Jesus Now*, Fount Paperbacks 1977, 95-8.

4. Don Cupitt, *The Long-Legged Fly*, SCM Press 1987; id., *The New Christian Ethics*, SCM Press 1988.

5. See above, Chapter 10. For a thorough discussion of cultural relativism see D.E.Nineham, *The Use and Abuse of the Bible*, Macmillan 1976, reissued SPCK 1978, 1-39; the position does not seem to me to be substantially altered by the two articles by John Barton, 'Reflections on Cultural Relativism', *Theology* 1979, 103-9, 191-8.

6. See above, 31 and 213 n.31.

7. Ian T.Ramsey, *On Being Sure in Religion*, Athlone Press 1963, 3.

8. Ibid., 90.

9. For further discussion see my 'Vision', *Theology*, January 1980, 4-12.

10. The parable first appeared in 'Theology and Verification', *Theology Today* 17, 1960, 18f.; it has often been quoted, e.g. in John Bowden and James Richmond (eds.), *A Reader in Contemporary Theology*, SCM Press and Westminster Press 1967, 149f. Cf. more recently John Hick,

'Eschatological Verification Reconsidered', in *Problems of Religious Pluralism*, Macmillan 1985, 110-25.

11. In *The Good and the True*, see above, 110f.

12. Tom Driver, *Christ in a Changing World*, SCM Press and Crossroad Publishing Company 1981.

13. Stewart Sutherland, *God, Jesus and Belief*, Blackwell 1984, 16.

14. See Alasdair MacIntyre, *After Virtue*, Duckworth [2]1985, 1-5.

15. Ibid., 226ff.

16. Renford Bambrough, *Moral Scepticism and Moral Knowledge*, Routledge and Kegan Paul 1979, 15.

17. Ibid., 33: 'The fact that a tailor needs to make a different suit for each of us, and that no non-trivial specification of what a suit has to be like in order to fit its wearer will be without exceptions, does not mean that there are no rights and wrongs about the question whether your suit or mine is a good fit.'

18. Ibid., 107ff.

19. See Lucas Grollenberg, *Unexpected Messiah*, SCM Press 1988.

20. Galatians 3.28.

21. *English Hymnal* 405, *Hymns Ancient and Modern Revised* 192. For John Newton see Bernard Martin, *John Newton*, Heinemann 1950.

22. See E. Royston Pike, *Human Documents of the Industrial Revolution in Britain*, Allen and Unwin 1966.

23. See Kenneth Slack, *Martin Luther King*, SCM Press 1970, 85ff.

24. David E. Jenkins in his unpublished Ferguson lectures has drawn attention to the way in which while Marxism offers an important critique of Christianity, it (like other ideologies) has a tendency to draw on the capital of the religious tradition to lend support to its theses, giving many of its statements a quasi-religious tone. See also Alistair Kee's introduction to the reissue of his *The Way of Transcendence*, SCM Press 1980, 2-5.

25. See e.g. Edward Schillebeeckx, *Christ. The Christian Experience in the Modern World*, SCM Press and Crossroad Publishing Company 1980, 27-64; id., *Interim Report on the Books Jesus and Christ*, SCM Press and Crossroad Publishing Company 1980, 10-19.

26. See e.g. Schillebeeckx, *Christ*, 744-839, and on the whole issue my *Edward Schillebeeckx. Portrait of a Theologian* (US title *Edward Schillebeeckx: In Search of the Kingdom of God*), SCM Press and Crossroad Publishing Company 1983, 90-103.

27. I have taken these phrases from David E. Jenkins, *God, Politics and the Future*, SCM Press 1988, 28, 34.

28. See above, 150.

29. Gerd Theissen, *On Having a Critical Faith*, SCM Press and Fortress Press 1979, vii.

30. Ibid., viif.

31. See again David E. Jenkins, *God, Politics and the Future*, 112.

32. Philip Toynbee, *Towards the Holy Spirit*, SCM Press [2]1982, 15-27.

33. Ibid., 31-41.
34. Ibid,. 50.
35. Ibid., 63.
36. In addition to *Towards the Holy Spirit* see also his *Part of a Journey*, Fount Books 1981, and especially 'A Marriage of Heaven and Earth', 199-207: the latter is also included in the second edition of *Towards the Holy Spirit*, 77-86. Having finished with the proofs of my own book, I now look forward to reading his *End of a Journey* ed. John Bullimore, Bloomsbury Publishing 1988.
37. 'A Marriage of Heaven and Earth', *Towards the Holy Spirit*, 82f.; *Part of a Journey*, 204f.
38. For a discussion specifically in relation to music see my article 'Music and Spirituality' in *A Dictionary of Christian Spirituality* ed. Gordon S.Wakefield, SCM Press and Westminster Press 1983, 271f., and the bibliography there.
39. John 13.17.
40. For an important discussion of this see Melvyn Thompson, *Cancer and the God of Love*, SCM Press 1976, 68-82.

13. Living with Questions

1. See below, 202f.
2. This decline, at any rate within Western Christianity, is documented in all the statistics, most noticeably those for clergy and religious. For the Roman Catholic church where this latter problem is acute see e.g. Jan Kerkhofs, 'From Frustration to Liberation? A Factual Approach to Numbers in the Church' in Lucas Grollenberg et al., *Minister, Pastor, Prophet*, SCM Press and Crossroad Publishing Company 1980, 5-20, especially the table of clergy replacement-rate on p.10, which in most Western European countries it is under 50%, in Holland as low as 7.7%. For the anti-intellectualism of the churches and the refusal to adjust church organization to meet modern demands see Robin Gill, *Beyond Decline*, SCM Press 1988.
3. H.Richard Niebuhr, *Radical Monotheism and Western Culture*, Faber 1961, 89f.
4. Jean Milet, *God or Christ*, SCM Press 1981, 2f.
5. Quoted by W.Cantwell Smith, *Towards a World Theology*, Macmillan 1981, 177.
6. See above, 167f.
7. This begins in the Old Testament with e.g. Amos 9.7; Isa. 45.1.
8. G.W.H.Lampe, *God as Spirit*, Oxford University Press 1977, reissued SCM Press 1983, 2.
9. For conversion see the famous A.D.Nock, *Conversion*, Oxford University Press 1933, especially 193ff.; A.J.Krailsheimer, *Conversion*, SCM Press 1980, which is an account of a series of conversions and unfortunately does not consider the point discussed here.

10. See Michael Paffard, *The Unattended Moment*, SCM Press 1976, 8.

11. Dag Hammarskjøld, *Markings*, Faber 1964, 169.

12. Paffard, op.cit., 10ff.

13. See the discussion in Chapter 11 above, 177f.

14. It is disturbing that W.Sargant's book *Battle for the Mind*, Pan Books 1959, which with its accounts of 'brainwashing' was perceived to have such damaging implications for some facets of evangelical Christianity, now seems to have been so completely forgotten.

15. S.W. Sykes, *The Identity of Christianity*, SPCK 1984, 282f.

16. See T.G.A.Baker, *Questioning Worship*, SCM Press 1977 and more recently his article 'Is Liturgy in Good Shape?' in *God's Truth* ed. Eric James 1988, 1-14.

17. Geoffrey Ahern and Grace Davie, *Inner City God*, Hodder 1987, 101. Compare Peter Brook, *The Empty Space*, Penguin Books 1972, 67: 'The Theatre is holy because its purpose is holy. It has a clearly defined place in the community and it responds to a need the churches can no longer fill.' The same thing can be said of the concert hall.

18. Stewart Sutherland, *God, Jesus and Belief*, Blackwell 1984, 142f.

19. See above, 192f.

20. W.Cantwell Smith, *Towards a World Theology*, 154ff.

21. See Dietrich Ritschl, *The Logic of Theology*, SCM Press and Fortress Press, 218: 'Today the common dangers which jeopardize the survival of humanity, the shortage of raw materials and energy sources, problems of over-population and hunger, permanent damage as a result of the pollution of the atmosphere, and above all the danger of nuclear war, are the strongest expression of the unity of humanity...The imperative of anxiety is beginning to have more significance than a common heritage.'

22. Ibid., 290.

23. See John Kent, *The End of the Line. The Development of Christian Theology in the Last Two Centuries*, SCM Press and Fortress Press 1982, and *The Unacceptable Face. The Modern Church in the Eyes of the Historian*, SCM Press 1987.

24. Albert Schweitzer, *The Quest of the Historical Jesus*, A.& C.Black ³1954, reissued SCM Press 1981, 4.

25. *By Heart. A Lifetime Companion*, selected and edited by John Bowden, SCM Press 1984.

26. The Collect for the Sixth Sunday after Trinity, *Book of Common Prayer*.

Indexes

Index of Names

Index of Subjects